POLITICAL CHRISTIANITY:
A READER

Books of Essential Readings published by SPCK:

POLITICAL CHRISTIANITY: A READER

Edited by David McLellan

First published in Great Britain 1997
Society for Promoting Christian Knowledge
Holy Trinity Church
Marylebone Road
London NW1 4DU

Introduction, compilation and editorial matter
copyright © David McLellan 1997

British Library Cataloguing-in-Publication Data

A catalogue record of this book is available from
the British Library

ISBN 0-281-04921-1

Typeset by Pioneer Associates, Perthshire.
Printed in Great Britain by
Redwood Books, Trowbridge, Wiltshire

For Nathanael and Madeline

CONTENTS

Contents

INTRODUCTION

This book covers an enormous amount of time and space: 2,000 years of history in very diverse parts of the world. It is therefore extremely selective. My aim is to give the reader a taste of the breadth and complexity of the subject. And given the necessarily introductory nature of the book, I have appended lists of further reading (with commentary) supported by a large general bibliography.

The reader is divided into three parts. The first is historical, for Christianity is nothing if not a historical, incarnate religion. To understand its contemporary situation and meaning, an acquaintance (at least) with its past is necessary. So I have included in this part a survey of what the Christian tradition, from the New Testament to John Paul II, has had to say about its relation to politics. The second part contains four case studies to give the reader a glimpse of the very different roles played by Christianity in various parts of the world – its impact on United States politics, liberation theology in South America, the influence of Christianity on the conflict in Northern Ireland and on the collapse of Communism in Eastern Europe. Finally, the third part deals with the use which past and contemporary politics have been able to make of Christianity. Here I deal with the relationship which conservatism, liberalism, socialism and Marxism have entertained towards Christianity – before looking at the more focused question of what succour feminist, green and race politics can find in the Christian religion. The book closes with two classic passages from Weber on the distinctiveness of the Christian attitude to politics.

In traditional, polite English society, the two subjects *never* to be discussed at a dinner table were politics and religion. Too controversial for genteel society, their relationship is nevertheless vital to a comprehensive understanding of the contemporary world. The intertwining of politics and religion is an essential element of the crisis in which we

1

find ourselves. Some see this intertwining as the bane of current politics, others as its potential salvation. However that may be, it is too late to be merely polite. And an enhanced understanding of the nature of the problems confronting us is at least a necessary condition for solving them.

PART ONE

Christianity and politics

Chapter One

THE BIBLE

Introduction

Virtually all readers of the New Testament would agree that it contains *some* political message, in the sense of a message that has a bearing on politics, but it has proved notoriously difficult to decipher.

In the first place, it is important to remember that Jesus's life and death was seen by himself and his followers as the culmination of a long line of Jewish prophetic teaching. These prophecies not only foretold the coming of a Messiah or Saviour: they also contained highly political statements about justice and the abuse of power. An example is the passage from Isaiah: 'Ah, you who make iniquitous decrees, who write oppressive statutes, to turn aside the needy from justice and to rob the poor of my people of their right, that widows may be your spoil, and that you may make the orphans your prey!'

When Jesus began his preaching, he chose a passage from the same prophet which declared 'The Spirit of the Lord is upon me, because he has anointed me to bring good news to the poor. He has sent me to proclaim release to the captives, and recovery of sight to the blind, to let the oppressed go free, to proclaim the year of the Lord's favour', and declared that 'today this scripture has been fulfilled in your hearing' (Luke 4.18–19, 21).

But in spite of seeing himself as inaugurating a Kingdom of God in line with the Jewish prophetic tradition and his consequent criticism of contemporary authoritarian and patriarchal attitudes, Jesus did not align himself with any of the political movements of his time. He was fiercely opposed to the political conformism of the Herodians, to the compromising religious establishment of the Sadducees, and to the narrow, reactionary stance of the Pharisees. He was also dubious about the withdrawal and quietism of the Essenes and the opposite policy of

5

active struggle for liberation from Roman rule, a policy with which four or five of Jesus's disciples sympathized: choosing as a close follower the tax-collector Matthew and the story of the good Samaritan do not fit with the strict nationalism of these so-called Zealots. But if Jesus was opposed to Jewish authorities, he was no less critical of the Romans. God and Caesar were firmly distinguished (in contrast to the ruling conceptions of later Christendom) and there was no doubt where the priority lay. It was the Roman state which condemned Jesus to death by crucifixion, its own favoured method of execution.

If we turn to the attitudes evident in the records of the early Christian communities, we find the same tensions and ambiguities. In the Acts of the Apostles, we are told that the community 'had all things in common; they would sell their possessions and goods and distribute the proceeds to all as any had need' (Acts 2.44–5). This distributive communism is accompanied by a more ambivalent political message. St Paul took a critical stance towards the 'powers' of this world and declared that 'God chose what is weak in the world to shame the strong' (1 Cor. 1.27). But at the same time he was loath to disturb existing social institutions such as slavery and wrote, in a passage naturally much quoted down the centuries by more conservative Christians, that 'those authorities that exist have been instituted by God. Therefore whoever resists authority resists what God has appointed' (Rom. 13.1–2). St Paul may have been doing little more here than warning the Christians in Rome to adopt a low profile in the face of Nero's persecutions. This is in sharp contrast to the violently anti-Roman imagery in the Book of Revelation and the prediction of the thousand year reign of the martyrs with Christ which has inspired millenarian movements from Thomas Münzer to the Mormons.

The writings of the New Testament contain texts written by many hands, in different genres, in widely separate places, and spread over at least two generations. It is not surprising that during later centuries material could be found to justify almost any political position.

(a) Mary

And Mary said,

> 'My soul magnifies the Lord,
> and my spirit rejoices in God my Savior,
> for he has looked with favor on the lowliness of his servant.
> Surely, from now on all generations will call me blessed;
> for the Mighty One has done great things for me,
> and holy is his name.

His mercy is for those who fear him
from generation to generation.
He has shown strength with his arm;
he has scattered the proud in the thoughts of their hearts.
He has brought down the powerful from their thrones,
and lifted up the lowly;
he has filled the hungry with good things,
and sent the rich away empty.
He has helped his servant Israel,
in remembrance of his mercy,
according to the promise he made to our ancestors,
to Abraham and to his descendants forever.'

(Luke 1.46–55)

(b) Jesus

Then he began to speak, and taught them, saying:

'Blessed are the poor in spirit, for theirs is the kingdom of heaven.
Blessed are those who mourn, for they will be comforted.
Blessed are the meek, for they will inherit the earth.
Blessed are those who hunger and thirst for righteousness, for they
will be filled.
Blessed are the merciful, for they will receive mercy.
Blessed are the pure in heart, for they will see God.
Blessed are the peacemakers, for they will be called children of God.
Blessed are those who are persecuted for righteousness' sake, for
theirs is the kingdom of heaven.
Blessed are you when people revile you and persecute you and utter
all kinds of evil against you falsely on my account. Rejoice and be
glad, for your reward is great in heaven, for in the same way they
persecuted the prophets who were before you.'

(Matt. 5.2–12)

Do not think that I have come to bring peace to the earth; I have not
come to bring peace, but a sword.

For I have come to set a man against his father,
and a daughter against her mother,
and a daughter-in-law against her mother-in-law;
and one's foes will be members of one's own household.

Whoever loves father or mother more than me is not worthy of me; and
whoever loves son or daughter more than me is not worthy of me; and

7

whoever does not take up his cross and follow me is not worthy of me. Those who find their life will lose it, and those who lose their life for my sake will find it.

(Matt. 10.34–9)

He said to them, 'When I sent you out without a purse, bag or sandals, did you lack anything?' They said, 'No, not a thing.' He said to them, 'But now, the one who has a purse must take it, and likewise a bag. And the one who has no sword must sell his cloak and buy one. For I tell you, this scripture must be fulfilled in me, "And he was counted among the lawless"; and indeed what is written about me is being fulfilled.'

They said, 'Lord, look, here are two swords.' He replied, 'It is enough.'

(Luke 22.35–8)

Then Jesus entered the temple and drove out all who were selling and buying in the temple, and he overturned the tables of the money changers and the seats of those who sold doves. He said to them, 'It is written,

> "My house shall be called a house of prayer";
>   but you are making it a den of robbers,'

The blind and the lame came to him in the temple, and he cured them. But when the chief priests and the scribes saw the amazing things that he did, and heard the children crying out in the temple, 'Hosanna to the Son of David,' they became angry and said to him, 'Do you hear what these are saying?' Jesus said to them, 'Yes; have you never read,

> "Out of the mouths of infants and nursing babies
>   you have prepared praise for yourself"?'

(Matt. 21.12–16)

Then the Pharisees went and plotted to entrap him in what he said. So they sent their disciples to him, along with the Herodians, saying, 'Teacher, we know that you are sincere, and teach the way of God in accordance with truth, and show deference to no one; for you do not regard people with partiality. Tell us, then, what you think. Is it lawful to pay taxes to the emperor, or not?' But Jesus, aware of their malice, said, 'Why are you putting me to the test, you hypocrites? Show me the coin used for the tax.' And they brought him a denarius. Then he said to them, 'Whose head is this, and whose title?' They answered, 'The emperor's.' Then he said to them, 'Give therefore to the emperor the things that are the emperor's, and to God the things that are God's.'

(Matt. 22.15–21)

'When the Son of Man comes in his glory, and all the angels with him, then he will sit on the throne of his glory. All the nations will be gathered before him, and he will separate people one from another as a shepherd separates the sheep from the goats, and he will put the sheep at his right hand and the goats at the left. Then the king will say to those at his right hand, "Come, you that are blessed by my Father, inherit the kingdom prepared for you from the foundation of the world; for I was hungry and you gave me food, I was thirsty and you gave me something to drink, I was a stranger and you welcomed me, I was naked and you gave me clothing, I was sick and you took care of me, I was in prison and you visited me." Then the righteous will answer him, "Lord, when was it that we saw you hungry and gave you food, or thirsty and gave you something to drink? And when was it that we saw you a stranger and welcomed you, or naked and gave you clothing? And when was it that we saw you sick or in prison and visited you?" And the king will answer them, "Truly I tell you, just as you did it to one of the least of these who are members of my family, you did it to me." Then he will say to those at his left hand, "You that are accursed, depart from me into the eternal fire prepared for the devil and his angels; for I was hungry and you gave me no food, I was thirsty and you gave me nothing to drink, I was a stranger and you did not welcome me, naked and you did not give me clothing, sick and in prison and you did not visit me." Then they also will answer, "Lord, when was it that we saw you hungry or thirsty or a stranger or naked or sick or in prison, and did not take care of you?" Then he will answer them, "Truly I tell you, just as you did not do it to one of the least of these, you did not do it to me." And these will go away into eternal punishment, but the righteous into eternal life.'

(Matt. 25.31–46)

Then Pilate entered the headquarters again, summoned Jesus, and asked him, 'Are you the King of the Jews?' Jesus answered, 'Do you ask this on your own, or did others tell you about me?' Pilate replied, 'I am not a Jew, am I? Your own nation and the chief priests have handed you over to me. What have you done?' Jesus answered, 'My kingdom is not from this world. If my kingdom were from this world, my followers would be fighting to keep me from being handed over to the Jews. But as it is, my kingdom is not from here.' Pilate asked him, 'So you are a king?' Jesus answered, 'You say that I am a king. For this I was born, and for this I came into the world, to testify to the truth. Everyone who belongs to the truth listens to my voice.' Pilate asked him, 'What is truth?'

After he had said this, he went out to the Jews again and told them,

'I find no case against him. But you have a custom that I release some-
one for you at the Passover. Do you want me to release for you the
King of the Jews?' They shouted in reply, 'Not this man, but Barabbas!'
Now Barabbas was a bandit.

(John 18.33–40)

(c) Acts

Now the whole group of those who believed were of one heart and
soul, and no one claimed private ownership of any possessions, but
everything they owned was held in common. With great power the
apostles gave their testimony to the resurrection of the Lord Jesus, and
great grace was upon them all. There was not a needy person among
them, for as many as owned lands or houses sold them and brought the
proceeds of what was sold. They laid it at the apostles' feet, and it was
distributed to each as any had need.

(Acts 4.33–5)

(d) Paul

Let every person be subject to the governing authorities; for there is no
authority except from God, and those authorities that exist have been
instituted by God. Therefore whoever resists authority resists what
God has appointed, and those who resist will incur judgment. For rulers
are not a terror to good conduct, but to bad. Do you wish to have no
fear of the authority? Then do what is good, and you will receive its
approval; for it is God's servant for your good. But if you do what is
wrong, you should be afraid, for the authority does not bear the sword
in vain! It is the servant of God to execute wrath on the wrongdoer.
Therefore one must be subject, not only because of wrath but also
because of conscience. For the same reason you also pay taxes, for the
authorities are God's servants, busy with this very thing. Pay to all what
is due them – taxes to whom taxes are due, revenue to whom revenue
is due, respect to whom respect is due, honor to whom honor is due.

(Rom. 13.1–7)

Let each of you remain in the condition in which you were called.
    Were you a slave when called? Do not be concerned about it. Even
if you can gain your freedom, make use of your present condition now
more than ever. For whoever was called in the Lord as a slave is a freed
person belonging to the Lord, just as whoever was free when called is
a slave of Christ. You were bought with a price; do not become slaves

of human masters. In whatever condition you were called, brothers and sisters, there remain with God.

(1 Cor. 7.20–4)

(e) *James*

Come now, you rich people, weep and wail for the miseries that are coming to you. Your riches have rotted, and your clothes are moth-eaten. Your gold and silver have rusted, and their rust will be evidence against you, and it will eat your flesh like fire. You have laid up treasure for the last days. Listen! The wages of the laborers who mowed your fields, which you kept back by fraud, cry out, and the cries of the harvesters have reached the ears of the Lord of hosts. You have lived on the earth in luxury and in pleasure; you have fattened your hearts in a day of slaughter. You have condemned and murdered the righteous one, who does not resist you.

(f) *Revelation*

And war broke out in heaven; Michael and his angels fought against the dragon. The dragon and his angels fought back, but they were defeated, and there was no longer any place for them in heaven. The great dragon was thrown down, that ancient serpent, who is called the Devil and Satan, the deceiver of the whole world – he was thrown down to the earth, and his angels were thrown down with him.

Then I heard a loud voice in heaven, proclaiming,

'Now have come the salvation and the power
and the kingdom of our God
and the authority of his Messiah,
for the accuser of our comrades has been thrown down,
who accuses them day and night before our God.
But they have conquered him by the blood of the Lamb
and by the word of their testimony,
for they did not cling to life even in the face of death.
Rejoice then, you heavens
and those who dwell in them!
But woe to the earth and the sea,
for the devil has come down to you
with great wrath,
because he knows that his time is short!'

So when the dragon saw that he had been thrown down to the earth, he pursued the woman who had given birth to the male child. But the woman was given the two wings of the great eagle, so that she could fly from the serpent into the wilderness, to her place where she is nourished for a time, and times, and half a time. Then from his mouth the serpent poured water like a river after the woman, to sweep her away with the flood. But the earth came to the help of the woman; it opened on the sand of the seashore. And I saw a beast rising out of the sea, having ten horns and seven heads; and on its horns were ten diadems, and on its heads were blasphemous names. And the beast that I saw was like a leopard, its feet were like a bear's, and its mouth was like a lion's mouth. And the dragon gave it his power and his throne and great authority. One of its heads seemed to have received a death-blow, but its mortal wound had been healed. In amazement the whole earth followed the beast. They worshipped the dragon, for he had given his authority to the beast, and they worshipped the beast, saying, 'Who is like the beast, and who can fight against it?'

The beast was given a mouth uttering haughty and blasphemous words, and it was allowed to exercise authority for forty-two months. It opened its mouth to utter blasphemies against God, blaspheming his name and his dwelling, that is, those who dwell in heaven. Also it was allowed to make war on the saints and to conquer them. It was given authority over every tribe and people and language and nation, and all the inhabitants of the earth will worship it, everyone whose name has not been written from the foundation of the world in the book of life of the Lamb that was slaughtered.

Let anyone who has an ear listen:

> If you are to be taken captive,
>   into captivity you go;
> if you kill with the sword,
>   with the sword you must be killed.

Here is a call for the endurance and faith of the saints.

Then I saw another beast that rose out of the earth; it had two horns like a lamb and it spoke like a dragon. It exercises all the authority of the first beast on its behalf, and it makes the earth and its inhabitants worship the first beast, whose mortal wound had been healed. It performs great signs, even making fire come down from heaven to earth in the sight of all; and by the signs that it is allowed to perform on behalf of the beast, it deceives the inhabitants of earth, telling them to make an image for the beast that had been wounded by the sword and yet lived; and it was allowed to give breath to the image of the beast so that the image of the beast could even speak and cause those who would not worship the image of the beast to be killed. Also it causes all, both small and great, both rich and poor, both free and slave, to be marked on the right hand or the forehead, so that no one can buy or sell who does not have the mark, that is, the name of the beast or the number of its name. This calls for wisdom: let anyone with understanding calculate the number of the beast, for it is the number of a person. Its number is six hundred sixty-six.

(Rev. 13.7 13.18)

Further reading

Two good overviews can be found in Cullman's classic *The State in the New Testament*. There are collections on restricted topics by Bammel and by Barbour. The thesis that Jesus was a Zealot is argued in Brandon's *Jesus and the Zealots* while the opposite view of Jesus as a pacifist is argued in the books by Ellul, Yoder and McClendon. The antiestablishment view of Jesus is well brought out in Myers' *Binding the Strong Man* and in Part 3 of Rowland and Corner's *Liberating Exegesis*. See also Wink's *Naming the Powers*. The social background to the early Christian community is discussed in the two books by Douglas and Wayne Meeks, in Fiorenza's *In Memory of Her* and in Rowland's *Christian Origins*. There is a brief discussion of the historical importance of Revelation in Rowland and Corner Chapter 4 and a lengthier treatment in Court Chapter 1.

Chapter Two

EARLY CHRISTIANITY

Introduction

During the first three centuries after the death of Jesus, the Christian Church lived in an ambivalent relationship to the Roman Empire. This ambivalence, though not entirely removed, was largely suppressed by the recognition by Constantine of Christianity as the official religion of the Empire.

Christianity undoubtedly benefited from the *Pax Romana* which gave a sense of unity to the countries around the Mediterranean, fostered good communications, and gave a sense of common order to very diverse societies. All this helped the expansion of the Church which was occupied in creating its own forms of organization, with its centre emerging in Rome, and in working out what were the essential elements of the Christian faith as distinct from the deviations that later came to be known as heresies. But difficulties arose when the authorities insisted that Christians subscribe to the civil religion of the Roman Empire. It was refusal to do this that earned Christians the reputation of atheism. This problem often occurred in the context of military service – not for reasons of conscientious objection but because of the apparently idolatrous character of the oaths in which it involved the conscript. Irenaeus, Bishop of Lyon, writing in the late second century, insists that secular authority has its origins in God's designs and not those of the devil. By contrast, the most striking example of antipathy towards political power is provided by the writings of Tertullian around AD 200 who saw the Christian Church as a kind of rigorous counter-culture set over against the practices and ethos of the Roman State. This attitude was reiterated by Origen, writing around AD 250, and reinforced by the persecution of Christians under emperors such as Marcus Aurelius, Decius, and particularly Diocletian.

The reversal of this policy came with the 'conversion' of the Emperor Constantine to Christianity and his decision in the Edict of Milan in AD 312 to recognize the legal personality of the Christian churches and to tolerate all religions equally. Although this did not 'establish' the Church, it did lead to a growing intimacy of Church and State. Some think that the history of institutional Christianity has been downhill ever since.

The sack of Rome in AD 410 by Alaric the Goth was attributed by many to the abandonment by the Empire of its traditional deities. This prompted the most influential of all political theologians, St Augustine, to write his *City of God* in refutation of this view. Augustine constructs his book in terms of two cities, the heavenly and the earthly, which are in fact two societies, that of the sacred and of the reprobate. The fact that these two cities are by no means co-extensive with Church and State makes Augustine's views capable of many interpretations. Although he was not above calling in the secular power to suppress the Donatist heretics (whom he regarded with some justification as terrorists), Augustine's writings give little support to the 'political Augustinianism' of the Middle Ages which conferred on the Church a sort of universal political sovereignty. The claims of the City of God relativize those of any earthly power. Nevertheless, the resilience and stability of the Church as the one institution which could hold the ruins of the Roman Empire together did mean the increasing politicization of the Church and the sacralization of secular powers that came to be characteristic of the Middle Ages.

(a) *Irenaeus:* Against the Heresies

The devil lied at the beginning, and he was lying again at the end when he said, 'All these things have been delivered to me, and I give them to whom I will' (Luke 4.6). It is not the devil who has fixed the bounds of the kingdom of this world, but God. For 'the king's heart is in the hand of God' (Prov. 21.1). Through Solomon the Word also says: 'By me kings reign and rulers exercise justice; by me princes are raised up and by me monarchs govern the earth' (Prov. 8.15–16). Moreover Paul the apostle speaks to the same effect: 'Be subject to all the higher powers; for there is no power except from God. Those that exist have been instituted by God' (Rom. 13.1). And later on he says of them: 'He does not bear the sword in vain; he is the minister of God to execute his wrath on the evildoer' (Rom. 13.4). Some people are rash enough to expound this passage as speaking of angelic powers and invisible rulers; but Paul is not talking about them but about human powers. This is clear from his going on to say: 'For the same reason you also pay taxes, since they are God's ministers, serving for this very purpose' (Rom. 13.6). The Lord himself confirmed this by not doing what the devil tried to persuade him to do, but giving instructions that the tribute-money was to be paid to the tax-collectors for himself and for Peter, his reason being that 'they are God's ministers, serving for this very purpose'.

By departing from God, men reached such a pitch of savagery that they came to treat even blood-relations as enemies and to practise all kinds of violence, murder and greed without any sense of fear. Since they knew no fear of God, God imposed on them a human fear. The aim was that by being subjected to the authority of men and educated by human laws, they might achieve some measure of justice and exercise restraint towards one another through fear of the sword so clearly held before them. This is what the apostle means when he says: 'He does not bear the sword in vain; he is the minister of God to execute his wrath on the evildoer.' For the magistrates themselves the laws provide a cloak of righteousness. As long as they act justly and in accordance with the laws, they will not be interrogated about what they do; but if ever they do anything to subvert justice, if they act unjustly, illegally or tyrannically, they too will perish for their actions. God's just judgement falls equally on all men, and never fails.

So then earthly authority has been established by God for the benefit of the nations. It has not been established by the devil, who is never at peace himself and has no wish to see the nations living in peace. God's purpose is that men should fear this authority and so not consume one another as fish do; his intention is that the imposition of laws should hold in check the great wickedness to be found among the nations. It is in this sense that they 'are God's ministers'.

If then those who demand taxes of us 'are God's ministers, serving for this very purpose', and if 'the powers that exist have been instituted by God', it is clear that the devil is lying when he says: 'All these things have been delivered to me, and I give them to whom I will.' It is by God's decree that men are born and it is by that same God's decree that rulers are set up – rulers appropriate to the people to be ruled over by them at that particular time. Thus some rulers are given by God with a view to the improvement and benefit of their subjects and the preservation of justice; others are given with a view to producing fear, punishment and reproof; yet others are given with a view to displaying mockery, insult and pride – in each case in accordance with the deserts of the subjects. Thus, as we have already said, God's just judgement falls equally on all men.

(V, 24, 1–3)
Source: *Documents in Early Christian Thought*, ed. M. Wiles and M. Santer, Cambridge University Press, 1975, pp. 225–6.

(b) *Tertullian:* Letter to Scapula

For us, the things that we suffer at the hands of ignorant men are not a source of great fear or dread. When we joined this sect we plainly undertook to accept the conditions this involved. So we come to these contests as men who have already hired themselves out for them. Our hope is to attain the promises of God; our fear is lest we should have to undergo the punishments with which he threatens those who live otherwise. When you turn on us with your utmost ferocity we are quite ready to do battle with you; indeed we enter the fray of our own accord. We find more cause for joy in condemnation than in acquittal. So it is not fear for ourselves that makes us send you this pamphlet, but fear for you and for all our enemies, or I should rather say, our friends, since it is the teaching of our faith that we are to love even our enemies and pray for those who persecute us (see Matt. 5.44). Here lies the perfection and distinctiveness of Christian goodness. Ordinary goodness is different; for all men love their friends but only Christians love their enemies. We are moved with sorrow at your ignorance and with pity for the errors of men's ways, and, as we look to the future, we see signs of impending disasters every day. In such circumstances we have no choice but to take the initiative and lay before you those things which you refuse to listen to openly and publicly.

We worship the one God. He it is whom you all know by the light of nature. His is the lightning and thunder at which you tremble. His is the bounty at which you rejoice. There are others whom you regard as gods; we know them to be demons. Nevertheless it is a basic human right that everyone should be free to worship according to his own convictions. No one is either harmed or helped by another man's religion. It is no part of the practice of religion to compel others to the practice of religion. Religion must be practised freely, not by coercion; even animals for sacrifice must be offered with a willing heart. So even if you compel us to sacrifice, you will not be providing your gods with any worthwhile service. They will not want sacrifices from unwilling offerers – unless they are perverse, which God is not. In fact the true God gives all that is his as freely to the irreligious as to his own; furthermore he has established an eternal judgement to distinguish the grateful from the ungrateful. Yet it is us whom you regard as sacrilegious, even though you have never found us guilty of theft – let alone of sacrilege. Those who actually rob temples are people who swear by the gods and worship them; in spite of not being Christians, they are still found guilty of sacrilege! It would take too long to describe the other ways in which all the gods are ridiculed and despised by their own worshippers.

Another charge against us concerns treason with respect to the person of the Emperor. Yet Christians have never been found among the followers of Albinus or Niger or Cassius. Those who have actually been found in practice to be enemies of the Emperor are the very same people who only a day before had been swearing by his genius, had been solemnly offering sacrifices for his safety, and not infrequently had been condemning Christians as well. A Christian is an enemy to no man – certainly not to the Emperor, for he knows that it is by his God that the Emperor has been appointed. He is bound therefore to love him, to revere him, to honour him and to desire the safety not only of the Emperor but of the whole Roman empire as long as the world endures – for as long as the world endures, so also will the Roman empire. So then we do 'worship' the Emperor in such manner as is both permissible to us and beneficial to him, namely as a man second only to God. All that he is he has received from God, and it is God alone whom he ranks below. This surely is what the Emperor himself will desire. He ranks above all else; it is the true God alone whom he ranks below. This means that he is above even the gods themselves and they come within his sovereignty. So also we 'offer sacrifices' for the safety of the Emperor, but we do so to our God – and his – and we do it in the way that God has ordained, namely by the offering simply of prayers. (For God, being the creator of the whole Universe, is in no need of smells or of blood. That is the fodder of petty demons. We do not merely despise these demons; we subdue them; we put them to daily disgrace; we drive them out of people, as multitudes can testify.) So then our prayers for the safety of the Emperor are all the more real as we offer them to the one who is able to grant them.

Our religion teaches a divine patience and it is on this basis that we conduct our lives. You can see this clearly enough from the fact that although we are such a large company of men (almost a majority in fact of every city) yet we live out our lives quietly and temperately; we are probably better known individually than as a corporate entity, since the only way we can be distinguished is by the way we get rid of our former vices. Far be it from us to react with indignation when we suffer things which in fact we welcome or in any way to plot the vengeance at our own hands which we confidently await from God.

(1–2)

Source: *Documents in Early Christian Thought*, ed. M. Wiles and M. Santer, Cambridge University Press, 1975, pp. 226–8.

(c) Origen: Against Celsus

In the next place, Celsus urges us 'to help the king with all our might, and to labour with him in the maintenance of justice, to fight for him; and if he requires it, to fight under him, or lead an army along with him.' To this our answer is, that we do, when occasion requires, give help to kings, and that, so to say, a divine help, 'putting on the whole armour of God'. And this we do in obedience to the injunction of the apostle, 'I exhort, therefore, that first of all, supplications, prayers, intercessions, and giving of thanks, be made for all men; for kings, and for all that are in authority'; and the more any one excels in piety, the more effective help does he render to kings, even more than is given by soldiers, who go forth to fight and slay as many of the enemy as they can. And to those enemies of our faith who require us to bear arms for the commonwealth, and to slay men, we can reply: 'Do not those who are priests at certain shrines, and those who attend on certain gods, as you account them, keep their hands free from blood, that they may with hands unstained and free from human blood offer the appointed sacrifices to your gods; and even when war is upon you, you never enlist the priests in the army. If that, then, is a laudable custom, how much more so, that while others are engaged in battle, these too should engage as the priests and ministers of God, keeping their hands pure, and wrestling in prayers to God on behalf of those who are fighting in a righteous cause, and for the king who reigns righteously, that whatever is opposed to those who act righteously may be destroyed!' And as we by our prayers vanquish all demons who stir up war, and lead to the violation of oaths, and disturb the peace, we in this way are much more helpful to the kings than those who go into the field to fight for them. And we do take our part in public affairs, when along with righteous prayers we join self-denying exercises and meditations, which teach us to despise pleasures, and not to be led away by them. And none fight better for the king than we do. We do not indeed fight under him, although he require it; but we fight on his behalf, forming a special army – an army of piety – by offering our prayers to God.

And if Celsus would have us to lead armies in defence of our country, let him know that we do this too, and that not for the purpose of being seen by men, or of vainglory. For 'in secret', and in our own hearts, there are prayers which ascend as from priests in behalf of our fellow-citizens. And Christians are benefactors of their country more than others. For they train up citizens, and inculcate piety to the Supreme Being; and they promote those whose lives in the smallest cities have been good and worthy, to a divine and heavenly city, to whom it may be said, 'Thou hast been faithful in the smallest city, come into a great one', where 'God standeth in the assembly of the gods, and judgeth the gods in the midst'; and he reckons thee among them, if thou no more 'die as a man, or fall as one of the princes'.

Celsus also urges us to 'take office in the government of the country, if that is required for the maintenance of the laws and the support of religion'. But we recognize in each state the existence of another national organization, founded by the Word of God, and we exhort those who are mighty in word and of blameless life to rule over churches. Those who are ambitious of ruling we reject; but we constrain those who, through excess of modesty, are not easily induced to take a public charge in the Church of God. And those who rule over us well are under the constraining influence of the great King, whom we believe to be the Son of God, God the Word. And if those who govern in the Church, and are called rulers of the divine nation – that is, the Church – rule well, they rule in accordance with the divine commands, and never suffer themselves to be led astray by worldly policy. And it is not for the purpose of escaping public duties that Christians decline public offices, but that they may reserve themselves for a diviner and more necessary service in the Church of God – for the salvation of men. And this service is at once necessary and right. They take charge of all – of those that are within, that they may day by day lead better lives, and of those that are without, that they may come to abound in holy words and in deeds of piety; and that, while thus worshipping God truly, and training up as many as they can in the same way, they may be filled with the word of God and the law of God, and thus be united with the Supreme God through his Son the Word, Wisdom, Truth, and Righteousness, who unites to God all who are resolved to conform their lives in all things to the law of God.

(VIII, 73–5)

Source: *The Ante-Nicene Fathers*, Eerdmans, 1956, vol. 4, pp. 667–8.

(d) Augustine: The City of God

The two cities were created by two kinds of love: the earthly city was created by self-loving reaching the point of contempt for God, the Heavenly City by the love of God carried as far as contempt of self. In fact, the earthly city glories in itself, the Heavenly City glories in the Lord. The former looks for glory from men, the latter finds its highest glory in God, the witness of a good conscience. The earthly lifts up its head in its own glory, the Heavenly City says to its God: 'My glory; you lift up my head.' In the former, the lust for domination lords it over its princes as over the nations it subjugates; in the other both those put in authority and those subject to them serve one another in love, the rulers by their counsel, the subjects by obedience. The one city loves its own strength shown in its powerful leaders; the other says to its God, 'I will love you, my Lord, my strength.'

Consequently, in the earthly city its wise men who live by men's standards have pursued the goods of the body or of their own mind, or of both. Or those of them who were able to know God 'did not honour him as God, nor did they give thanks to him, but they dwindled into futility in their thoughts, and their senseless heart was darkened: in asserting their wisdom' – that is, exalting themselves in their wisdom, under the domination of pride – 'they became foolish, and changed the glory of the imperishable God into an image representing a perishable man, or birds or beasts or reptiles' – for in the adoration of idols of this kind they were either leaders or followers of the general public – 'and they worshipped and served created things instead of the Creator, who is blessed for ever'. In the Heavenly City, on the other hand, man's only wisdom is the devotion which rightly worships the true God, and looks for its reward in the fellowship of the saints, not only holy men but also holy angels, 'so that God may be all in all'.

(Bk 14, ch. 28)

The good that God imparts, which the Devil has in his nature, does not withdraw him from God's justice by which his punishment is ordained. But God, in punishing, does not chastise the good which he created, but the evil which the Devil has committed. And God does not take away all that he gave to that nature; he takes something, and yet he leaves something, so that there may be some being left to feel pain at the deprivation.

Now this pain is in itself evidence of the good that was taken away and the good that was left. In fact, if no good had been left there could have been no grief for lost good. For a sinner is in a worse state if he rejoices in the loss of righteousness; but a sinner who feels anguish, though he may gain no good from his anguish, is at least grieving at the loss of salvation. And since righteousness and salvation are both good, and the loss of any good calls for grief rather than for joy (assuming that there is no compensation for the loss in the shape of a higher good – for example, righteousness of character is a higher good than health of body), the unrighteous man's grief in his punishment is more appropriate than his rejoicing in sin. Hence, just as delight in the abandonment of good, when a man sins, is evidence of a bad will, so grief at the loss of good, when a man is punished, is evidence of a good nature. For when a man grieves at the loss of the peace of his nature, his grief arises from some remnants of that peace, which ensure that his nature is still on friendly terms with itself. Moreover, it is entirely right that in the last punishment the wicked and ungodly should bewail in their agonies the loss of their 'natural' goods, and realize that he who divested them of

21

these goods with perfect justice is God, whom they despised when with supreme generosity he bestowed them.

God then, created all things in supreme wisdom and ordered them in perfect justice; and in establishing the mortal race of mankind as the greatest ornament of earthly things, he has given to mankind certain good things suitable to this life. These are: temporal peace, in proportion to the short span of a mortal life – the peace that consists in bodily health and soundness, and in fellowship with one's kind; and everything necessary to safeguard or recover this peace – those things, for example, which are appropriate and accessible to our senses: light, speech, air to breathe, water to drink, and whatever is suitable for the feeding and clothing of the body, for the care of the body and the adornment of the person. And all this is granted under the most equitable condition: that every mortal who uses aright such goods, goods designed to serve the peace of mortal men, shall receive goods greater in degree and superior in kind, namely, the peace of immortality, and the glory and honour appropriate to it in a life which is eternal for the enjoyment of God and of one's neighbour in God, whereas he who wrongly uses those mortal goods shall lose them, and shall not receive the blessings of eternal life.

We see, then, that all man's use of temporal things is related to the enjoyment of earthly peace in the earthly city; whereas in the Heavenly City it is related to the enjoyment of eternal peace. Thus, if we were irrational animals, our only aim would be the adjustment of the parts of the body in due proportion, and the quieting of the appetites – only, that is, the repose of the flesh, and an adequate supply of pleasures, so that bodily peace might promote the peace of the soul. For if bodily peace is lacking, the peace of the irrational soul is also hindered, because it cannot achieve the quieting of its appetites. But the two together promote that peace which is a mutual concord between soul and body, the peace of an ordered life and of health. For living creatures show their love of bodily peace by their avoidance of pain, and by their pursuit of pleasure to satisfy the demands of their appetites they demonstrate their love of peace of soul. In just the same way, by shunning death they indicate quite clearly how great is their love of the peace in which soul and body are harmoniously united.

But because there is in man a rational soul, he subordinates to the peace of the rational soul all that part of his nature which he shares with the beasts, so that he may engage in deliberate thought and act in accordance with this thought, so that he may thus exhibit that ordered agreement of cognition and action which we called the peace of the rational soul. For with this end in view he ought to wish to be spared the distress of pain and grief, the disturbances of desire, the dissolution of death, so that he may come to some profitable knowledge and may order his life and his moral standards in accordance with this knowledge. But he needs divine direction, which he may obey with resolution, and divine assistance that he may obey it freely, to prevent him from falling, in his enthusiasm for knowledge, a victim to some fatal error, through the weakness of the human mind. And so long as he is in this mortal body, he is a pilgrim in a foreign land, away from God; therefore he walks by faith, not by sight. That is why he views all peace, of body or of soul, or of both, in relation to that peace which exists between mortal man and immortal God, so that he may exhibit an ordered obedience in faith in subjection to the everlasting Law.

Now God, our master, teaches two chief precepts, love of God and love of neighbour; and in them man finds three objects for his love: God, himself, and his neighbour; and a man who loves God is not wrong in loving himself. It follows, therefore, that he will be concerned also that his neighbour should love God, since he is told to love his neighbour as himself, and the same is true of his concern for his wife, his children, for the members of his household, and for all other men, so far as is possible. And, for the same end, he will wish his neighbour to be concerned for him, if he happens to need that concern. For this reason he will be at peace, as far as lies in him, with all men, in that peace among men, that ordered harmony; and the basis of this order is the observance of two rules: first, to do no harm to anyone, and, secondly, to help everyone whenever possible. To begin with, therefore, a man has a responsibility for his own household – obviously, both in the order of nature and in the framework of human society, he has easier and more immediate contact with them; he can exercise his concern for them. That is why the Apostle says, 'Anyone who does not take care of his own people, especially those in his own household, is worse than an unbeliever – he is a renegade.' This is where domestic peace starts, the ordered harmony about giving and obeying orders among those who live in the same house. For the orders are given by those who are concerned for the interests of others; thus the husband gives orders to the wife, parents to children, masters to servants. While those who are the objects of this concern obey orders; for example, wives obey husbands, the children obey their parents, the servants their masters. But in the household of the just man who 'lives on the basis of faith' and who is still on pilgrimage, far from that Heavenly City, even those who give orders are the servants of those whom they appear to command. For they do not give orders because of a lust for domination but from a

23

dutiful concern for the interests of others, not with pride in taking precedence over others, but with compassion in taking care of others.

This relationship is prescribed by the order of nature, and it is in this situation that God created man. For he says, 'Let him have lordship over the fish of the sea, the birds of the sky . . . and all the reptiles that crawl on the earth.' He did not wish the rational being, made in his own image, to have dominion over any but irrational creatures, not man over man, but man over the beasts. Hence the first just men were set up as shepherds of flocks, rather than as kings of men, so that in this way also God might convey the message of what was required by the order of nature, and what was demanded by the deserts of sinners – for it is understood, of course, that the condition of slavery is justly imposed on the sinner. That is why we do not hear of a slave anywhere in the Scriptures until Noah, the just man, punished his son's sin with this word; and so that son deserved this name because of his misdeed, not because of his nature. The origin of the Latin word for slave, *servus*, is believed to be derived from the fact that those who by the laws of war could rightly be put to death by the conquerors, became *servi*, slaves, when they were preserved, receiving this name from their preservation. But even this enslavement could not have happened, if it were not for the deserts of sin. For even when a just war is fought it is in defence of his sin that the other side is contending; and victory, even when the victory falls to the wicked, is a humiliation visited on the conquered by divine judgement, either to correct or to punish their sins. We have a witness to this in Daniel, a man of God, who in captivity confesses to God his own sins and the sins of his people, and in devout grief testifies that they are the cause of that captivity. The first cause of slavery, then, is sin, whereby man was subjected to man in the condition of bondage; and this can only happen by the judgement of God, with whom there is no injustice, and who knows how to allot different punishments according to the deserts of the offenders.

Now, as our Lord above says, 'Everyone who commits sin is sin's slave', and that is why, though many devout men are slaves to unrighteous masters, yet the masters they serve are not themselves free men; 'for when a man is conquered by another he is also bound as a slave to his conqueror'. And obviously it is a happier lot to be slave to a human being than to a lust; and, in fact, the most pitiless domination that devastates the hearts of men, is that exercised by this very lust for domination, to mention no others. However, in that order of peace in which men are subordinate to other men, humility is as salutary for the servants as pride is harmful to the masters. And yet by nature, in the condition in which God created man, no man is the slave either of man or of sin. But it remains true that slavery as a punishment is also ordained by that law which enjoins the preservation of the order of nature, and forbids its disturbance; in fact, if nothing had been done to contravene that law, there would have been nothing to require the discipline of slavery as a punishment. That explains also the Apostle's admonition to slaves, that they should be subject to their masters, and serve them loyally and willingly. What he means is that if they cannot be set free by their masters, they themselves may thus make their slavery, in a sense, free, by serving not with the slyness of fear, but with the fidelity of affection, until all injustice disappears and all human lordship and power is annihilated, and God is all in all.

This being so, even though our righteous fathers had slaves, they so managed the peace of their households as to make a distinction between the situation of children and the condition of slaves in respect of the temporal goods of this life; and yet in the matter of the worship of God – in whom we must place our hope of everlasting goods – they were concerned, with equal affection, for all the members of their household. This is what the order of nature prescribes, so that this is the source of the name *paterfamilias*, a name that has become so generally used that even those who exercise unjust rule rejoice to be called by this title. On the other hand, those who are genuine 'fathers of their household' are concerned for the welfare of all in their households in respect of the worship and service of God, as if they were all their children, longing and praying that they may come to the heavenly home, where it will not be a necessary duty to give orders to men, because it will no longer be a necessary duty to be concerned for the welfare of those who are already in the felicity of that immortal state. But until that home is reached, the fathers have an obligation to exercise the authority of masters greater than the duty of slaves to put up with their condition as servants.

However, if anyone in the household is, through his disobedience, an enemy to the domestic peace, he is reproved by a word, or by a blow, or any other kind of punishment that is just and legitimate, to the extent allowed by human society; but this is for the benefit of the offender, intended to readjust him to the domestic peace from which he had broken away. For just as it is not an act of kindness to help a man, when the effect of the help is to make him lose a greater good, so it is not a blameless act to spare a man, when by so doing you let him fall into a greater sin. Hence the duty of anyone who would be blameless includes not only doing no harm to anyone but also restraining a man from sin or punishing his sin, so that either the man who is chastised may be corrected by his experience, or others may be deterred by

25

his example. Now a man's house ought to be the beginning, or rather a small component part of the city, and every beginning is directed to some end of its own kind, and every component part contributes to the completeness of the whole of which it forms a part. The implication is quite apparent, that domestic peace contributes to the peace of the city – that is, the ordered harmony of those who live together in a house in the matter of giving and obeying orders, contributes to the ordered harmony concerning authority and obedience obtaining among the citizens. Consequently it is fitting that the father of a household should take his rules from the law of the city, and govern his household in such a way that it fits in with the peace of the city.

But a household of human beings whose life is not based on faith is in pursuit of an earthly peace based on the things belonging to this temporal life, and on its advantages, whereas a household of human beings whose life is based on faith looks forward to the blessings which are promised as eternal in the future, making use of earthly and temporal things like a pilgrim in a foreign land, who does not let himself be taken in by them or distracted from his course towards God, but rather treats them as supports which help him more easily to bear the burden of 'the corruptible body which weighs heavy on the soul'; they must on no account be allowed to increase the load. Thus both kinds of men and both kinds of households alike make use of the things essential for this mortal life; but each has its own very different end in making use of them. So also the earthly city, whose life is not based on faith, aims at an earthly peace, and it limits the harmonious agreement of citizens concerning the giving and obeying of orders to the establishment of a kind of compromise between human wills about the things relevant to mortal life. In contrast, the Heavenly City – or rather that part of it which is on pilgrimage in this condition of mortality, and which lives on the basis of faith – must needs make use of this peace also, until this mortal state, for which this kind of peace is essential, passes away. And therefore, it leads what we may call a life of captivity in this earthly city as in a foreign land, although it has already received the promise of redemption, and the gift of the Spirit as a kind of pledge of it; and yet it does not hesitate to obey the laws of the earthly city by which those things which are designed for the support of this mortal life are regulated; and the purpose of this obedience is that, since this mortal condition is shared by both cities, a harmony may be preserved between them in things that are relevant to this condition.

But this earthly city has had some philosophers belonging to it whose theories are rejected by the teaching inspired by God. Either led astray by their own speculation or deluded by demons, these thinkers reached the belief that there are many gods who must be won over to serve human ends, and also that they have, as it were, different departments with different responsibilities attached. Thus the body is the department of one god, the mind that of another; and within the body itself, one god is in charge of the head, another of the neck and so on with each of the separate members. Similarly, within the mind, one is responsible for natural ability, another for learning, another for anger, another for lust, and in the accessories of life there are separate gods over the departments of flocks, grain, wine, oil, forests, coinage, navigation, war and victory, marriage, birth, fertility, and so on. The Heavenly City, in contrast, knows only one God as the object of worship, and decrees, with faithful devotion, that he only is to be served with that service which the Greeks call *latreia*, which is due to God alone. And the result of this difference has been that the Heavenly City could not have laws of religion common with the earthly city, and in defence of her religious laws she was bound to dissent from those who thought differently and to prove a burdensome nuisance to them. Thus she had to endure their anger and hatred, and the assaults of persecution; until at length that City shattered the morale of her adversaries by the terror inspired by her numbers, and by the help she continually received from God.

While this Heavenly City, therefore, is on pilgrimage in this world, she calls out citizens from all nations and so collects a society of aliens, speaking all languages. She takes no account of any difference in customs, laws, and institutions, by which earthly peace is achieved and preserved – not that she annuls or abolishes any of those, rather, she maintains them and follows them (for whatever divergences there are among the diverse nations, those institutions have one single aim – earthly peace), provided that no hindrance is presented thereby to the religion which teaches that the one supreme and true God is to be worshipped. Thus even the Heavenly City in her pilgrimage here on earth makes use of the earthly peace and defends and seeks the compromise between human wills in respect of the provisions relevant to the mortal nature of man, so far as may be permitted without detriment to true religion and piety. In fact, that City relates the earthly peace to the heavenly peace, which is so truly peaceful that it should be regarded as the only peace deserving the name, at least in respect of the rational creation; for this peace is the perfectly ordered and completely harmonious fellowship in the enjoyment of God, and of each other in God. When we arrive at that state of peace, there will be no longer a life that ends in death, but a life that is life in sure and sober truth; there will be no animal body to 'weigh down the soul' in its process of corruption; there will be a spiritual body with no cravings, a body subdued in every part to the will. This peace the Heavenly City possesses in faith while on its pilgrimage, and it lives a life of righteousness, based on this faith, having the attainment of that peace in view in every good action it performs in relation to God, and in relation to a neighbour, since the life of a city is inevitably a social life.

(Bk 19, chs 13–17)

Justice is found where God, the one supreme God, rules an obedient City according to his grace, forbidding sacrifice to any being save himself alone; and where in consequence the soul rules the body in all men who belong to this City and obey God, and the reason faithfully rules the vices in a lawful system of subordination; so that just as the individual righteous man lives on the basis of faith which is active in love, so the association, or people, of righteous men lives on the same basis of faith, active in love, the love with which a man loves God as God ought to be loved, and loves his neighbour as himself. But where this justice does not exist, there is certainly no 'association of men united by a common sense of right and by a community of interest'. Therefore there is no commonwealth; for where there is no 'people', there is no 'weal of the people'.

If, on the other hand, another definition than this is found for a 'people', for example, if one should say, 'A people is the association of a multitude of rational beings united by a common agreement on the objects of their love', then it follows that to observe the character of a particular people we must examine the objects of its love. And yet, whatever those objects, if it is the association of a multitude not of animals but of rational beings, and is united by a common agreement about the objects of its love, then there is no absurdity in applying to it the title of a 'people'. And, obviously, the better the objects of this agreement, the better the people; the worse the objects of this love, the worse the people. By this definition of ours, the Roman people is a people and its estate is indubitably a commonwealth. But as for the objects of that people's love – both in the earliest times and in subsequent periods – and the morality of that people as it proceeded to bloody strife of parties and then to the social and civil wars, and corrupted and disrupted that very unity which is, as it were, the health of a people – for all this we have the witness of history; and I have had a great deal to say about it in my preceding books. And yet I shall not make that a reason for asserting that a people is not really a people or that a state is not a commonwealth, so long as there remains an association of some kind or other between a multitude of rational beings united by a common agreement on the objects of its love. However, what I have said about

the Roman people and the Roman commonwealth I must be understood to have said and felt about those of the Athenians and of any
other Greeks, or of that former Babylon of the Assyrians, when they
exercised imperial rule, whether on a small or a large scale, in their
commonwealths – and indeed about any other nation whatsoever. For
God is not the ruler of the city of the impious, because it disobeys his
commandment that sacrifice should be offered to himself alone. The
purpose of this law was that in that city the soul should rule over the
body and reason over the vicious elements, in righteousness and faith.
And because God does not rule there the general characteristic of that
city is that it is devoid of true justice.

The fact is that the soul may appear to rule the body and the reason to
govern the vicious elements in the most praiseworthy fashion; and yet
if the soul and reason do not serve God as God himself has commanded that he should be served, then they do not in any way exercise
the right kind of rule over the body and the vicious propensities. For
what kind of a mistress over the body and the vices can a mind be that
is ignorant of the true God and is not subjected to his rule, but instead
is prostituted to the corrupting influence of vicious demons? Thus the
virtues which the mind imagines it possesses, by means of which it
rules the body and the vicious elements, are themselves vices rather
than virtues, if the mind does not bring them into relation with God in
order to achieve anything whatsoever and to maintain that achievement.
For although the virtues are reckoned by some people to be genuine
and honourable when they are related only to themselves and are
sought for no other end, even then they are puffed up and proud, and
so are to be accounted vices rather than virtues. For just as it is not
something derived from the physical body itself that gives life to that
body, but something above it, so it is not something that comes from
man, but something above man, that makes his life blessed; and this is
true not only of man but of every heavenly dominion and power
whatsoever.

Thus, as the soul is the life of the physical body, so God is the blessed-
ness of man's life. As the holy Scriptures of the Hebrews say, 'Blessed
is the people, whose God is the Lord.' It follows that a people alienated
from that God must be wretched. Yet even such a people loves a peace
of its own, which is not to be rejected; but it will not possess it in
the end, because it does not make good use of it before the end.
Meanwhile, however, it is important for us also that this people should
possess this peace in this life, since so long as the two cities are inter-
mingled we also make use of the peace of Babylon – although the

People of God is by faith set free from Babylon, so that in the mean-time they are only pilgrims in the midst of her. That is why the Apostle instructs the Church to pray for kings of that city and those in high positions, adding these words: 'that we may lead a quiet and peaceful life with all devotion and love'. And when the prophet Jeremiah pre-dicted to the ancient People of God the coming captivity, and bade them, by God's inspiration, to go obediently to Babylon, serving God even by their patient endurance, he added his own advice that prayers should be offered for Babylon, 'because in her peace is your peace' – meaning, of course, the temporal peace of the meantime, which is shared by good and bad alike.

In contrast, the peace which is our special possession is ours even in this life, a peace with God through faith; and it will be ours for ever, a peace with God through open vision. But peace here and now, whether the peace shared by all men or our own special possession, is such that it affords a solace for our wretchedness rather than the joy of blessed-ness. Our righteousness itself, too, though genuine, in virtue of the genuine Ultimate Good to which it is referred, is nevertheless only such as to consist in the forgiveness of sins rather than in the perfection of virtues. The evidence for this is in the prayer of the whole City of God on pilgrimage in the world, which, as we know, cries out to God through the lips of all its members: 'Forgive us our debts, as we forgive our debtors.' And this prayer is not effective for those whose 'faith, without works, is dead' but only for those whose 'faith is put into action through love'. For such a prayer is needed by righteous men because the reason, though subjected to God, does not have complete command over the vices in this mortal state and in the 'corruptible body which weighs heavy on the soul'. In fact, even though command be exercised over the vices it is assuredly not by any means without a conflict. And even when a man fights well and even gains the mastery by conquering and subduing such foes, still in this situation of weakness something is all too likely to creep in to cause sin, if not in hasty action, at least in a casual remark or a fleeting thought.

For this reason there is no perfect peace so long as command is exercised over the vicious propensities, because the battle is fraught with peril while those vices that resist are being reduced to submission, while those which have been overcome are not yet triumphed over in peaceful security, but are repressed under a rule still troubled by anxieties. Thus we are in the midst of these temptations, about which we find this brief saying amongst the divine oracles: 'Is a man's life on earth anything but temptation?'; and who can presume that his life is of such a kind that he has no need to say to God, 'Forgive us our debts', unless he is a man of overwhelming conceit, not a truly great man, but one puffed up and swollen with pride, who is with justice resisted by him who gives grace to the humble, as it says in the Scriptures, 'God resists the proud, but he gives his favour to the humble.' In this life, therefore, justice in each individual exists when God rules and man obeys, when the mind rules the body and reason governs the vices even when they rebel, either by subduing them or by resisting them, while from God himself favour is sought for good deeds and pardon for offences, and thanks are duly offered to him for benefits received. But in that ultimate peace, to which this justice should be related, and for the attainment of which this justice is to be maintained, our nature will be healed by immortality and incorruption and will have no perverted elements, and nothing at all, in ourselves or any other, will be in conflict with any one of us. And so reason will not need to rule the vices, since there will be no vices, but God will hold sway over man, and the soul over the body, and in this state our delight and facility in obeying will be matched by our felicity in living and reigning. There, for each and every one, this state will be eternal, and its eternity will be assured; and for that reason the peace of this blessedness, or the blessedness of this peace, will be the Supreme Good.

(Bk 19, chs 23–7)

Source: Augustine, *The City of God*, tr. H. Bettenson, Penguin, 1972

Further reading

Detailed historical background is to be found in Frend's *The Rise of Christianity*. Succinct accounts of the intellectual scene are provided by the articles of Chadwick and Markus in Burns's *Mediaeval Political Thought*. A more detailed discussion is contained in the scholarly works by Cochrane and by Dvornik. On Augustine, read the splendid biography by Brown and the two studies of his political thought by Markus and by Deane.

Chapter Three

MEDIEVAL CHRISTIANITY

Introduction

With the collapse of the Roman Empire and the onset of the Dark Ages, the power of the Church, the main organ of social and cultural cohesion, increased substantially. The Church became, in the words of Hobbes, 'the ghost of the Roman Empire, sitting crowned upon the grave thereof'. The most striking example of this ecclesiastical supremacy was the public humiliation and submission of the Emperor Henry IV to Pope Gregory VII at Canossa in 1077. The power of the medieval papacy reached its climax with the reign of Innocent III (1198–1216) whose forceful personality and genius in organization enabled him briefly to put into practice his view that 'no king can rightly reign unless he devoutly serve Christ's vicar'.

The most reflective account of the relation of religious to secular authority in this period is that of Thomas Aquinas. Strongly influenced by the thought of Aristotle, Aquinas saw each sphere of human activity as enjoying its own autonomy, which was, nevertheless, not complete: 'The spiritual power and the temporal power both derive from divine power ... In things which concern civic goods, it is better to obey the secular than the spiritual power.' He favoured a balance of monarchy, aristocracy and democracy which, it has been claimed, is not unlike the relationship of executive, judicial and legislative power in the United States. This idea of balance ran through all Aquinas's views on major political questions. He advocated the idea of a just price as a combination of a just wage and a just profit with production for use and only secondarily for profit, and was firm about the duty of those in authority to make provision for those in need. His comments here are obviously relevant to the contemporary debate about the role of the State in ensuring the welfare of its citizens – comments which have been elaborated in the twentieth century through the social teaching of the Catholic Church. Similar contemporary relevance can be found in Aquinas's teaching on the limits of the obligation to obey unjust laws and the circumstances which could justify tyrannicide – in other words, under what conditions violence is justified to obtain legitimate political ends. Finally, Aquinas attempted to codify the principles of a 'just war', principles which formed the framework for the recent debate about the moral justification of the Gulf War.

The synthesis of Aquinas, however, proved, like all balances, to be vulnerable to the forces of history. In the early fourteenth century Boniface VIII proclaimed in his *Unam Sanctum* the two swords of the New Testament to be the spiritual and temporal powers with the latter clearly subordinate to the former. This arrogance inevitably produced a profound reaction supported by the first stirrings of ideas of individual rights and the birth of the nation-state. These ideas find expression in the writings of such thinkers as William of Ockham, who advocated a radical separation of the Church from political concerns and denied the Pope any temporal authority. They were carried further by Marsilius of Padua who maintained that the State, which derived its authority ultimately from the people, was the supreme power in society to which the Church should be subordinate. These attitudes were to find their fulfilment two centuries later in the Reformation.

Aquinas: Summa Theologiae

Should human law be framed for the community
rather than for the individual?
Objection 1. It would seem that human law should be framed not for the community, but rather for the individual. For the Philosopher says that 'the legal just . . . includes all particular acts of legislation . . . and all those matters which are the subject of decrees', which are also individual matters, since decrees are framed about individual actions. Therefore law is framed not only for the community, but also for the individual.

Obj. 2. Further, law is the director of human acts . . . But human acts are about individual matters. Therefore human laws should be framed, not for the community, but rather for the individual.

Obj. 3. Further, law is a rule and measure of human acts . . . But a measure should be most certain, as stated in Metaphysics x. Since therefore in human acts no general proposition can be so certain as not to fail in some individual cases, it seems that laws should be framed not in general but for individual cases.

On the contrary, the jurist says that 'laws should be made to suit the majority of instances; and they are not framed according to what may possibly happen in an individual case'.

I answer that, whatever is for an end should be proportionate to that end. Now the end of law is the common good; because, as Isidore says, 'law should be framed, not for any private benefit, but for the common good of all the citizens'. Hence human laws should be proportionate to the common good. Now the common good comprises many things. Wherefore law should take account of many things, as to persons, as to matters, and as to times. Because the community of the state is composed of many persons; and its good is procured by many actions; nor is it established to endure for only a short time, but to last for all time by the citizens succeeding one another, as Augustine says.

Reply Obj. 1. The Philosopher divides the legal just, i.e., positive law, into three parts. For some things are laid down simply in a general way: and these are the general laws. Of these he says that 'the legal is that which originally was a matter of indifference, but which, when enacted, is so no longer': as the fixing of the ransom of a captive. Some things affect the community in one respect, and individuals in another. These are called 'privileges', i.e., 'private laws', as it were, because they regard private persons, although their power extends to many matters; and in regard to these, he adds, 'and further, all particular acts of legislation'. Other matters are legal, not through being laws, but through being applications of general laws to particular cases: such are decrees which have the force of law; and in regard to these, he adds 'all matters subject to decrees'.

Reply Obj. 2. A principle of direction should be applicable to many; wherefore the Philosopher says that all things belonging to one genus, are measured by one, which is the principle in that genus. For if there were as many rules or measures as there are things measured or ruled, they would cease to be of use, since their use consists in being applicable to many things. Hence law would be of no use, if it did not extend further than to one single act. Because the decrees of prudent men are made for the purpose of directing individual actions; whereas law is a general precept.

Reply Obj. 3. 'We must not seek the same degree of certainty in all things.' Consequently in contingent matters, such as natural and human things, it is enough for a thing to be certain, as being true in the greater number of instances, though at times and less frequently it fail.

Does human law bind a man in conscience?

Objection 1. It would seem that human law does not bind a man in conscience. For an inferior power has no jurisdiction in a court of higher power. But the power of man, which frames human law, is beneath the divine power. Therefore human law cannot impose its precept in a divine court, such as is the court of conscience.

Obj. 2. Further, the judgment of conscience depends chiefly on the commandments of God. But sometimes God's commandments are made void by human laws, according to Matt. 15.6: 'You have made void the commandment of God for your tradition.' Therefore human law does not bind a man in conscience.

Obj. 3. Further, human laws often bring loss of character and injury on man, according to Isa. 10.1ff.: 'Woe to them that make wicked laws, and when they write, write injustice, to oppress the poor in judgment, and do violence to the cause of the humble of My people.' But it is lawful for anyone to avoid oppression and violence. Therefore human laws do not bind man in conscience.

On the contrary, it is written (1 Pet. 2.19): 'This is thanksworthy, if for conscience . . . a man endure sorrows, suffering wrongfully.'

I answer that, laws framed by man are either just or unjust. If they be just, they have the power of binding in conscience, from the eternal law whence they are derived, according to Prov. 8.15: 'By Me kings reign, and lawgivers decree just things.' Now laws are said to be just, both from the end, when, to wit, they are ordained to the common good, and from their author, that is to say, when the law that is made does not exceed the power of the lawgiver, and from their form, when, to wit, burdens are laid on the subjects, according to an equality of proportion and with a view to the common good. For, since one man is a part of the community, each man, in all that he is and has, belongs to the community; just as a part, in all that it is, belongs to the whole; wherefore nature inflicts a loss on the part, in order to save the whole; so that on this account, such laws as these, which impose proportionate burdens, are just and binding in conscience, and are legal laws.

On the other hand laws may be unjust in two ways: first, by being contrary to human good, through being opposed to the things mentioned above – either in respect of the end, as when an authority imposes on his subjects burdensome laws, conducive, not to the common good, but rather to his own cupidity or vainglory – or in respect of the author, as when a man makes a law that goes beyond the power committed to him – or in respect of the form, as when burdens are imposed unequally on the community, although with a view to the common good. The like are acts of violence rather than laws; because, as Augustine says, 'a law that is not just, seems to be no law at all'. Wherefore such laws do not bind in conscience, except perhaps in order to avoid scandal or disturbance, for which cause a man should even yield his right, according to Matt. 5.40, 41: 'If a man . . . take away thy coat, let go thy cloak also unto him; and whosoever will force thee one mile, go with him other two.'

Secondly, laws may be unjust through being opposed to the divine good: such are the laws of tyrants inducing to idolatry, or to anything else contrary to the divine law: and laws of this kind must nowise be observed, because, as stated in Acts 5.29, 'we ought to obey God rather than men'.

Reply Obj. 1. As the Apostle says (Rom. 8.1, 2), all human power is from God . . . 'therefore he that resisteth the power', in matters that are within its scope, 'resisteth the ordinance of God'; so that he becomes guilty according to his conscience.

Reply Obj. 2. This argument is true of laws that are contrary to the commandments of God, which is beyond the scope of (human) power. Wherefore in such matters human law should not be obeyed.

Reply Obj. 3. This argument is true of a law that inflicts unjust hurt on its subjects. The power that man holds from God does not extend to this: wherefore neither in such matters is man bound to obey the law, provided he avoid giving scandal or inflicting a more grievous hurt.

Are all subject to the law?

Objection 1. It would seem that not all are subject to the law. For those alone are subject to a law for whom a law is made. But the Apostle says (1 Tim. 1.9): 'The law is not made for the just man.' Therefore the just are not subject to the law.

Obj. 2. Further, Pope Urban says: 'He that is guided by a private law need not for any reason be bound by the public law.' Now all spiritual men are led by the private law of the Holy Ghost, for they are the sons of God, of whom it is said (Rom. 8.14): 'Whosoever are led by the Spirit of God, they are the sons of God.' Therefore not all men are subject to human law.

Obj. 3. Further, the jurist says that 'the sovereign is exempt from the laws'. But he that is exempt from the law is not bound thereby. Therefore not all are subject to the law.

On the contrary, the Apostle says (Rom. 8.1): 'Let every soul be subject to the higher powers.' But subjection to a power seems to imply subjection to the laws framed by that power. Therefore all men should be subject to human law.

I answer that, the notion of law contains two things; first, that it is a rule of human acts; secondly, that it has coercive power. Wherefore a man may be subject to law in two ways. First, as the regulated is subject to the regulator: and, in this way, whoever is subject to a power, is subject to the law framed by that power. But it may happen in two ways that one is not subject to a power. In one way, by being altogether free from its authority: hence the subjects of one city or kingdom are not bound by the laws of the sovereign of another city or kingdom, since they are not subject to his authority. In another way, by being under a yet higher law; thus the subject of a proconsul should be ruled by his command, but not in those matters in which the subject receives his orders from the emperor: for in these matters, he is not bound by the mandate of the lower authority, since he is directed by that of a higher. In this way, one who is simply subject to a law, may not be subject thereto in certain matters, in respect of which he is ruled by a higher law.

Secondly, a man is said to be subject to a law as the coerced is subject to the coercer. In this way the virtuous and righteous are not subject to the law, but only the wicked. Because coercion and violence are contrary to the will: but the will of the good is in harmony with the law, whereas the will of the wicked is discordant from it. Wherefore in this sense the good are not subject to the law, but only the wicked.

Reply Obj. 1. This argument is true of subjection by way of coercion: for, in this way, 'the law is not made for the just men': because 'they are a law to themselves', since they 'shew the work of the law written in their hearts', as the Apostle says (Rom. 2.14, 15). Consequently the law does not enforce itself upon them as it does on the wicked.

Reply Obj. 2. The law of the Holy Ghost is above all law framed by man: and therefore spiritual men, in so far as they are led by the law of the Holy Ghost, are not subject to the law in those matters that are inconsistent with the guidance of the Holy Ghost. Nevertheless the very fact that spiritual men are subject to law, is due to the leading of the Holy Ghost, according to 1 Pet. 2.13: 'Be ye subject . . . to every human creature for God's sake.'

Reply Obj. 3. The sovereign is said to be 'exempt from the law' as to its coercive power; since, properly speaking, no man is coerced by himself, and law has no coercive power save from the authority of the sovereign. Thus then is the sovereign said to be exempt from the law, because none is competent to pass sentence on him, if he acts against the law. Wherefore on Ps. 50.6: 'To Thee only have I sinned', a gloss says that 'there is no man who can judge the deeds of a king'. But as to the directive force of law, the sovereign is subject to the law by his own will, according to the statement that 'whatever law a man makes for another, he should keep himself'. And a wise authority says: 'Obey the law that thou makest thyself.' Moreover the Lord reproaches those who 'say and do not'; and who 'bind heavy burdens and lay them on men's shoulders, but with a finger of their own they will not move them' (Matt. 23.3, 4). Hence, in the judgment of God, the sovereign is not exempt from the law, as to its directive force; but he should fulfil it of his own free-will and not of constraint. Again the sovereign is above the law, in so far as, when it is expedient, he can change the law, and dispense in it according to time and place.

May he who is under a law act beside the letter of the law?

Objection 1. It seems that he who is subject to a law may not act beside the letter of the law. For Augustine says: 'Although men judge about temporal laws when they make them, yet when once they are made they must pass judgment not on them, but according to them.' But if anyone disregarded the letter of the law, saying that he observes the intention of the lawgiver, he seems to pass judgment on the law. Therefore it is not right for one who is under a law to disregard the letter of the law, in order to observe the intention of the lawgiver.

Obj. 2. Further, he alone is competent to interpret the law who can make the law. But those who are subject to the law cannot make the law. Therefore they have no right to interpret the intention of the lawgiver, but should always act according to the letter of the law.

Obj. 3. Further, every wise man knows how to explain his intention by words. But those who framed the laws should be reckoned wise: for Wisdom says (Prov. 8.15): 'By Me kings reign, and lawgivers decree just things.' Therefore we should not judge of the intention of the lawgiver otherwise than by the words of the law.

On the contrary, Hilary says: 'The meaning of what is said is according to the motive for saying it: because things are not subject to speech, but speech to things.' Therefore we should take account of the motive of the lawgiver, rather than to his very words.

I answer that, every law is directed to the common weal of men, and derives the force and nature of law accordingly. Hence the jurist says: 'By no reason of law, or favour of equity, is it allowable for us to interpret harshly, and render burdensome, those useful measures which have been enacted for the welfare of man.' Now it happens often that the observance of some point of law conduces to the common weal in the majority of instances, and yet, in some cases, is very hurtful. Since then the lawgiver cannot have in view every single case, he shapes the law according to what happens most frequently, by directing his attention to the common good. Wherefore if a case arise wherein the observance of that law would be hurtful to the general welfare, it should not be observed. For instance, suppose that in a besieged city it be an established law that the gates of the city are to be kept closed, this is good for public welfare as a general rule: but, if it were to happen that the enemy are in pursuit of certain citizens, who are defenders of the city, it would be a great loss to the city, if the gates were not opened to them: and so in that case the gates ought to be opened, contrary to the letter of the law, in order to maintain the common weal, which the lawgiver had in view.

Nevertheless it must be noted, that if the observance of the law according to the letter does not involve any sudden risk needing instant remedy, it is not competent for everyone to expound what is useful and what is not useful to the state: those alone can do this who are in authority, and who, on account of suchlike cases, have the power to dispense from the laws. If, however, the peril be so sudden as not to allow of the delay involved by referring the matter to authority, the mere necessity brings with it a dispensation, since necessity knows no law.

Reply Obj. 1. He who in a case of necessity acts beside the letter of the law, does not judge of the law; but of a particular case in which he sees that the letter of the law is not to be observed.

Reply Obj. 2. He who follows the intention of the lawgiver, does not interpret the law simply; but in a case in which it is evident, by reason of the manifest harm, that the lawgiver intended otherwise. For if it be a matter of doubt, he must either act according to the letter of the law, or consult those in power.

Reply Obj. 3. No man is so wise as to be able to take account of every single case; wherefore he is not able sufficiently to express in words all those things that are suitable for the end he has in view. And even if a lawgiver were able to take all the cases into consideration, he ought not to mention them all, in order to avoid confusion: but should frame the law according to that which is of most common occurrence.

(Ia IIae, Q.96, arts. 1, 4, 5 and 6)

Is sedition a special sin distinct from other sins?

Objection 1. It would seem that sedition is not a special sin distinct from other sins. For, according to Isidore, 'a seditious man is one who sows dissent among minds, and begets discord'. Now, by provoking the commission of a sin, a man sins by no other kind of sin than that which he provoked. Therefore it seems that sedition is not a special sin distinct from discord.

Obj. 2. Further, sedition denotes a kind of division. Now schism takes its name from scission. Therefore, seemingly, the sin of sedition is not distinct from that of schism.

Obj. 3. Further, every special sin that is distinct from other sins, is either a capital vice, or arises from some capital vice. Now sedition is reckoned neither among the capital vices, nor among those vices which arise from them, as appears from *Moralium* 31.45, where both kinds of vice are enumerated. Therefore sedition is not a special sin, distinct from other sins.

On the contrary, seditions are mentioned as distinct from other sins (2 Cor. 12.20).

I answer that, sedition is a special sin, having something in common with war and strife, and differing somewhat from them. It has something in common with them, in so far as it implies a certain antagonism, and it differs from them in two points. First, because war and strife denote actual aggression on either side, whereas sedition may be said to denote either actual aggression, or the preparation for such aggression. Hence a gloss on 2 Cor. 12.20 says that 'seditions are tumults tending to fight', when, to wit, a number of people make preparations with the intention of fighting. Secondly, they differ in that war is, properly speaking, carried on against external foes, being as it were between one people and another, whereas strife is between one individual and another, or between few people on one side and few on the other, while sedition, in its proper sense, is between the mutually dissentient parts of one people, as when one part of the state rises in tumult against another part. Wherefore, since sedition is opposed to a special kind of good, namely the unity and peace of a people, it is a special kind of sin.

Reply Obj. 1. A seditious man is one who incites others to sedition, and since sedition denotes a kind of discord, it follows that a seditious man is one who creates discord, not of any kind, but between the parts of a multitude. And the sin of sedition is not only in him who sows discord, but also in those who dissent from one another inordinately.

Reply Obj. 2. Sedition differs from schism in two respects. First, because schism is opposed to the spiritual unity of the multitude, viz. ecclesiastical unity, whereas sedition is contrary to the temporal or secular unity of the multitude, for instance of a city or kingdom. Secondly, schism does not imply any preparation for a material fight as sedition does, but only a spiritual dissent.

Reply Obj. 3. Sedition, like schism, is contained under discord, since each is a kind of discord, not between individuals, but between the parts of a multitude.

Is sedition always a mortal sin?

Objection 1. It would seem that sedition is not always a mortal sin. For sedition denotes 'a tumult tending to fight', according to the gloss quoted above. But fighting is not always a mortal sin, indeed it is sometimes just and lawful. Much more, therefore, can sedition be without a mortal sin.

Obj. 2. Further, sedition is a kind of discord. Now discord can be without mortal sin, and sometimes without any sin at all. Therefore sedition can be also.

Obj. 3. Further, it is praiseworthy to deliver a multitude from a tyrannical rule. Yet this cannot easily be done without some dissension in the multitude, if one part of the multitude seeks to retain the tyrant, while the rest strive to dethrone him. Therefore there can be sedition without mortal sin.

On the contrary, the Apostle forbids seditions together with other things that are mortal sins (2 Cor. 12.20).

I answer that, sedition is contrary to the unity of the multitude, viz. the people of a city or kingdom. Now Augustine says that 'wise men understand the word people to designate not any crowd of persons, but the assembly of those who are united together in fellowship recognized by law and for the common good'. Wherefore it is evident that the unity to which sedition is opposed is the unity of law and common good: whence it follows manifestly that sedition is opposed to justice and the common good. Therefore by reason of its genus it is a mortal sin, and its gravity will be all the greater according as the common good which it assails surpasses the private good which is assailed by strife.

Accordingly the sin of sedition is first and chiefly in its authors, who sin most grievously; and secondly it is in those who are led by them to disturb the common good. Those, however, who defend the common good, and withstand the seditious party, are not themselves seditious, even as neither is a man to be called quarrelsome because he defends himself.

Reply Obj. 1. It is lawful to fight, provided it be for the common good. But sedition runs counter to the common good of the multitude, so that it is always a mortal sin.

Reply Obj. 2. Discord from what is not evidently good, may be without sin, but discord from what is evidently good, cannot be without sin: and sedition is discord of this kind, for it is contrary to the unity of the multitude, which is a manifest good.

Reply Obj. 3. A tyrannical government is not just, because it is directed, not to the common good, but to the private good of the ruler, as the Philosopher states. Consequently there is no sedition in disturbing a government of this kind, unless indeed the tyrant's rule be disturbed so inordinately, that his subjects suffer greater harm from the consequent disturbance than from the tyrant's government. Indeed it is the tyrant rather that is guilty of sedition, since he encourages discord and sedition among his subjects, that he may lord over them more securely; for this is tyranny, being conducive to the private good of the ruler, and to the injury of the multitude.

(IIa IIae, Q.42, arts. 1 and 2)

Are subjects bound to obey their superiors in all things?

Objection 1. It seems that subjects are bound to obey their superiors in all things. For the Apostle says: 'Children, obey your parents in all things'; and farther on: 'Servants, obey in all things your masters according to the flesh.' Therefore in like manner other subjects are bound to obey their superiors in all things.

Obj. 2. Further, superiors stand between God and their subjects, according to Deuteronomy 5.5: 'I was the mediator and stood between the Lord and you at that time, to show you His words.' Now there is no going from extreme to extreme, except through that which stands between. Therefore the commands of a superior must be esteemed the commands of God, wherefore the Apostle says: 'You . . . received me as an angel of God, even as Christ Jesus'; and: 'When you had received of us the word of the hearing of God, you received it, not as the word of men, but, as it is indeed, the word of God.' Therefore as man is bound to obey God in all things, so is he bound to obey his superiors.

Obj. 3. Further, just as religious in making their profession take vows of chastity and poverty, so do they also vow obedience. Now a religious is bound to observe chastity and poverty in all things. Therefore he is also bound to obey in all things.

On the contrary, it is written: 'We ought to obey God rather than men.' Now sometimes the things commanded by a superior are against God. Therefore superiors are not to be obeyed in all things.

I answer that, he who obeys is moved at the bidding of the person who commands him by a certain necessity of justice, even as a natural thing is moved through the power of its mover by a natural necessity. That a natural thing be not moved by its mover may happen in two ways. First on account of a hindrance arising from the stronger power of some other mover; thus wood is not burned by fire if a stronger force of water intervene. Secondly, through lack of order in the movable with regard to its mover, since, though it is subject to the latter's action in one respect, yet it is not subject thereto in every respect. Thus a humour is sometimes subject to the action of heat as regards being heated, but not as regards being dried up or consumed. In like manner there are two reasons for which a subject may not be bound to obey his superior in all things. First on account of the command of a higher power. For as a gloss says on Romans 13.2, 'They that resist the power, resist the ordinance of God. If a commissioner issue an order, are you to comply if it is contrary to the bidding of the proconsul? Again if the proconsul command one thing and the emperor another, will you hesitate to disregard the former and serve the latter? Therefore if the emperor commands one thing and God another, you must disregard the former and obey God.' Secondly, a subject is not bound to obey his superior if the latter command him to do something wherein he is not subject to him. For Seneca says: 'It is wrong to suppose that slavery falls upon the whole man; for the better part of him is excepted. His body is subjected and assigned to his master, but his soul is his own.' Consequently in matters touching the internal movement of the will man is not bound to obey his fellow man, but God alone.

Nevertheless man is bound to obey his fellow man in things that have to be done externally by means of the body; and yet, since by nature all men are equal, he is not bound to obey another man in matters touching the nature of the body, for instance, in those relating to the support of his body or the begetting of his children. Wherefore servants are not bound to obey their masters, nor children their parents, in the question of contracting marriage or of remaining in the state of virginity or the like. But in matters concerning the disposal of actions and human affairs a subject is bound to obey his superior within the sphere of his authority; for instance, a soldier must obey his general in matters relating to war, a servant his master in matters touching the execution of the duties of his service, a son his father in matters relating to the conduct of his life and the care of the household, and so forth.

Reply Obj. 1. When the Apostle says 'in all things', he refers to matters within the sphere of a father's or master's authority.

Reply Obj. 2. Man is subject to God simply as regards all things, both internal and external, wherefore he is bound to obey him in all things. On the other hand inferiors are not subject to their superiors in all things, but only in certain things and in a particular way, in respect of which the superior stands between God and his subjects; whereas in respect of other matters the subject is immediately under God, by whom he is taught either by the natural or by the written law.

Reply Obj. 3. Religious profess obedience as to the regular mode of life, in respect of which they are subject to their superiors; wherefore they are bound to obey in those matters only which may belong to the regular mode of life, and this obedience suffices for salvation. If they be willing to obey even in other matters, this will belong to the super-abundance of perfection, provided, however, such things be not contrary to God or to the rule they profess, for obedience in this case would be unlawful.

Accordingly we may distinguish a threefold obedience: one, sufficient for salvation and consisting in obeying when one is bound to obey; secondly, perfect obedience, which obeys in all things lawful; thirdly, indiscreet obedience, which obeys even in matters unlawful.

Are Christians bound to obey the secular power?

Objection 1. It seems that Christians are not bound to obey the secular power. For a gloss on Matthew 17.25, 'Then the children are free', says: 'If in every kingdom the children of the king who holds sway over that kingdom are free, then the children of that King, under whose sway are all kingdoms, should be free in every kingdom.' Now Christians, by their faith in Christ, are made children of God, according to John 1.12: 'He gave them power to be made the sons of God, to them that believe in His name.' Therefore they are not bound to obey the secular power.

Obj. 2. Further, it is written: 'You . . . are become dead to the law by the body of Christ', and the law mentioned here is the divine law of the Old Testament. Now human law whereby men are subject to the secular power is of less account than the divine law of the Old Testament. Much more, therefore, since they have become members of Christ's body, are men freed from the law of subjection, whereby they were under the power of secular princes.

Obj. 3. Further, men are not bound to obey robbers, who oppress them with violence. Now Augustine says: 'Without justice, what else is a kingdom but a huge robbery?' Since therefore the authority of secular princes is frequently exercised with injustice or owes its origin to some unjust usurpation, it seems that Christians ought not to obey secular princes.

On the contrary, it is written: 'Admonish them to be subject to princes and powers'; and 'Be ye subject . . . to every human creature for God's sake, whether it be to the king as excelling or to governors as sent by him.'

I answer that, faith in Christ is the origin and cause of justice, according to Romans 3.22: 'The justice of God by faith of Jesus Christ'; wherefore faith in Christ does not void the order of justice, but strengthens it. Now the order of justice requires that subjects obey their superiors, else the stability of human affairs would cease. Hence faith in Christ does not excuse the faithful from the obligation of obeying secular princes.

Reply Obj. 1. As stated above, the subjection whereby one man is bound to another regards the body, not the soul, which retains its liberty. Now, in this state of life we are freed by the grace of Christ from defects of the soul, but not from defects of the body, as the Apostle declares by saying of himself that in his mind he served the law of God, but in his flesh the law of sin. Wherefore those that are made children of God by grace are free from the spiritual bondage of sin, but not from the bodily bondage, whereby they are held bound to earthly masters, as a gloss observes on 1 Timothy 6.1, 'Whosoever are servants under the yoke', etc.

Reply Obj. 2. The Old Law was a figure of the New Testament, and therefore it had to cease on the advent of truth. And the comparison with human law does not stand, because thereby one man is subject to another. Yet man is bound by divine law to obey his fellow man.

Reply Obj. 3. Man is bound to obey secular princes in so far as this is required by the order of justice. Wherefore if the prince's authority is not just but usurped, or if he commands what is unjust, his subjects are not bound to obey him, except perhaps accidentally, in order to avoid scandal or danger.

(IIa IIae, Q.104, arts. 5 and 6)

Source: *The Political Ideas of St Thomas Aquinas: Representative Selections,*
ed. O. Bigongiari, Hafner, 1953, pp. 65–7, 70–7, 92–5, 168–72.

Further reading

A lucid short overview is to be found in Plamenatz, Chapter 1, while Burns's *Mediaeval Political Thought* is an excellent work of reference. Black's *Political Thought in Europe 1250–1450* is a good introduction to the Middle Ages. Ullmann's *A History of Political Thought: The Middle Ages* traces the medieval origins of modern constitutionalism. On Aquinas, see the editions by d'Entrèves and by Baumgart and Regan, and Gilby's *Principality and Pity*. There are general selections of medieval political thinkers in the books edited by Lerner and Mahdi and by Lewis.

Chapter Four

REFORMATION CHRISTIANITY

Introduction

When the medieval synthesis finally fell apart, the reformulation of the Christian religion was led by two thinkers, Luther and Calvin, whose contrasting views on religion and politics have had a profound influence which continues to the present day.

In Luther's rather pessimistic view, the Christian was subject to two very different kingdoms. In the affairs of the sinful secular world God's role was represented by the State; the Church embodied the reign of God in spiritual matters. This stark separation matched Luther's view that human nature was profoundly corrupt and that salvation could be gained by faith alone and not by 'good works'. This attitude has led to a greater political passivity in the Lutheran tradition than in most other branches of Christianity. Luther himself did not elaborate a consistent attitude to politics. In particular, when some of his more enthusiastic followers joined the Peasants' Revolt of 1525, Luther supported the efforts of the German princes to suppress these 'heretical' views. Chief among these heretical revolutionaries was Thomas Munzer whose millennial views argued for the immediate reign of Christ on earth when all goods would be held in common. Munzer was executed but his brand of Christian utopianism was to have a continued, though always marginal, existence.

In sharp contrast to Luther, the more activist Calvin was quite happy to advocate what he called a 'Christian polity'. The original version of his major work *Institution of the Christian Religion* taught unquestioning obedience to secular authority whose duty it was to safeguard external manifestations of righteousness while true, i.e. internal, religion was left in the hands of the Church. In his later years, Calvin saw the relation of civil to spiritual authority as potentially one of close co-operation. This was partly due to his emerging as the leading figure in Geneva which was an amalgam of a Church and State – like Savonarola's Florence the preceding century or the later Paraguayan Reductions of the Jesuits. In this theocracy, which effectively subordinated State to Church, both magistrates and pastors derived their authority from God and were called to close co-operation in the building up of God's Kingdom. This monolithic approach, together with the idea of 'calling', found an even more powerful expression in the Puritan tradition of Cromwell and, in a less rigid form, the founders of the United States of America. Moreover, if we follow the arguments of Max Weber (see the extract in Chapter 15 below), Calvinism was responsible for something even more momentous: the rise of capitalism. In Weber's much controverted thesis, Calvinism's emphasis on worldly success as evidence of God's predestinatory choice together with the asceticism which precluded the wasteful spending of the fruits of this success were necessary preconditions for the emergence of the capitalist spirit.

(a) *Luther:* On Secular Authority

We now come to the main part of this sermon. We have learnt that there must be secular authority on this earth and how a Christian and salutary use may be made of it. Now we must establish how long its reach is, and how far it may stretch out its arm without overreaching itself and trenching upon God's kingdom and government. This is something about which we need to be quite clear. When [secular government] is given too much freedom of action, the harm that results is unbearable and horrifying, but to have it confined within too narrow a compass is also harmful. In the one case there is too much punishment, in the other too little. But it is more tolerable to err on the side of the latter: it is always better that a villain should live than that a just man should be killed. There always are, and always must be, villains in the world, but there are few just men.

The first point to be noted is that the two parts into which the children of Adam are divided (as we have said above), the one the kingdom of God under Christ, the other the kingdom of the world under [secular] authority, have each their own kind of law. Everyday experience sufficiently shows us that every kingdom must have its own laws and that no kingdom or government can survive without law. Secular government has laws that extend no further than the body, goods and outward, earthly matters. But where the soul is concerned, God neither can nor will allow anyone but himself to rule. And so, where secular authority takes it upon itself to legislate for the soul, it trespasses on [what belongs to] God's government, and merely seduces and ruins souls. I

47

intend to make this so unambiguously clear that no one can fail to grasp it, in order that our lords the princes and bishops may see the folly of trying to compel belief in this or that by means of laws and commands.

If someone imposes a man-made law on souls, compelling belief in what he wants to be believed, then there will probably be no word of God to justify it. If there is nothing in God's Word about it, then it is uncertain whether this is what God wants. If he himself has not commanded something, there is no way of establishing that it is pleasing to him. Or rather, we can be sure that it is not pleasing to him, for he will have our faith grounded solely in his divine Word; as he says in Matthew 18 [in fact 16.18]: 'On this rock I will build my church.' And John 10[27]: 'My sheep hear my voice and know me, but the strangers' voice they hear not, but flee from them.' From this it follows that secular authority drives souls to eternal damnation with such blasphemous commands. For this is to compel people to believe that something is certain to please God, when it is not certain at all; on the contrary, it is certain that it displeases God, since there is no clear [text in] God's Word to warrant it. For whosoever believes something to be right, which is in fact wrong or uncertain, denies the truth, which is God himself, and believes lies and error . . .

It is therefore utter folly for them to order us to believe the Church, the [Church] Fathers and the Councils, even though there is no [express] Word of God [for what they tell us to believe]. It is the apostles of the devil that issue that sort of command, not the Church. The Church commands nothing except what it is certain is God's Word. As St Peter says [1 Pet. 4.11]: 'Whoever speaks, let him speak according to God's word.' But they will never be able to show that the decrees of Councils are the Word of God. And what is even more ridiculous is when it is argued that, after all, this is what kings and princes and people generally believe. But, my friends, we are not baptized in the name of kings and princes and people in general, but in the name of Christ and of God himself. And our title is not 'kings' or 'princes' or 'people in general', but Christians. No one can or should lay down commandments for the soul, except those who can point it on the way to heaven. But no human being can do that; only God. And therefore in those things which concern the salvation of souls, nothing is to be taught or accepted except God's Word.

Another important point is this. However stupid they are, they must admit that they have no power over the soul. For no human being can kill the soul or bring it to life, or lead it to heaven or to hell. And if they will not believe us, then Christ will show it clearly enough when he says in Matthew 10[28]: 'Do not be afraid of those that kill the body and after that can do nothing more. Fear rather him who, after he kills the body, has the power to condemn to hell.' Surely that is clear enough: the soul is taken out of the hands of any human being whatsoever, and is placed exclusively under the power of God. Now tell me this: would anyone in his right mind give orders where he has no authority? You might as well command the moon to shine at your behest. What sense would there be in it, if the people of Leipzig were to lay down laws for us here in Wittenberg, or vice versa? Anyone who tried it, would be sent a dose of hellebore by way of thanks, to clear their heads and cure their cold. But this is just what our Emperor and our prudent princes are doing; they let the Pope, the bishops and the sophists lead them, the blind leading the blind, commanding their subjects to believe as they see fit, without God's Word. And then they still want to retain the title of 'Christian Princes', which God forbid.

Another way of understanding this point is that each and every authority can only act, and ought only to act, where it can see, know, judge, adjudicate and change things. What kind of judge would it be that judges blindly in matters where he can neither hear nor see? But tell me this: how can a human being see, know, judge and change hearts? That is reserved to God alone. As Psalm 7[10] says: 'God searches the heart and bowels.' And again [Ps. 7.9]: 'The Lord is judge over the people', and Acts 10 [in fact 1.24; 15.8]: 'God knows the heart.' And Jeremiah 1 [in fact 17.9]: 'Wicked and unsearchable is the human heart. Who can search it? I the Lord, who search hearts and bowels.' A court has to have an exact knowledge of what it is to judge. But people's thoughts and minds cannot be manifest to anyone but God. And therefore it is impossible and futile to command or coerce someone to believe this or that. A different skill is needed here; force will not do. I am surprised at these lunatics, seeing that they themselves have a saying: *De occultis non iudicat ecclesia*; the Church does not judge in secret matters. Now, if [even] the Church, the spiritual government, only rules over matters that are public and open, by what right does secular authority, in its folly, presume to judge a thing as secret, spiritual, hidden as faith?

Each must decide at his own peril what he is to believe, and must see to it that he believes rightly. Other people cannot go to heaven or hell on my behalf, or open or close [the gates to either] for me. And just as little can they believe or not believe on my behalf, or force my faith or unbelief. How he believes is a matter for each individual's conscience, and this does not diminish [the authority of] secular governments. They ought therefore to content themselves with attending to their own business, and allow people to believe what they can, and what they want, and they must use no coercion in this matter against anyone.

Faith is free, and no one can be compelled to believe. More precisely, so far from being something secular authority ought to create and enforce, faith is something that God works in the spirit. Hence that common saying which also occurs in Augustine: no one can or ought to be forced to believe anything against his will.

[. . .]

Now that we know how far [the competence of] secular authority extends, it is time to consider how a prince should go about exercising it. [I am writing this] for the sake of those who want to be Christian rulers and lords, and who give some thought to their own salvation; there are very few of that sort. Christ himself describes the character of secular princes when he says in Luke 22[25]: 'The secular princes rule, and those who are superiors use force.' For when they are born or chosen as rulers, they imagine themselves entitled to be served, and to rule by force. Now, whoever wants to be a Christian prince must abandon any intention of lording it over people and using force. For all life that is lived and sought after for one's own benefit is cursed and damned: damned are all the works that do not come from love. And the works that spring from love are those that are not done for one's own pleasure, benefit, honour, comfort and well-being, but rather those which are aimed wholly at the benefit, honour and well-being of others.

And hence I shall say nothing here about worldly matters and laws. There are far too many law-books already and the topic is [too] broad. In any case, if a prince is not himself more prudent than those who advise him about the law, and does not understand more than is to be found in the texts of the law, he will surely govern as the proverb (Prov. 28[16]) says: 'A prince who lacks prudence shall oppress many with injustice.' For however good or equitable the laws might be, they are all subject to this exception: they cannot prevail against necessity. Therefore the prince must keep the laws as firmly under his own control as he does the Sword, and use his own reason to judge when and where the law should be applied in its full rigour, and when it should be moderated. So that reason remains the ruler at all times, the supreme law and master of all the laws. In the same way, the father of a household will no doubt establish times and amounts of work and food for his servants and his children. But he must nevertheless maintain his power over these rules he has made, so that he can alter or suspend them, if it should happen that the servants are sick, or are taken prisoner, are detained, deceived or hindered in some way. He must not [for example] treat both the sick and the healthy with the same strictness. I say this so that people will not think it a precious thing, and enough by itself, to follow the written laws or the counsel of those learned in the law. More is needed.

But what is a prince to do if he is not as wise or as prudent as this,

and must [therefore] allow himself to be governed by lawyers and by the letter of the law. It is precisely with reference to this that I said that the prince's office is beset by dangers, and if the prince is not wise enough to rule over both his laws and his counsellors, then what will happen is what Solomon says: 'Woe to the land that has a child for its prince.' And because Solomon knew it, he despaired of all the laws, even though God [himself] had laid them down for him through [the agency of] Moses, and of all his princes and counsellors, and turned to God himself, asking him for a wise heart with which to rule the people. And a prince must follow his example: he must act in fear, and rely neither on dead books nor on living heads, but on God alone, pestering him for right understanding, greater than all books and teachers, with which to govern his subjects wisely. In short, I know nothing about what laws to recommend to a prince; I want only to instruct him how to dispose his heart with regard to whatever laws, counsels, verdicts and cases he has to deal with. If he does that, God will surely give him [the capacity] to use all laws, advice and actions to good effect.
[. . .]
Let a prince take care how he metes out justice to wrongdoers. Punishing some without ruining others [who are innocent] calls for the greatest prudence and wisdom. Once again, I know of no better model than David. He once had a captain named Joab, who treacherously murdered two other captains, both just men, and so he deserved death twice over. And yet David, while he lived, did not kill him, but ordered his son Solomon to do it [after David's death]. This was doubtlessly because David could not do it himself without causing even more harm and upheaval. A prince must punish the wicked in such a way that in 'picking up the spoon he does not tread on the plate and break it', and does not plunge his whole country and its people into chaos for the sake of one [person's] head, and fill the land with widows and orphans. For the same reason, he must not follow those advisers and 'armchair soldiers' that would push him into wars with arguments like: are we to put up with such insults and injustice? It is a very bad Christian who will put a whole country at risk for the sake of a castle. In short, the prince in such cases must act after the maxim: a person who can't wink at faults, doesn't know how to govern. So let this be his rule of conduct: where an injustice cannot be punished without a greater injustice, he should not insist on his rights, however just his cause. He is to look to the injustices suffered by others and not the damage he suffers himself, considering what others will suffer if he exacts punishments. What have all those women and children done to deserve becoming widows and orphans, just so that you can take your revenge against a worthless mouth or a wicked hand that has done you harm?

Here you may ask: is a prince not to wage war [at all]? And are his subjects not to follow him into battle? That is a broad question, but the short answer is this. The Christian way is that no ruler is to wage war against his overlord, be he the King, the Emperor or any other liege-lord. If one of these takes something, let him take it. For superiors are not to be resisted by force, but only by witnessing to the truth. If they take any notice, well and good. If not, you are guiltless and you suffer injustice for God's sake. But if your opponent is your equal or your inferior, or a foreign ruler, then you should first offer him justice and peace, as Moses taught the children of Israel. If he will not settle, then do the best you can and resist force with force, as Moses well describes in Deuteronomy 20[10ff.]. But here you are not to consider your own advantage, and how you can remain ruler, but your subjects, whom you owe help and protection, so that the work is done out of love. Since your whole country is placed in danger [by war], you must consider whether God will help you, so that everything does not go to wrack and ruin; and even if you cannot help making some widows and some orphans, you must at least prevent total ruin, and nothing but widows and orphans [being left].

The subjects for their part owe obedience and must set their lives and goods to it. For in such a case everyone must risk his goods and even himself, for the sake of his neighbour. And in such a war, it is a Christian act, and an act of love, to kill enemies without scruple, to rob and to burn, and to do whatever damages the enemy, according to the usages of war, until he is defeated. But beware of sins and of violating women and maidens. And when the enemy is defeated, then those who surrender and submit are to be shown mercy and granted peace. In other words, act according to the maxim 'God helps the strongest.' Abraham did so when he defeated the four kings (Genesis 14[15]). Of course, he killed many and did not show much mercy until the victory was his. A case like this should be regarded as something sent by God, so that for once the land is swept clean of villains.

But what if a prince is in the wrong? Are his people obliged to obey him even then? No, because no one has a duty to act unjustly; we must obey God (who will have justice prevail), rather than men [Acts 5.29]. But what if subjects do not know whether their ruler is in the right or not? As long as they do not know and cannot find out, although they have made every effort, they may obey without danger to their souls. For in such cases, one must follow the Law of Moses in Exodus 21[13], where he writes that a murderer who has unknowingly and unintentionally killed someone shall flee to a free city and there be absolved by the courts. And whichever side is beaten, whether it be in the right or the wrong, must take it as a punishment from God, but the side that fights and wins, in such a state of ignorance, must regard the battle as if someone fell from a roof and killed someone, and leave the matter with God. To God it is all one whether he deprives you of your goods or life by a just or an unjust lord. You are God's creature, and he may do with you as he pleases, as long as your conscience is innocent. And thus God himself excuses King Abimelech (Genesis 20[6]), when the latter took Abraham's wife. Not that the act was right, but he did not know that she was Abraham's wife.

Fourth, and this should perhaps have been the first point: as we have said above, a prince must also act like a Christian towards God. That is, he ought to subject himself to him in complete confidence and ask him for the wisdom to rule well, as Solomon did. But I have written a great deal elsewhere about faith and confidence in God and there is therefore no need to say any more now. And so we shall leave it at that and sum up. A prince ought to comfort himself in four different ways. First: towards God with real confidence and heartfelt prayer. Second: to his subjects with love and Christian service. Third: towards his counsellors and great men, with free reason and unbound understanding. Fourth: towards evil-doers with condign gravity and severity. In that way his condition will be outwardly and inwardly right, pleasing to God and men. But he must anticipate a great deal of envy and suffering. As illustrious a man as this will soon feel the cross lying on his neck.

Source: *Luther and Calvin on Secular Authority*, ed. H. Höpfl, Cambridge University Press, 1991, pp. 22–3, 25–6, 34–5, 38–41.

(b) *Calvin:* On Civil Government

And make no mistake: it is impossible to resist the magistrate without also resisting God. Even if it appears possible to defy an unarmed magistrate with impunity, God is armed and his vengeance for any contempt shown him is harsh. The obedience [of which I am speaking] also includes that self-restraint which private persons ought to impose on themselves in public [matters], neither meddling in public matters, nor intruding rashly on the magistrate's preserve, nor undertaking anything whatever of a public nature. If there is something in need of correction in the public order, private men are not to create disturbances, or take matters into their own hands, for these hands ought here to be tied. Instead, they should submit the matter to the cognizance of the magistrate, whose hand alone is free. What I mean is that they should do nothing, unless they have a specific right or command to do so. For where a superior lends them his authority, then they too are invested with public authority. The ruler's advisers are commonly described as his 'eyes and ears'; it would not be inappropriate to call those whom he has commissioned to act for him his 'hands'.

Up to this point we have been considering magistrates who live up to the titles given to them: fathers of their country, or (as the poet puts it) shepherds of the people, guardians of the peace, upholders of justice, defenders of the innocent. And anyone who thinks the authority of such persons unacceptable deserves to be considered a madman. But we find in almost every age another sort of prince. Some of them live lives of indolence and pleasure, not in the least concerned about all those duties to which they ought to attend. Others, intent only on their own profit, prostitute every right, privilege, judgement and charter by putting them up for sale. Others again drain the poor people of their money, only to squander it in wild prodigality. Yet others pillage homes, violate wives and maidens, slaughter the innocent; in short, they engage in what can only be called criminality. And there are many people who cannot be convinced that these too ought to be acknowledged as princes, and as being endowed with an authority which is to be obeyed, as far as is permissible. For they cannot see any semblance of that image of God which ought to shine forth from magistrates, nor any vestige of that 'minister of God' who is given to the righteous in praise and to the wicked for their punishment. Faced with such lack of dignity and with criminal conduct so remote from the duties of a magistrate, indeed so remote from the duties of ordinary humanity, they cannot recognize the kind of superior whose dignity and authority Scripture commends to us. Mankind has always had an innate hatred and detestation of tyrants, just as it loves and venerates lawful kings.

But reflection on the Word of God will carry us beyond [the ordinary sentiments of mankind]. For we are to be subject not only to the authority of those princes who do their duty towards us as they should, and uprightly, but to all of them, however they came by their office, even if the very last thing they do is to act like [true] princes. For even though the Lord declares that the [office of] magistrate is the greatest gift of his goodness for the preservation of mankind, and although he himself sets the boundaries within which they are to confine themselves, nonetheless he also declares at the same time that whatever they are, it is from him alone that they derive their authority. Those who govern for the public good are true examples and signs of his goodness; those who govern unjustly and intemperately have been raised up by him to punish the iniquity of the people. Both are equally furnished with that sacred majesty, with which he has endowed legitimate authority. I shall not continue without offering some proof-texts for my point: Job 34.30; Hosea 13.11; Isaiah 3.4 and 10.5; Deuteronomy 28.29. We need not devote much effort to proving that an ungodly king is the wrath of God on the land; there is no one (I imagine) who will deny it, and in any case this says no more about kings than might equally be said of a robber who steals your goods, or an adulterer who defiles your marriage-bed, or a murderer who encompasses your death; all these calamities are counted by Scripture amongst God's curses (Deut. 28.29). What however does require more proof, because people are much less ready to accept it, is that even the worst of them, and those entirely undeserving of any honour, provided they have public authority, are invested with that splendid and sacred authority which God's Word bestows on the ministers of his justice and judgement. And hence, as far as public obedience is concerned, they are to be held in the same honour and reverence as would be accorded an excellent king, if they had such a one.

So that in the first place I would have my readers note and meditate on this: it is not without good reason that Scripture so often reminds us of God's providence and his special operation in distributing kingdoms and setting up such kings as he sees fit. As it says in Daniel (2.21 and 37): 'The Lord changes the times and the diversity of times; he overthrows kings and sets them up.' And again: 'Let the living know that the Most High is mighty in the kingdom of men and gives [the kingship] to whomever he wishes.' The whole of Scripture abounds in such passages, but they are especially frequent in the prophets. Everyone knows what sort of a king Nebuchadnezzar was, the man who took Jerusalem and who was always bent on invading and ravaging other men's lands. And yet in Ezekiel (29.19) the Lord affirms that it was he himself who gave him the land of Egypt, in return for the service he had rendered him in laying it waste. And Daniel said to him (Ezek. 2.37): 'You O King are the king of kings, to whom the Lord of heaven has given a kingdom powerful, strong and glorious; to you I say he gave it, and all the lands inhabited by the sons of men, the beasts of the forest and the birds of the air; he gave them into your hand and made you to rule over them.' And again to his son Belshazzar (Dan. 5.18): 'The Lord the Most High gave to your father Nebuchadnezzar kingship and magnificence, honour and glory; and on account of the greatness he conferred on him, all peoples, tribes and tongues were fearful and trembled in his sight.' When we hear that God established such a king, we must also recall to mind the divine ordinances about honouring and fearing kings, nor must we be in any doubt that we must honour [even] the worst tyrant in the office in which the Lord has seen fit to set him. When Samuel proclaimed to the people of Israel what they would have to endure from their kings, he said (1 Sam. 8.11): 'This will be the right (*ius*) of the king who will reign over you: he will take your sons and put them to his chariots to be his horsemen, to work his fields and gather in his harvest, and to make him weapons. He will take your daughters to make perfumes, to cook and to bake. He will take your fields and your vineyards and your best olive-groves and give them to his servants. He will take tithes of your seed and your grape-harvest and give them to his eunuchs and servants. He will take your servants, handmaidens and asses and apply them to his work and will take tithes of your flocks besides, and you shall be his servants.' Kings will not indeed do all this by right; on the contrary, God's law fully instructs them in temperance and self-restraint. But Samuel calls it a right (*ius*) over the people, because they must obey the king and are not allowed to resist him. It is as if Samuel had said: kings will be carried away by their licentiousness, but it will not be for you to restrain them; all that will remain for you will be to hear what they command, and obey.

One passage stands out as especially important and memorable: Jeremiah 27.5ff. I am prepared to quote it because, although it is some-what long, it resolves the question in the clearest possible fashion. [It reads:] 'The Lord says: I have made heaven, and mankind, and the ani-mals who are on the surface of the earth, in the greatness of my power and by my outstretched arm, and have handed them over to whoever is pleasing in my sight. And now therefore I have given all these lands into the hands of my servant Nebuchadnezzar; let all the peoples and the [great] kings serve him until the time of his land shall come. And it shall come to pass that every people and kingdom which has not served the king of Babel, I shall visit that people with sword, hunger and pestilence; therefore serve the king of Babel and live.' We see here the degree of obedience and honour the Lord wished to be accorded to that loathsome and cruel tyrant, and merely because he was in possession of the kingship. It was this [possession] alone which showed that he had been placed on the royal throne by divine decree, and had been vested with royal majesty, which must remain inviolate. If we keep firmly in mind that even the very worst kings are appointed by this same decree which establishes the authority of kings [in general], then we will never permit ourselves the seditious idea that a king is to be treated according to his deserts, or that we need not obey a king who does not conduct himself towards us like a king.

There is no force either in the objection that this precept was exclusively for the Israelites. We must consider the reason God himself gave to support it. What he says is: 'I have given the kingdom to Nebuchadnezzar; therefore serve him and live' (Jer. 27.17). Thus we cannot doubt that we must serve anyone who has manifestly had king-ship conferred on him. In the very act of raising someone to the exalted rank of king, the Lord thereby reveals to us that it is his will that that person should rule. And there are general testimonies to the truth of this to be found in Scripture. In Solomon (Prov. 28.1): 'Because of the iniquity of the land there are many princes.' And Job 12.18: 'He takes away dominion from princes, and then girds them again with a girdle.' When that is admitted, there remains nothing for us but to serve and live. And in the Prophet Jeremiah (29.7) we find another command of the Lord. There he orders his people to seek peace in Babylon, to which they had been taken by force as captives, and to pray to him for Babylon, for in its peace would be their peace. Notice how the Israelites, despoiled of all their goods, expelled from their homes, carried off into exile, cast down into a wretched bondage, are [yet] commanded to pray for the prosperity of their conqueror. And not merely in the sense that we are elsewhere commanded to pray for those who persecute us, but rather, to pray for the peace and safety of his reign, so that they too might live prosperously under him. And in the same way David, already designated king by God's ordinance and anointed with his holy oil, when he was persecuted by Saul without having done anything to deserve it, nonetheless treated the person of his ambusher as sacrosanct, because God had honoured Saul with the royal dignity. 'Far be it from me,' he said (1 Sam. 24.6 and 11), 'that I should do this thing to my lord, the Anointed of the Lord, in the sight of the Lord my God: that I should lay my hands on him; for he is the Lord's Anointed.' And again (1 Sam. 26.9): 'My soul has spared you and I have said: I shall not lay hands on my lord, since he is the Anointed of the Lord.' And again: 'Who shall lay hands on the Anointed of the Lord and remain guiltless? The Lord lives, and unless the Lord strikes him down, or his day comes and he dies, or is laid low in battle, far be it from me that I should lay hands on the Anointed of the Lord' (1 Sam. 24.7–11; 26.9 and 10).

This is the kind of reverence and dutifulness that we all owe to our superiors, whoever they are. I say this often, so that we might learn not to consider the persons and conduct [of rulers], but be content with the person they represent, by the will of God, and with whose inviolable majesty they have been inscribed and stamped. But, you will reply, superiors in their turn reciprocally owe duties to their subjects. I have already acknowledged it. But if you go on to infer that only just governments are to be repaid by obedience, your reasoning is stupid. Husbands and wives owe each other mutual duties; so do parents and children. But what if husbands or parents do not do their duty? What if parents, although forbidden to provoke their children to anger (Eph. 6.4), are instead hard and intractable and weary their children beyond measure by their peevishness? What if husbands treat their wives with great abusiveness, even though they have been commanded to love and spare them, as weak vessels (Eph. 5.25; 1 Pet. 3.7)? Shall children then be less obedient to their parents, or wives to their husbands on that account? But [children and wives] are subject to the wicked and the undutiful just as much [as to the upright and dutiful]. No: all are to act in such a way as not to look at the bag hanging from the backs of other people; that is, they are not to ask about the duties of others, but only to consider their own, and especially when they are placed in subjection to the power of others. Hence, if we are tormented by a cruel ruler, if we are fleeced by a rapacious and extravagant one, if we suffer neglect from an indolent one or are afflicted for [our] godliness by an impious and sacrilegious one, let us first recall to mind our sins, for it is those without a doubt which God is punishing by such scourges. Then humility will bridle our impatience. And let us all summon this reflection to our assistance: it is not for us to remedy such evils; all that is left to us is to implore the help of the Lord, for the hearts of princes and alterations of kingdoms are in his hands (Prov. 21.1). It is God who will stand in the assembly of the gods and will give judgement in their midst (Ps. 82.1). Before his face all kings will fall down and be terrified, and the judges who had not kissed his Anointed (Ps. 2.12); those who wrote unjust laws to oppress the poor by their judgements and to do violence to the cause of the humble; to prey on widows and rob orphans (Isa. 10.1–2).

And in all this is revealed God's admirable goodness, might and providence. For sometimes he raises up avengers from amongst his servants, designated and commanded by him to punish the tyranny of vicious men and to deliver the oppressed from their wretched calamities; at other times he turns the frenzy of men who intended something quite different to the same end. In the former manner he freed the people of Israel from Pharaoh's tyranny by means of Moses, from the violence of Chusan, King of Syria, by Othoniel, and from other servitudes by other kings or judges (Exod. 3.8; Judg. 3.9 and ff. chs). And by the latter means he overcame the pride of Tyre by means of the Egyptians, the haughtiness of the Egyptians by the Assyrians, the ferocity of the Assyrians by the Chaldeans, the overweening pride of Babylon by the Medes and Persians, when Cyrus had already subjugated the Medes. On occasion, he punished the ingratitude shown him by the kings of Israel and Judah for his many mercies, and their contempt to him, by means of the Assyrians, on other occasions by the Babylonians, though in quite different ways. The former [i.e. the avengers] were summoned to punish these crimes by a lawful calling from God; they did not in the least violate the majesty with which kings are endowed by divine ordinance when they took up arms against kings. Armed by heaven, they subjugated a lesser power by a greater, in just the same way that kings are entitled to punish their own officials. The latter, by contrast, did

God's work without knowing it, for all that they intended to do was to commit crimes. All the same, it was the hand of God that directed them do to his bidding.

But irrespective of what may be thought about the actions themselves, it was the Lord who by these instruments carried out his just purpose, when he broke the bloodstained sceptres of insolent kings and overturned unbearable tyrannies. Let princes hear and be afraid. As for us, however, let us take the greatest possible care never to hold in contempt, or trespass upon, that plenitude of authority of magistrates whose majesty it is for us to venerate and which God has confirmed by the most weighty pronouncements, even when it is exercised by individuals who are wholly unworthy of it and who do their best to defile it by their wickedness. And even if the punishment of unbridled tyranny is the Lord's vengeance [on tyrants], we are not to imagine that it is we ourselves who have been called upon to inflict it. All that has been assigned to us is to obey and suffer. Here as always, I am speaking about private persons. It may be that there are in our days popular magistrates established to restrain the licentiousness of kings, corresponding to those 'Ephors', which were set against the authority of the kings of the Spartans, or the 'Tribunes of the People, set over against the Roman consuls, or the 'Demarchs', set up against the Council of the Athenians. And perhaps, in current circumstances, the authority exercised by the three estates in individual kingdoms when they hold their principal assemblies is of the same kind. If there are such [popular magistrates established], then it is no part of my intention to prohibit them from acting in accordance with their duty, and resisting the licentiousness and frenzy of kings; on the contrary, if they connive at their unbridled violence and insults against the poor common people, I say that such negligence is a nefarious betrayal of their oath; they are betraying the people and defrauding them of that liberty which they know they were ordained by God to defend.

But there is always one exception to that obedience which, as we have established, is due to the authority of superiors, and it is this that must be our principal concern: we must never allow ourselves to be diverted from our obedience to the one to whose will the desires of every king must be subjected, to whose decrees all their commands give place, and before whose majesty they must lay down their own insignia. Would it not be an absurdity to give contentment to [mere] men [by obeying them], but thereby to incur the wrath of him on whose account alone [any human being at all] must be obeyed? The Lord is the king of kings. When his sacred mouth has spoken, it alone and no one else is to be heard. We are subject to those who have been placed over us, but only in him. If they command anything against [his will], it must be as nothing to us. And in this instance we must ignore all that dignity that magistrates possess. There is no injustice in compelling it to be subordinate to the true, unique and supreme power of God. It is for this reason that Daniel (Dan. 6.22) denied that he was guilty of any offence against the king when he disobeyed an ungodly law the latter had made: for the king had transgressed the bounds set to him [by God] and had not only wronged men, but had raised his horns against God, thereby abrogating his own power. By contrast, the Israelites are condemned for their excessive readiness to submit to an ungodly law of their king. For when Jeroboam had had the golden calves cast, they defected from the temple of God and went over to new superstitions (1 Kings 12.30), in order to please him. Their descendants were just as ready to accommodate themselves to the will and pleasure of their kings. They too were sharply reproved by the prophet for submitting to the king's commands. Thus there is nothing at all to praise in that pretended 'humble submission' which the flatterers at court invoke to cover themselves and deceive the simple, when they claim that it is wrong for them to refuse obedience to anything their kings command. As if God had surrendered his own rights to the mortal men he has placed in authority over the human race. Or as if earthly power suffered diminution by being subjected to God's, who is its author and in whose sight even the celestial principalities tremble in fear and supplication. I recognize full well the gravity and the immediacy of the perils which threaten [those who show] the constancy I demand; I know that kings are not prepared to tolerate any defiance and that their anger is a messenger of death, as Solomon says (Prov. 16.14). But heaven's messenger Peter (in Acts 5.29) proclaims this commandment: 'We must obey God rather than men.' Let us therefore derive consolation from the thought that we are rendering to God the obedience he demands when we rather suffer all things than to depart from our duty to him. And so that our courage may not fail us, Paul (1 Cor. 7, 23) adduces something else to spur us on: our redemption has been purchased at so high a price in order that we might not become slaves to the wicked desires of men; still less should we submit to their ungodliness.

Source: *Luther and Calvin on Secular Authority*, ed. H. Höpfl,
Cambridge University Press, 1991, pp. 75–84.

Further reading

There is a short account in Plamenatz, Vol. 1, Chapter 3 and a detailed survey of the intellectual climate in Skinner, *The Foundations of Modern Political Thought*. See also, the magisterial survey by Burns and Goldie,

The Cambridge History of Modern Political Thought 1450–1700, especially the articles by Oakley and Kingdon. On Luther, see the biography by Dickens and study of his political thought by Cargill Thompson. On Calvin's politics, see the old study by Bieler and the more recent works of Bowsma and of Höpfl. Also the provocative sociological approach of Walzer's *The Revolution of the Saints*.

Chapter Five

CONTEMPORARY CATHOLIC CHRISTIANITY

Introduction

While the ideals of the Protestant Reformation, particularly those of Calvin, continued to exert a radical influence on politics, the Roman Catholic Church adopted a firmly conservative stance. It is only over the last century or so that Catholicism has ceased to be an automatically reactionary force and even, in some areas, been on the side of profound political reform. Faced with the prospect of losing touch altogether with the modern world, the Catholic Church has revived and elaborated its traditional teachings to produce an impressive body of social and political thought.

This process was begun by Leo XIII whose most famous encyclical *Rerum Novarum* of 1891 addressed itself to questions of social justice and avoided a narrow individualism in social questions. Leo was profoundly conservative, particularly on strictly political questions. His encyclical attacked socialism (by which he understood the abolition of all private property), questioned the right to strike, and extolled the blessings of private property. Nevertheless, he was also violent in his criticism of the greed and concentration of wealth promoted by capitalism and advocated state intervention to prevent and repair the more flagrant forms of social injustice.

The ideas of Leo XIII were built upon by Pius XI in his encyclical *Quadragesimo Anno* published in 1931 at the height of the depression. It reflected the widespread dissatisfaction with the current concentration and abuse of economic power and advocated a reconstruction of the economic order combining representatives of labour, management, and the State in a system that could be regarded as close to socialism or fascism according to one's point of view. In the post-war world, there is a steady radicalization of Catholic social and political teaching through Paul VI's *Populorum Progressio* and John XXIII's *Pacem in Terris* to the encyclicals of John Paul II. *Laborem Exercens* of 1981 insists on the priority of labour over capital and the responsibility of the State for alleviating unemployment, themes taken up in *Centesimus Annus* of 1991. With the collapse of Communist regimes the Catholic Church has grown more critical of the *laissez-faire* attitudes of liberal democracy. The reactionary (in the literal sense) nature of much traditional Catholic thought has enabled much trenchant criticism of contemporary trends. This tends to be conservative on matters of personal morality – and thus, on abortion, for instance, to question some of the fundamental tenets of liberal democracy as in *Evangelium Vitae* of 1995 – while in economic and political areas the pervasive anti-individualism is decidedly more progressive.

(a) *John Paul II:* Laborem Exercens

The structure of the present-day situation is deeply marked by many conflicts caused by man, and the technological means produced by human work play a primary role in it. We should also consider here the prospect of worldwide catastrophe in the case of a nuclear war, which would have almost unimaginable possibilities of destruction. In view of this situation we must first of all recall a principle that has always been taught by the Church: the principle of the priority of labour over capital. This principle directly concerns the process of production: in this process labour is always a primary efficient cause, while capital, the whole collection of means of production, remains a mere instrument or instrumental cause. This principle is an evident truth that emerges from the whole of man's historical experience.

[. . .]

Further consideration of this question should confirm our conviction of the priority of human labour over what in the course of time we have grown accustomed to calling capital. Since the concept of capital includes not only the natural resources placed at man's disposal but also the whole collection of means by which man appropriates natural resources and transforms them in accordance with his needs (and thus in a sense humanizes them), it must immediately be noted that all these means are the results of the historical heritage of human labour. All the means of production, from the most primitive to the ultramodern ones – it is man that has gradually developed them: man's experience and intellect. In this way there have appeared not only the simplest instruments for cultivating the earth but also, through adequate progress in science and technology, the more modern and complex ones: machines, factories, laboratories, and computers. Thus everything that is at the service of work, everything that in the present state of technology constitutes its ever more highly perfected 'instrument', is the result of work.

This gigantic and powerful instrument – the whole collection of means of production that in a sense are considered synonymous with 'capital' – is the result of work and bears the signs of human labour. At the present stage of technological advance, when man, who is the subject of work, wishes to make use of this collection of modern instruments, the means of production, he must first assimilate cognitively the result of the work of the people who invented those instruments, who planned them, built them and perfected them, and who continue to do so. Capacity for work – that is to say, for sharing efficiently in the modern production process – demands greater and greater preparation and, before all else, proper training. Obviously, it remains clear that every human being sharing in the production process, even if he or she is only doing the kind of work for which no special training or qualifications are required, is the real efficient subject in this production process, while the whole collection of instruments, no matter how perfect they may be in themselves, are only a mere instrument subordinate to human labour.

This truth, which is part of the abiding heritage of the Church's teaching, must always be emphasized with reference to the question of the labour system and with regard to the whole socio-economic system. We must emphasize and give prominence to the primacy of man in the production process, the primacy of man over things. Everything contained in the concept of capital in the strict sense is only a collection of things. Man, as the subject of work, and independently of the work that he does – man alone is a person. This truth has important and decisive consequences.

It is obvious that, when we speak of opposition between labour and capital, we are not dealing only with abstract concepts or 'impersonal forces' operating in economic production. Behind both concepts there are people, living, actual people: on the one side are those who do the work without being the owners of the means of production, and on the other side those who act as entrepreneurs and who own these means or represent the owners. Thus the issue of ownership or property enters from the beginning into the whole of this difficult historical process. The Encyclical *Rerum Novarum*, which has the social question as its theme, stresses this issue also, recalling and confirming the Church's teaching on ownership, on the right to private property even when it is a question of the means of production. The Encyclical *Mater et Magistra* did the same.

The above principle, as it was then stated and as it is still taught by the Church, diverges radically from the programme of collectivism as proclaimed by Marxism and put into practice in various countries in the decades following the time of Leo XIII's Encyclical. At the same time it differs from the programme of capitalism practised by liberalism and by the political systems inspired by it. In the latter case, the difference consists in the way the right to ownership or property is understood. Christian tradition has never upheld this right as absolute and untouchable. On the contrary, it has always understood this right within the broader context of the right common to all to use the goods of the whole of creation: the right to private property is subordinated to the right to common use, to the fact that goods are meant for everyone.

Furthermore, in the Church's teaching, ownership has never been understood in a way that could constitute grounds for social conflict in labour. As mentioned above, property is acquired first of all through work in order that it may serve work. This concerns in a special way ownership of the means of production. Isolating these means as a separate property in order to set it up in the form of 'capital' in opposition to 'labour' – and even to practise exploitation of labour – is contrary to the very nature of these means and their possession. They cannot be possessed against labour, they cannot even be possessed for possession's sake, because the only legitimate title to their possession – whether in the form of private ownership or in the form of public or collective ownership – is that they should serve labour, and thus, by serving labour, that they should make possible the achievement of the first principle of this order, namely, the universal destination of goods and the right to common use of them. From this point of view, therefore, in consideration of human labour and of common access to the goods meant for man, one cannot exclude the socialization, in suitable conditions, of certain means of production. In the course of the decades since the publication of the Encyclical *Rerum Novarum*, the Church's teaching has always recalled all these principles, going back to the arguments formulated in a much older tradition, for example, the well-known arguments of the *Summa Theologiae* of Saint Thomas Aquinas.

In the present document, which has human work as its main theme, it is right to confirm all the effort with which the Church's teaching has striven and continues to strive always to ensure the priority of work and, thereby, man's character as a subject in social life and, especially, in the dynamic structure of the whole economic process. From this point of view the position of 'rigid' capitalism continues to remain unacceptable, namely the position that defends the exclusive right to private ownership of the means of production as an untouchable 'dogma' of economic life. The principle of respect for work demands that this right should undergo a constructive revision, both in theory and in practice. If it is true that capital, as the whole of the means of production, is at the same time the product of the work of generations, it is equally true that capital is being unceasingly created through the work done with the help of all these means of production, and these means can be seen as a great workbench at which the present generation of workers is working day after day. Obviously we are dealing here with different kinds of work, not only so-called manual labour but also the many forms of intellectual work, including white-collar work and management.

In the light of the above, the many proposals put forward by experts in Catholic social teaching and by the highest Magisterium of the Church take on special significance: proposals for joint ownership of the means of work, sharing by the workers in the management and/or profits of businesses, so-called shareholding by labour, etc. Whether these various proposals can or cannot be applied concretely, it is clear that recognition of the proper position of labour and the worker in the production process demands various adaptations in the sphere of the right to ownership of the means of production. This is so not only in view of older situations but also, first and foremost, in view of the whole of the situation and the problems in the second half of the present century with regard to the so-called Third World and the various new independent countries that have arisen, especially in Africa but elsewhere as well, in place of the colonial territories of the past.

[. . .]

In order to meet the danger of unemployment and to ensure employment for all, the agents defined here as 'indirect employer' must make provision for overall planning with regard to the different kinds of work by which not only the economic life, but also the cultural life of a given society is shaped; they must also give attention to organizing that work in a correct and rational way. In the final analysis this overall concern weighs on the shoulders of the State, but it cannot mean one-sided centralization by the public authorities. Instead, what is in question is a just and rational co-ordination, within the framework of which the initiative of individuals, free groups and local work centres and complexes must be safeguarded, keeping in mind what has been said above with regard to the subject character of human labour.

The fact of the mutual dependence of societies and states and the need to collaborate in various areas mean that, while preserving the sovereign rights of each society and state in the field of planning and organizing labour in its own society, action in this important area must also be taken in the dimension of international collaboration by means of the necessary treaties and agreements. Here too the criterion for these pacts and agreements must more and more be the criterion of human work considered as a fundamental right of all human beings, work which gives similar rights to all those who work in such a way that the living standard of the workers in the different societies will less and less show those disturbing differences which are unjust and are apt to provoke even violent reactions. The international organizations have an enormous part to play in this area. They must let themselves be guided by an exact diagnosis of the complex situations and of the influence exercised by natural, historical, civil and other such circumstances. They must also be more highly operative with regard to plans for action jointly decided on, that is to say, they must be more effective in carrying them out.

In this direction, it is possible to actuate a plan for universal and proportionate progress by all in accordance with the guidelines of Paul VI's encyclical *Populorum Progressio*. It must be stressed that the constitutive element in this progress and also the most adequate way to verify it in a spirit of justice and peace, which the Church proclaims and for which she does not cease to pray to the Father of all individuals and of all peoples, is the continual reappraisal of man's work, both in the aspect of its objective finality and in the aspect of the dignity of the subject of all work, that is to say, man. The progress in question must be made through man and for man and it must produce its fruit in man. A test of this progress will be the increasingly mature recognition of the purpose of work and increasingly universal respect for the rights inherent in work in conformity with the dignity of man, the subject of work.

Rational planning and the proper organization of human labour in keeping with individual societies and states should also facilitate the discovery of the right proportions between the different kinds of employment: work on the land, in industry, in the various services, white-collar work and scientific or artistic work, in accordance with the capacities of individuals and for the common good of each society and of the whole of mankind. The organization of human life in accordance with the many possibilities of labour should be matched by a suitable system of instruction and education aimed first of all at developing mature human beings, but also aimed at preparing people specifically for assuming to good advantage an appropriate place in the vast and socially differentiated world of work.

As we view the whole human family throughout the world, we cannot fail to be struck by a disconcerting fact of immense proportions:

67

the fact that while conspicuous natural resources remain unused there are huge numbers of people who are unemployed or underemployed and countless multitudes of people suffering from hunger. This is a fact that without any doubt demonstrates that both within the individual political communities and in their relationships on the continental and world levels there is something wrong with the organization of work and employment, precisely at the most critical and socially most important points.

After outlining the important role that concern for providing employment for all workers plays in safeguarding respect for the inalienable rights of man in view of his work, it is worth while taking a closer look at these rights, which in the final analysis are formed within the relationship between worker and direct employer. All that has been said above on the subject of the indirect employer is aimed at defining these relationships more exactly, by showing the many forms of conditioning within which these relationships are indirectly formed. This consideration does not however have a purely descriptive purpose; it is not a brief treatise on economics or politics. It is a matter of highlighting the deontological and moral aspect. The key problem of social ethics in this case is that of just remuneration for work done. In the context of the present there is no more important way of securing a just relationship between the worker and the employer than that constituted by remuneration for work. Whether the work is done in a system of private ownership of the means of production or in a system where ownership has undergone a certain 'socialization', the relationship between the employer (first and foremost the direct employer) and the worker is resolved on the basis of the wage, that is, through just remuneration of the work done.

It should also be noted that the justice of a socio-economic system and, in each case, its just functioning, deserve in the final analysis to be evaluated by the way in which man's work is properly remunerated in the system. Here we return once more to the first principle of the whole ethical and social order, namely the principle of the common use of goods. In every system, regardless of the fundamental relationships within it between capital and labour, wages, that is to say remuneration for work, are still a practical means whereby the vast majority of people can have access to those goods which are intended for common use: both the goods of nature and manufactured goods. Both kinds of goods become accessible to the worker through the wage which he receives as remuneration for his work. Hence in every case a just wage is the concrete means of verifying the justice of the whole socio-economic system and, in any case, of checking that it is functioning justly. It is not the only means of checking, but it is a particularly important one and in a sense the key means.

(Paragraphs 18.1–19.1)

Source: Catholic Truth Society, 1981, pp. 41, 43–4, 50–3, 63–5.

(b) *John Paul II:* Centesimus Annus

Pope Leo XIII was aware of the need for a sound *theory of the State* in order to ensure the normal development of man's spiritual and temporal activities, both of which are indispensable. For this reason, in one passage of *Rerum Novarum* he presents the organization of society according to the three powers – legislative, executive and judicial – something which at the time represented a novelty in Church teaching. Such an ordering reflects a realistic vision of man's social nature, which calls for legislation capable of protecting the freedom of all. To that end, it is preferable that each power be balanced by other powers and by other spheres of responsibility which keep it within proper bounds. This is the principle of the 'rule of law', in which the law is sovereign, and not the arbitrary will of individuals.

In modern times, this concept has been opposed by totalitarianism, which, in its Marxist-Leninist form, maintains that some people, by virtue of a deeper knowledge of the laws of the development of society, or through membership of a particular class or through contact with the deeper sources of the collective consciousness, are exempt from error and can therefore arrogate to themselves the exercise of absolute power. It must be added that totalitarianism arises out of a denial of truth in the objective sense. If there is no transcendent truth, in obedience to which man achieves his full identity, then there is no sure principle for guaranteeing just relations between people. Their self-interest as a class, group or nation would inevitably set them in opposition to one another. If one does not acknowledge transcendent truth, then the force of power takes over, and each person tends to make full use of the means at his disposal in order to impose his own interests or his own opinion, with no regard for the rights of others. People are then respected only to the extent that they can be exploited for selfish ends. Thus, the root of modern totalitarianism is to be found in the denial of the transcendent dignity of the human person who, as the visible image of the invisible God, is therefore by his very nature the subject of rights which no one may violate – no individual group, class, nation or State. Not even the majority of a social body may violate these rights, by going against the minority, by isolating, oppressing, or exploiting it, or by attempting to annihilate it.

The culture and praxis of totalitarianism also involve a rejection of the Church. The State or the party which claims to be able to lead history towards perfect goodness, and which sets itself above all values, cannot tolerate the affirmation of an *objective criterion of good and evil* beyond the will of those in power, since such a criterion, in given circumstances, could be used to judge their actions. This explains why totalitarianism attempts to destroy the Church, or at least to reduce her to submission, making her an instrument of its own ideological apparatus.

Furthermore, the totalitarian State tends to absorb within itself the nation, society, the family, religious groups and individuals themselves. In defending her own freedom, the Church is also defending the human person, who must obey God rather than men (cf. Acts 5.29), as well as defending the family, the various social organizations and nations – all of which enjoy their own spheres of autonomy and sovereignty.

The Church values the democratic system inasmuch as it ensures the participation of citizens in making political choices, guarantees to the governed the possibility both of electing and holding accountable those who govern them, and of replacing them through peaceful means when appropriate. Thus she cannot encourage the formation of narrow ruling groups which usurp the power of the State for individual interests or for ideological ends.

Authentic democracy is possible only in a State ruled by law, and on the basis of a correct conception of the human person. It requires that the necessary conditions be present for the advancement both of the individual through education and formation in true ideals, and of the 'subjectivity' of society through the creation of structures of participation and shared responsibility. Nowadays there is a tendency to claim that agnosticism and sceptical relativism are the philosophy and the basic attitude which correspond to democratic forms of political life. Those who are convinced that they know the truth and firmly adhere to it are considered unreliable from a democratic point of view, since they do not accept that truth is determined by the majority, or that it is subject to variation according to different political trends. It must be observed in this regard that if there is no ultimate truth to guide and direct political activity, then ideas and convictions can easily be manipulated for reasons of power. As history demonstrates, a democracy without values easily turns into open or thinly disguised totalitarianism.

Nor does the Church close her eyes to the danger of fanaticism or fundamentalism among those who, in the name of an ideology which purports to be scientific or religious, claim the right to impose on others their own concept of what is true and good. *Christian truth* is not of this kind. Since it is not an ideology, the Christian faith does not presume to imprison changing socio-political realities in a rigid schema, and it recognizes that human life is realized in history in conditions that are diverse and imperfect. Furthermore, in constantly reaffirming the transcendent dignity of the person, the Church's method is always that of respect for freedom.

But freedom attains its full development only by accepting the truth. In a world without truth, freedom loses its foundation and man is exposed to the violence of passion and to manipulation, both open and hidden. The Christian upholds freedom and serves it, constantly offering to others the truth which he has known (cf. John 8.31–2), in accordance with the missionary nature of his vocation. While paying heed to every fragment of truth which he encounters in the life experience and in the culture of individuals and of nations, he will not fail to affirm in dialogue with others all that his faith and the correct use of reason have enabled him to understand.

Following the collapse of Communist totalitarianism and of many other totalitarian and 'national security' regimes, today we are witnessing a predominance, not without signs of opposition, of the democratic ideal, together with lively attention to and concern for human rights. But for this very reason it is necessary for peoples in the process of reforming their systems to give democracy an authentic and solid foundation through the explicit recognition of those rights. Among the most important of these rights, mention must be made of the right to life, an integral part of which is the right of the child to develop in the mother's womb from the moment of conception; the right to live in a united family and in a moral environment conducive to the growth of the child's personality; the right to develop one's intelligence and freedom in seeking and knowing the truth; the right to share in the work which makes wise use of the earth's material resources, and to derive from that work the means to support oneself and one's dependents; and the right freely to establish a family, to have and to rear children through the responsible exercise of one's sexuality. In a certain sense, the source and synthesis of these rights is religious freedom, understood as the right to live in the truth of one's faith and in conformity with one's transcendent dignity as a person.

Even in countries with democratic forms of government, these rights are not always fully respected. Here we are referring not only to the scandal of abortion, but also to different aspects of a crisis within democracies themselves, which seem at times to have lost the ability to make decisions aimed at the common good. Certain demands which arise within society are sometimes not examined in accordance with the criteria of justice and morality, but rather on the basis of the electoral or financial power of the groups promoting them. With time, such distortions of political conduct create distrust and apathy, with a sub-sequent decline in the political participation and civic spirit of the general population, which feels abused and disillusioned. As a result, there is a growing inability to situate particular interests within the framework of a coherent vision of the common good. The latter is not simply the sum total of particular interests; rather it involves an assessment and integration of those interests on the basis of a balanced hierarchy of values; ultimately, it demands a correct understanding of the dignity and the rights of the person.

The Church respects *the legitimate autonomy of the democratic order* and is not entitled to express preferences for this or that institutional or constitutional solution. Her contribution to the political order is precisely her vision of the dignity of the person revealed in all its fulness in the mystery of the Incarnate Word.

These general observations also apply to the *role of the State in the economic sector*. Economic activity, especially the activity of a market economy, cannot be conducted in an institutional, juridical or political vacuum. On the contrary, it presupposes sure guarantees of individual freedom and private property, as well as a stable currency and efficient public services. Hence the principal task of the State is to guarantee this security, so that those who work and produce can enjoy the fruits of their labours and thus feel encouraged to work efficiently and honestly. The absence of stability, together with the corruption of public officials and the spread of improper sources of growing rich and of easy profits derived from illegal or purely speculative activities, constitutes one of the chief obstacles to development and to the economic order.

Another task of the State is that of overseeing and directing the exercise of human rights in the economic sector. However, primary responsibility in this area belongs not to the State but to individuals and to the various groups and associations which make up society. The State could not directly ensure the right to work for all its citizens unless it controlled every aspect of economic life and restricted the free initiative of individuals. This does not mean, however, that the State has no competence in this domain, as was claimed by those who argued against any rules in the economic sphere. Rather, the State has a duty to sustain business activities by creating conditions which will ensure job opportunities, by stimulating those activities where they are lacking or by supporting them in moments of crisis.

The State has the further right to intervene when particular monop-olies create delays or obstacles to development. In addition to the tasks of harmonizing and guiding development, in exceptional circumstances the State can also exercise a *substitute function*, when social sectors or business systems are too weak or are just getting under way, and are not equal to the task at hand. Such supplementary interventions, which are justified by urgent reasons touching the common good, must be as brief as possible, so as to avoid removing permanently from society and business systems the functions which are properly theirs, and so as to avoid enlarging excessively the sphere of State intervention to the detriment of both economic and civil freedom.

In recent years the range of such intervention has vastly expanded, to the point of creating a new type of State, the so-called 'Welfare State'. This has happened in some countries in order to respond better to many needs and demands, by remedying forms of poverty and deprivation unworthy of the human person. However, excesses and abuses, especially in recent years, have provoked very harsh criticisms of the Welfare State, dubbed the 'Social Assistance State'. Malfunctions and defects in the Social Assistance State are the result of an inadequate understanding of the tasks proper to the State. Here again *the principle of subsidiarity* must be respected: a community of a higher order should not interfere in the internal life of a community of a lower order, depriving the latter of its functions, but rather should support it in case of need and help to coordinate its activity with the activities of the rest of society, always with a view to the common good.

By intervening directly and depriving society of its responsibility, the Social Assistance State leads to a loss of human energies and an inordinate increase of public agencies, which are dominated more by bureaucratic ways of thinking than by concern for serving their clients, and which are accompanied by an enormous increase in spending. In fact, it would appear that needs are best understood and satisfied by people who are closest to them and who act as neighbours to those in need. It should be added that certain kinds of demands often call for a response which is not simply material but which is capable of perceiving the deeper human need. One thinks of the condition of refugees, immigrants, the elderly, the sick, and all those in circumstances which call for assistance, such as drug abusers: all these people can be helped effectively only by those who offer them genuine fraternal support, in addition to the necessary care.

Faithful to the mission received from Christ her Founder, the Church has always been present and active among the needy, offering them material assistance in ways that neither humiliate nor reduce them to mere objects of assistance, but which help them to escape their precarious situation by promoting their dignity as persons. With heartfelt gratitude to God it must be pointed out that active charity has never ceased to be practised in the Church; indeed, today it is showing a manifold and gratifying increase. In this regard, special mention must be made of *volunteer work*, which the Church favours and promotes by urging everyone to cooperate in supporting and encouraging its undertakings.

In order to overcome today's widespread individualistic mentality, what is required is *a concrete commitment to solidarity and charity*, beginning in the family with the mutual support of husband and wife and the care which the different generations give to one another. In this sense the family too can be called a community of work and solidarity. It can happen, however, that when a family does decide to live up fully to its vocation, it finds itself without the necessary support from the State and without sufficient resources. It is urgent therefore to promote not only family policies, but also those social policies which have the family as their principal object, policies which assist the family by providing adequate resources and efficient means of support, both for bringing up children and for looking after the elderly, so as to avoid distancing the latter from the family unit and in order to strengthen relations between generations.

Apart from the family, other intermediate communities exercise primary functions and give life to specific networks of solidarity. These develop as real communities of persons and strengthen the social fabric, preventing society from becoming an anonymous and impersonal mass, as unfortunately often happens today. It is in interrelationships on many levels that a person lives, and that society becomes more 'personalized'. The individual today is often suffocated between two poles represented by the State and the marketplace. At times it seems as though he exists only as a producer and consumer of goods, or as an object of State administration. People lose sight of the fact that life in society has neither the market nor the State as its final purpose, since life itself has a unique value which the State and the market must serve. Man remains above all a being who seeks the truth and strives to live in that truth, deepening his understanding of it through a dialogue which involves past and future generations.

From this open search for truth, which is renewed in every generation, *the culture of a nation* derives its character. Indeed, the heritage of values which has been received and handed down is always challenged by the young. To challenge does not necessarily mean to destroy or reject *a priori*, but above all to put these values to the test in one's own life, and through this existential verification to make them more real, relevant and personal, distinguishing the valid elements in the tradition from false and erroneous ones, or from obsolete forms which can be usefully replaced by others more suited to the times.

In this context, it is appropriate *to recall that evangelization too plays a role in the culture of the various nations*, sustaining culture in its progress towards the truth, and assisting in the work of its purification and enrichment. However, when a culture becomes inward looking, and tries to perpetuate obsolete ways of living by rejecting any exchange or debate with regard to the truth about man, then it becomes sterile and is heading for decadence.

All human activity takes place within a culture and interacts with culture. For an adequate formation of a culture, the involvement of the whole man is required, whereby he exercises his creativity, intelligence, and knowledge of the world and of people. Furthermore, he displays his capacity for self-control, personal sacrifice, solidarity and readiness to promote the common good. Thus the first and most important task is accomplished within man's heart. The way in which he is involved in building his own future depends on the understanding he has of himself and of his own destiny. It is on this level that *the Church's specific and decisive contribution to true culture* is to be found. The Church promotes those aspects of human behaviour which favour a true culture of peace, as opposed to models in which the individual is lost in the crowd, in which the role of his initiative and freedom is neglected, and in which his greatness is posited in the arts of conflict and war. The Church renders this service to human society *by preaching the truth about the creation of the world,* which God has placed in human hands so that people may make it fruitful and more perfect through their work; and *by preaching the truth about the Redemption,* whereby the Son of God has saved mankind and at the same time has united all people, making them responsible for one another. Sacred Scripture continually speaks to us of an active commitment to our neighbour and demands of us a shared responsibility for all of humanity.

This duty is not limited to one's own family, nation or State, but extends progressively to all mankind, since no one can consider himself extraneous or indifferent to the lot of another member of the human family. No one can say that he is not responsible for the well-being of his brother or sister (cf. Gen. 4.9; Luke 10.29–37; Matt. 25.31–46). Attentive and pressing concern for one's neighbour in a moment of need – made easier today because of the new means of communication which have brought people closer together – is especially important with regard to the search for ways to resolve international conflicts other than by war. It is not hard to see that the terrifying power of the means of destruction – to which even medium and small-sized countries have access – and the ever closer links between the peoples of the whole world make it very difficult or practically impossible to limit the consequences of a conflict.

Pope Benedict XV and his successors clearly understood this danger. I myself, on the occasion of the recent tragic war in the Persian Gulf, repeated the cry: 'Never again war!' No, never again war, which destroys the lives of innocent people, teaches how to kill, throws into upheaval even the lives of those who do the killing and leaves behind a trail of resentment and hatred, thus making it all the more difficult to find a just solution of the very problems which provoked the war. Just as the time has finally come when in individual States a system of private vendetta and reprisal has given way to the rule of law, so too a similar step forward is now urgently needed in the international community. Furthermore, it must not be forgotten that at the root of war there are usually real and serious grievances: injustices suffered, legitimate aspirations frustrated, poverty, and the exploitation of multitudes of desperate people who see no real possibility of improving their lot by peaceful means.

For this reason, another name for peace is *development*. Just as there is a collective responsibility for avoiding war, so too there is a collective responsibility for promoting development. Just as within individual societies it is possible and right to organize a solid economy which will direct the functioning of the market to the common good, so too there is a similar need for adequate interventions on the international level. For this to happen, *a great effort must be made to enhance mutual understanding and knowledge, and to increase the sensitivity of consciences.* This is the culture which is hoped for, one which fosters trust in the human potential of the poor, and consequently in their ability to improve their condition through work or to make a positive contribution to economic prosperity. But to accomplish this, the poor – be they individuals or nations – need to be provided with realistic opportunities. Creating such conditions calls for a *concerted worldwide effort to promote development*, an effort which also involves sacrificing the positions of income and of power enjoyed by the more developed economies.

This may mean making important changes in established life-styles, in order to limit the waste of environmental and human resources, thus enabling every individual and all the peoples of the earth to have a sufficient share of those resources. In addition, the new material and spiritual resources must be utilized which are the result of the work and culture of peoples who today are on the margins of the international community, so as to obtain an overall human enrichment of the family of nations.

(Sections 44–52)
Source: Catholic Truth Society, 1991, pp. 33–8.

Further reading

See the useful collections by Dorr, *Option for the Poor: A Hundred Years of Vatican Social Teaching* and by Walsh and Davies, *Proclaiming Justice and Peace*. The nineteenth-century background is well covered in Misner's *Social Catholicism in Europe*. On Christian Democracy see the classic work by Fogarty and the more recent collection by Baum and Coleman, *The Church and Christian Democracy*, and the concise review by Hehir in Witte's *Christianity and Democracy in Global Context*. On Catholic social thought, see the book by Habiger, the article by Mitchell in Wood's *Readings on Church and State* and Coleman's collection of comment in *One Hundred Years of Catholic Social Thought*.

Chapter Six

CONTEMPORARY PROTESTANT CHRISTIANITY

Introduction

Modern Protestant thought on politics is more diffuse than its Roman Catholic counterpart. This is not surprising given the greater diversity of its traditions. Its central theme, however, is a return to neo-orthodoxy best exemplified by Reinhold Niebuhr who reacted against the optimistic assumptions of much previous liberal-Protestant social thinking. God's grace was seen by Niebuhr not as something which, in the traditional Catholic view, perfects nature and constitutes the power of God within human society but as something which acts in a power of forgiveness set over against humanity. For him, this was a truth rediscovered by the Reformation but immediately obscured by the Renaissance with its over-optimistic confidence in human capacities. The Renaissance eclipsed the Reformation because the vast expansion of human knowledge and capabilities of the time enabled the following centuries to combine the biblical idea of sanctification and fulfilment of life with a meaningful history and unbounded confidence in human capacities. To this optimism contemporary liberal Protestantism with its neglect of the notion of eschatological judgement had merely given a Christian tinge.

By contrast, the more relaxed mood of the 1960s saw a much more world-affirming theology of which the most popular example is Harvey Cox. This 'secular' theology claimed to be inspired partly by Dietrich Bonhoeffer's 'religionless' Christianity. In fact, Bonhoeffer's position was more complex: he wished to preserve Christian values, which he saw exemplified in the struggle for a new and just political order, without recourse to the traditional idea of a supernatural God. Previous emphases on the world to come, personal salvation and the schism between secular and Christian values could be overcome by a return to a biblical prophetic faith.

During the 1970s, a current of explicitly 'political' theology emerged whose leading exponent was Jürgen Moltmann. In contrast to more traditional Reformation ideas, society was seen not so much under God's judgement as orientated *towards* it. This forward-looking theology intended to be public and practical, critically engaged in political matters: theology was to be interpreted in its socio-political context often with a socialist orientation which was more marked in its more radical offspring, liberation theology.

The more troubled outlook of the 1980s has seen the emergence of a post-modern, post-liberal theology which rejects the universal view taken by the Enlightenment and is concerned with the moral principles and practice of the particular Christian community. On this view, represented, for example, by Stanley Hauerwas, the task of the Christian is not to work on the universal principle of some natural law but to build up a Christian community within which the practice of Christian morality is possible.

(a) *Niebuhr:* The Nature and Destiny of Man

The struggle for justice is as profound a revelation of the possibilities and limits of historical existence as the quest for truth. In some respects it is even more revealing because it engages all human vitalities and powers more obviously than the intellectual quest.

The obligation to build and to perfect communal life is not merely forced upon us by the necessity of coming to terms with the rather numerous hosts, whom it has pleased an Almighty Creator to place on this little earth beside us. Community is an individual as well as social necessity; for the individual can realize himself only in intimate and organic relation with his fellowmen. Love is therefore the primary law of his nature; and brotherhood the fundamental requirement of his social existence.

Since man is a unity of vitality and reason, the social coherence of life can never be purely rational. It includes an interpenetration of all powers and potencies, emotional and volitional as well as rational. But the power of rational freedom gives human communities a higher dimension than those of nature. Man's freedom over the limits of nature in indeterminate regression means that no fixed limits can be placed upon either the purity or the breadth of the brotherhood for which men strive in history. No traditional attainment of brotherhood is secure against criticism from a higher historical perspective or safe from corruption on each new level of achievement.

The indeterminate character of these possibilities of both good and evil in social and political relations justifies the dynamic interpretation of the social process. The facts of history may not support the conclusion that historical process has continually purified and perfected social relations; but they certainly prove that the breadth and extent of historical communities have been consistently increased. Every age, and more particularly the age of technics, has confronted men with the problem of relating their lives to a larger number of their fellowmen. The task of creating community and avoiding anarchy is constantly pitched on broader and broader levels.

These facts have presented modern culture with what seemed irrefutable proofs of its progressive view of the social task. The 'Kingdom of God' seemed to be an immanent force in history, culminating in a universal society of brotherhood and justice. The secular and liberal-Protestant approaches to the socio-moral problem, based upon this presupposition, are too numerous to mention. Modern sociological treatises are practically unanimous in assuming this view of history. The Marxist interpretation of history deviates from it. But the deviation is only provisionally radical. Its catastrophism is finally subordinated to a progressive and utopian concept of history. The liberal-Protestant version has added little but pious phrases to the interpretation.

The definition of the Christian view of human destiny as presented must lead to other, and partly contrary, conclusions. The conclusions are not completely contrary because they do not refute the dynamic character of history or the significance of its continually expanding tasks and obligations. They do, however, challenge the identification of historical growth with moral progress. According to our interpretation, 'grace' is related to 'nature' partly as fulfilment and partly as negation. If the contradiction between 'nature' and 'grace' is not recognized, and the continued power of 'nature' in the realm of 'grace' is not conceded, new sins are brought into history by the pretension that sin has been progressively eliminated.

The achievements of democracy have been tortuously worked out in human history partly because various schools of religious and political thought had great difficulty in fully comprehending the perils to justice in either one or the other instrument of justice – the organization of power and the balance of power. Usually the school of thought which comprehended the moral ambiguities of government did not understand the perils of anarchy inhering in uncontrolled social life; while those who feared this anarchy were uncritical of the claims and pretensions of government. History had to stumble by tortuous process upon the proper techniques for avoiding both anarchy and tyranny, against the illusions of idealists and of realists who understood only one or the other side of the problem. In this process the Christian tradition itself seldom stated the full truth of its twofold approach to the political order in such a way that it would give guidance in the complexities of political and social life. The mistakes which were made in comprehending the paradox in the political sphere conform to the limitations of the various Christian and secular traditions, which we have examined in other spheres. They can therefore be stated fairly briefly.

The development of Christian and of modern secular theories of politics is determined by an interplay of one classical and of two Biblical approaches to stuff of the political order. The Bible contains two approaches which, taken together and held in balance, do justice to the moral ambiguities of government. According to the one, government is an ordinance of God and its authority reflects the Divine Majesty. According to the other, the 'rulers' and 'judges' of the nations are particularly subject to divine judgment and wrath because they oppress the poor and defy the divine majesty. These two approaches do justice to the two aspects of government. It is a principle of order and its power prevents anarchy; but its power is not identical with divine power. It is wielded from a partial and particular locus and it cannot achieve the perfect union of goodness and power which characterizes divine power. The pretension that its power is perfectly virtuous represents its false claim of majesty. This claim elicits alternate moods of reverent obedience and resentful rebellion in history.

[. . .]

Whatever may be the source of our insights into the problems of the political order, it is important both to recognize the higher possibilities of justice in every historic situation, and to know that the twin perils of tyranny and anarchy can never be completely overcome in any political achievement. These perils are expressions of the sinful elements of conflict and dominion, standing in contradiction to the ideal of brotherhood on every level of communal organization. There is no possibility of making history completely safe against either occasional conflicts of vital interests (war) or against the misuse of the power which is intended to prevent such conflict of interests (tyranny). To understand this is to labour for higher justice in terms of the experience of justification by faith. Justification by faith in the realm of justice means that we will not regard the pressures and counter pressures, the tensions, the overt and the covert conflicts by which justice is achieved and maintained, as normative in the absolute sense; but neither will we ease our conscience by seeking to escape from involvement in them. We will know that we cannot purge ourselves of the sin and guilt in which we are involved by the moral ambiguities of politics without also disavowing responsibility for the creative possibilities of justice.

Source: Reinhold Niebuhr, *The Nature and Destiny of Man: A Christian Interpretation*, Nisbet, 1941, pp. 253–4, 278, 294.

(b) Bonhoeffer: Ethics

The dominion of Christ and the decalogue do not mean that the secular institutions are made subservient to a human ideal or 'natural law', nor yet to the Church (this being a contradiction of the medieval Thomist doctrine), but they mean their emancipation for true worldliness, for the state to *be* a state, etc. The primary implication for secular institutions of the dominion of Christ and of the decalogue is not, therefore, the conversion of the statesman or the economist, nor yet the elimination of the harshness and unmercifulness of the state for the sake of a falsely interpreted christianization of the state and its transformation into a part of the Church. It is precisely in the dispensation of strict justice and in the administration of the office of the sword, in maintaining the unmerciful character of the institutions of the state, that is to say, their genuine worldliness, that the dominion of Christ, i.e. the rule of mercy, is given its due. The incarnation of God, that is to say, the incarnation of love, would be misinterpreted if one were to fail to perceive that the worldly institutions of strict justice, of punishment and of the wrath of God are also a fulfilment of this incarnate love and that the commandment of the sermon on the mount is also observed in genuine action by the state. The purpose and aim of the dominion of Christ is not to make the worldly order godly or to subordinate it to the Church but to set it free for true worldliness.

The emancipation of the worldly order under the dominion of Christ takes concrete form not through the conversion of Christian statesmen, etc., but through the concrete encounter of the secular institutions with the Church of Jesus Christ, her proclamation and her life. By allowing this Church of Jesus Christ to continue, by making room for her and by enabling her proclamation of the dominion of Christ to take effect, the secular institutions attain to their own true worldliness and law which has its foundation in Christ. Their attitude to the Church of Jesus Christ will always be the measure of the true worldliness which is not impeded by any ideological and alien law or by any arbitrary autonomy. A false attitude to the Church will always have as its consequence a failure to achieve genuine worldliness on the part of the secular institutions, the state, etc., and *vice versa*.

With regard to the relationship of the secular institutions to one another and to the Church, the Lutheran doctrine of the three estates, *oeconomicus, politicus* and *hierarchicus,* has as its decisive characteristic and permanent significance that it is based on coordination rather than any kind of priority and subordination, so that the worldly order is safe-guarded against the alien rule of the Church, and *vice versa.* In my opinion this doctrine must be replaced by a doctrine which is drawn from the Bible, the doctrine of the four divine mandates, marriage and family, labour, government, and Church. These institutions are divine in that they possess a concrete divine commission and promise which has its foundation and evidence in the revelation. Amid the changes of all historical institutions these divine mandates continue until the end of the world. Their justification is not simply their historical existence; in this they differ from such institutions as the people, the race, the class, the masses, the society, the nation, the country, the Empire, etc. It is a positive divine mandate for the preservation of the world for the sake and purpose of Christ. It is perhaps not by chance that precisely these mandates seem to have their type in the celestial world. Marriage corresponds with Christ and the congregation; the family with God the Father and the Son, and with the brotherhood of men with Christ; labour corresponds with the creative service of God and Christ to the world, and of men to God; government corresponds with the dominion of Christ in eternity; the state corresponds with the πόλις of God.

A word of the Church with regard to the secular institutions will consequently have to place these divine mandates, in whatever may be their concrete form at the time, under the dominion of Christ and under the decalogue. In doing this it will not be subjecting the secular institutions to an alien law, but it will be setting them free for concrete and genuine worldly service. It will speak of the divine mandates of the worldly order in such a way that the dominion of Christ is maintained *over* them and the divine mandate of the Christian Church is main-tained *side by side* with them. It cannot deprive the secular institutions of their responsible decision and their service, but it can direct them to the only place at which they can decide and act responsibly.

It may be remarked that the secular institutions are able to perform their service even without the encounter with the world of the Church of Jesus Christ (cf. Luther and the Turks). First of all, there is never more than a limited truth in this observation; genuine worldliness is achieved only through emancipation by Christ; without this there is the rule of alien laws, ideologies and idols. Secondly, the very limited correctness of this remark can only afford the Church a thankfully accepted confirmation of the truth which is revealed to her; it cannot lead her to suppose that this is in itself sufficient, but it must lead her to proclaim the dominion of Christ as the full truth in the midst of all partial truths. When the Church perceives that a worldly order is on some few occasions possible without the preaching being heard (but still never without the existence of Jesus Christ), this will not impel her to disregard Christ, but it will elicit from her the full proclamation of the grace of the dominion of Christ. The unknown God will now be preached as the God who is known because he is revealed.

Government is instituted for the sake of Christ; it serves Christ, and consequently it also serves the Church. Yet the dominion of Christ over all government does not by any means imply the dominion of the Church over government. But the same Lord, whom government serves, is the Head of the congregation, the Lord of the Church. The service of government to Christ consists in the exercise of its commission to secure an outward justice by the power of the sword. This service is thus an indirect service to the congregation, which only by this is enabled to 'lead a quiet and peaceable life' (1 Tim. 2.2). Through its service towards Christ, government is ultimately linked with the Church. If it fulfils its mission as it should, the congregation can live in peace, for government and congregation serve the same Master.

The claim of government to obedience and deference extends also to the Church. With respect to the spiritual office, government can indeed only demand that this office shall not interfere in the secular office, but that it shall fulfil its own mission, which does, in fact, include the admonition to obey government. Government possesses no authority over this mission itself, as it is exercised in the pastoral office and in the office of Church management. So far as the spiritual office is an office which is exercised publicly, government has a claim to supervise it, to see that everything is done in an orderly manner, that is to say, in accordance with outward justice. It is only in this connexion that it has a claim to intervene in the question of appointments and organization within the office. The spiritual office itself is not subject to government. Yet government possesses a full claim to obedience with regard to the Christian members of the congregation. In this it does not appear as a second authority side by side with the authority of Christ, but its own authority is only a form of the authority of Christ. In his obedience to government the Christian is obedient to Christ. As a citizen the Christian does not cease to be a Christian, but he serves Christ in a different way. This in itself also provides an adequate definition of the contents of the authentic claim of government. It can never lead the Christian against Christ; on the contrary, it helps him to serve Christ in the world. The person who exercises government thus becomes for the Christian a servant of God.

The Church's claim on Government. The Church has the task of summoning the whole world to submit to the dominion of Jesus Christ.

She testifies before government to their common Master. She calls upon the persons who exercise government to believe in Christ for the sake of their own salvation. She knows that it is in obedience to Jesus Christ that the commission of government is properly executed. Her aim is not that government should pursue a Christian policy, enact Christian laws, etc., but that it should be true government in accordance with its own special task. Only the Church brings government to an understanding of itself. For the sake of their common Master the Church claims to be listened to by government; she claims protection for the public Christian proclamation against violence and blasphemy; she claims protection for the institution of the Church against arbitrary interference, and she claims protection for Christian life in obedience to Jesus Christ. The Church can never abandon these claims; and she must make them heard publicly so long as government itself maintains its claim to acknowledge the Church. Of course, if government opposes the Church, explicitly or in fact, there may come a time when the Church no longer wastes her words, even though she still does not give up her claim; for the Church knows that, whether government performs its mission well or badly, it must always serve only its Master, and therefore also the Church. The government which denies protection to the Church thereby places the Church all the more patently under the protection of her Master. The government which blasphemes its Master testifies thereby all the more evidently to the power of this Master who is praised and glorified in the torments and martyrdoms of the congregation.

The Ecclesiastical Responsibility of Government. To the claim of the Church there corresponds the responsibility of government. Here it becomes necessary to answer the question of the attitude of government to the first commandment. Must government make a religious decision, or does its task lie in religious neutrality? Is government responsible for maintaining the true Christian service of God, and has it the right to prohibit other kinds of divine service? Certainly the persons who exercise government ought also to accept belief in Jesus Christ, but the office of government remains independent of the religious decision. Yet it pertains to the responsibility of the office of government that it should protect the righteous, and indeed praise them, in other words that it should support the practice of religion. A government which fails to recognize this undermines the root of the true obedience and, therefore, also its own authority (e.g. France in 1905). At the same time the office of government as such remains religiously neutral and attends only to its own task. And it can, therefore, never become the originator in the foundation of a new religion; for if it does so it disrupts itself. It affords protection to every form of service of God which does not undermine the office of government. It takes care that the differences

85

between the various forms of service of God do not give rise to a conflict which endangers the order of the country. But it achieves this purpose not by suppressing one form of service of God, but by a clear adherence to its own governmental commission. It will thereby become evident that the true Christian service of God does not endanger this commission, but, on the contrary, continually establishes it anew. If the persons who exercise government are Christian they must know that the Christian proclamation is delivered not by means of the sword but by means of the word. The idea of *cuius regio eius religio* was possible only in certain quite definite political circumstances: namely, the agreement of the princes to admit each other's exiles; as a general principle it is incompatible with the office of government. In the case of some special situation of ecclesiastical emergency it would be the responsibility of the Christians who exercise government to make their power available, if the Church requests it, in order to remove the source of the disorder. This does not mean, however, that in such circumstances government as such would take over the functions of ecclesiastical control. It is here exclusively a matter of restoring the rightful order within which the spiritual office can be rightfully discharged and both government and Church can perform their own several tasks. Government will fulfil its obligation under the first commandment by being government in the rightful manner and by discharging its governmental responsibility also with respect to the Church. But it does not possess the office of confessing and preaching faith in Jesus Christ.

The Political Responsibility of the Church. If political responsibility is understood exclusively in the sense of governmental responsibility, then it is clearly only upon government that this responsibility devolves. But if the term is taken to refer quite generally to life in the *polis*, then there are a number of senses in which it is necessary to speak of political responsibility of the Church in answer to the claim of government upon the Church. Here again we distinguish between the responsibility of the spiritual office and the responsibility of the Christians. It is part of the Church's office of guardianship that she shall call sin by its name and that she shall warn men against sin; for 'righteousness exalteth a nation', both in time and in eternity, 'but sin is perdition for the people', both temporal and eternal perdition (Prov. 14.34). If the Church did not do this, she would be incurring part of the guilt for the blood of the wicked (Ezek. 3.17ff.). This warning against sin is delivered to the congregation openly and publicly, and whoever will not hear it passes judgement upon himself. The intention of the preacher here is not to improve the world, but to summon it to belief in Jesus Christ and to bear witness to the reconciliation which has been accomplished through him and to his dominion. The theme of the proclamation is not the wickedness of the world but the grace of Jesus Christ. It is part of the responsibility of the spiritual office that it shall devote earnest attention to the proclamation of the reign of Christ as King, and that it shall with all due deference address government directly in order to draw its attention to shortcomings and errors which must otherwise imperil its governmental office. If the word of the Church is, on principle, not received, then the only political responsibility which remains to her is in establishing and maintaining, at least among her own members, the order of outward justice which is no longer to be found in the *polis*, for by so doing she serves government in her own way.

Is there a political responsibility on the part of individual Christians? Certainly the individual Christian cannot be made responsible for the action of government, and he must not make himself responsible for it; but because of his faith and his charity he is responsible for his own calling and for the sphere of his own personal life, however large or however small it may be. If this responsibility is fulfilled in faith, it is effectual for the whole of the *polis*. According to Holy Scripture, there is no right to revolution; but there is a responsibility of every individual for preserving the purity of his office and mission in the *polis*. In this way, in the true sense, every individual serves government with his responsibility. No one, not even government itself, can deprive him of this responsibility or forbid him to discharge it, for it is an integral part of his life in sanctification, and it arises from obedience to the Lord of both Church and government.

Conclusions. Government and Church are connected in such various ways that their relationship cannot be regulated in accordance with any single general principle. Neither the separation of state and Church, nor the form of the state church can in itself constitute a solution of the problem. Nothing is more dangerous than to draw theoretical conclusions by generalizing from single particular experiences. The recommendation for a withdrawal of the Church from the world and from the relations which she still maintains with the state under the impact of an apocalyptic age is, in this general aspect, nothing but a somewhat melancholy interpretation of the times in terms of the philosophy of history. If it were really acted upon in earnest, it would necessarily lead to the most drastic consequences, which are described in Revelation 13. But, conversely, a philosophy of history may equally easily be the source for a scheme for a state church or a national church. No constitutional form can as such exactly represent the actual relative closeness and remoteness of government and Church. Government and Church are bound by the same Lord and are bound together. In their task government and Church are separate, but government and Church have the same field of action, man. No single one of these relationships must be isolated so

87

as to provide the basis for a particular constitutional form (for example in the sequence state church, free church, national church); the true aim is to provide room within every given form for the relationship which is, in fact, instituted by God and to entrust the further development to the Lord of both government and Church.

In both Protestant and Catholic political theory the question of the form of the state is always treated as a secondary problem. Certainly, so long as government fulfils its assigned mission, the form in which it does so is of no great importance for the Church. Still, there is justification for asking which form of the state offers the best guarantee for the fulfilment of the mission of government and should, therefore, be promoted by the Church. No form of the state is in itself an absolute guarantee for the proper discharge of the office of government. Only concrete obedience to the divine commission justifies a form of the state. It is, nevertheless, possible to formulate a few general propositions in order to discern those forms of the state which provide a relatively favourable basis for rightful governmental action and, therefore, also for a rightful relationship between church and state; precisely these relative differences may be of great practical consequence.

a That form of the state will be relatively the best in which it becomes most evident that government is from above, from God, and in which the divine origin of government is most clearly apparent. A properly understood divine right of government, in its splendour and in its responsibility, is an essential constituent of the relatively best form of the state. (Unlike other western royalty, the kings of the Belgians called themselves kings 'by the grace of the people'.)

b That form of the state will be relatively the best which sees that its power is not endangered but is sustained and secured

I   by the strict maintenance of an outward justice,
II by the right of the family and of labour, a right which has its foundation in God, and
III by the proclamation of the gospel of Jesus Christ.

c That form of state will be relatively the best which does not express its attachment to its subjects by restricting the divine authority which has been conferred upon it, but which attaches itself to its subjects in mutual confidence by just action and truthful speech. It will be found here that what is best for government is also best for the relationship between government and church.

Source: D. Bonhoeffer, *Ethics*, SCM Press, 1955, pp. 338–41, 346–52.

(c) *Moltmann:* Theology of Hope

In the contradiction between the word of promise and the experiential reality of suffering and death, faith takes its stand on hope and 'hastens beyond this world', said Calvin. He did not mean by this that Christian faith flees the world, but he did mean that it strains after the future. To believe does in fact mean to cross and transcend bounds, to be engaged in an exodus. Yet this happens in a way that does not suppress or skip the unpleasant realities. Death is real death, and decay is putrefying decay. Guilt remains guilt and suffering remains, even for the believer, a cry to which there is no ready-made answer. Faith does not overstep these realities into a heavenly utopia, does not dream itself into a reality of a different kind. It can overstep the bounds of life, with their closed wall of suffering, guilt and death, only at the point where they have in actual fact been broken through. It is only in following the Christ who was raised from suffering, from a god-forsaken death and from the grave that it gains an open prospect in which there is nothing more to oppress us, a view of the realm of freedom and of joy. Where the bounds that mark the end of all human hopes are broken through in the raising of the crucified one, there faith can and must expand into hope.

[. . .]

To believe means to cross in hope and anticipation the bounds that have been penetrated by the raising of the crucified. If we bear that in mind, then this faith can have nothing to do with fleeing the world, with resignation and with escapism. In this hope the soul does not soar above our vale of tears to some imagined heavenly bliss, nor does it sever itself from the earth. For, in the words of Ludwig Feuerbach, it puts 'in place of the beyond that lies above our grave in heaven the beyond that lies above our grave on earth, the historic *future*, the future of mankind'. It sees in the resurrection of Christ not the eternity of heaven, but the future of the very earth on which his cross stands. It sees in him the future of the very humanity for which he died. That is why it finds the cross the hope of the earth. This hope struggles for the obedience of the body, because it awaits the quickening of the body. It espouses in all meekness the cause of the devastated earth and of harassed humanity, because it is promised possession of the earth. *Ave crux – unica spes!*

But on the other hand, all this must inevitably mean that the man who thus hopes will never be able to reconcile himself with the laws and constraints of this earth, neither with the inevitability of death nor with the evil that constantly bears further evil. The raising of Christ is not merely a consolation to him in a life that is full of distress and doomed to die, but it is also God's contradiction of suffering and death, of humiliation and offence, and of the wickedness of evil. Hope finds in Christ not only a consolation *in* suffering, but also the protest of the divine promise *against* suffering. If Paul calls death the 'last enemy' (1 Cor. 15.26), then the opposite is also true: that the risen Christ, and with him the resurrection hope, must be declared to be the enemy of death and of a world that puts up with death. Faith takes up this contradiction and thus becomes itself a contradiction to the world of death. That is why faith, wherever it develops into hope, causes not rest but unrest, not patience but impatience. It does not calm the unquiet heart, but is itself this unquiet heart in man. Those who hope in Christ can no longer put up with reality as it is, but begin to suffer under it, to contradict it. Peace with God means conflict with the world, for the goad of the promised future stabs inexorably into the flesh of every unfulfilled present. If we had before our eyes only what we see, then we should cheerfully or reluctantly reconcile ourselves with things as they happen to be. That we do not reconcile ourselves, that there is no pleasant harmony between us and reality, is due to our unquenchable hope. This hope keeps man unreconciled, until the great day of the fulfilment of all the promises of God. It keeps him *in statu viatoris*, in that unresolved openness to world questions which has its origin in the promise of God in the resurrection of Christ and can therefore be resolved only when the same God fulfils his promise. This hope makes the Christian Church a constant disturbance in human society, seeking as the latter does to stabilize itself into a 'continuing city'. It makes the Church the source of continual new impulses towards the realization of righteousness, freedom and humanity here in the light of the promised future that is to come. This Church is committed to 'answer for the hope' that is in it (1 Peter 3.15). It is called in question 'on account of the hope and resurrection of the dead' (Acts 23.6). Wherever that happens, Christianity embraces its true nature and becomes a witness of the future of Christ.

[. . .]

A third role in which modern society expects the Christian religion to be effectual is, surprisingly enough, once more to be found today in the institution with all it involves in the way of officialdom and official claims. Modern, post-Enlightenment culture is again more ready to play into the hands of religion than was the pre-industrial age of the eighteenth century. After the hectic decades of the founding of industrialism, in which vast social dislocations made men uncertain in their behaviour and therefore also susceptible to ideologies, industrial society in the highly industrialized countries is today again consolidating itself in new institutions. These new institutions, however, in turn relieve man of the permanent pressure of decision to which he is subjected in times of uncertainty. Stereotyped patterns of conduct give them an enduring, stable and communal character. Thus there emerges a new store of unvarying customs and axioms in work, consumption and intercourse. A 'beneficial unquestioningness' (A. Gehlen) spreads over life. This kind of institutionalizing of official, social life certainly springs from the permanent need of security on the part of man, who experiences himself in history as a 'creature at risk' and therefore also endeavours to resolve the historic character of his history into a cosmos of institutions. This institutionalizing, however, brings about at the same time by an inner logic the suspension of the question of meaning. 'The conduct which they have made habitual has the purely factual result of suspending the question of meaning. To raise the question of meaning is either to have taken a wrong turning, or else to express consciously or unconsciously a need for something other than the existing institutions.' For the latter are of course relationships and modes of conduct which must be axiomatic and unquestioning. The institutionalizing of public life is today producing in the highly industrialized countries an everywhere perceptible disappearance of ideologies. Ideologies as a means of giving purpose and meaning to life are becoming increasingly superfluous. This makes them optional and private. To be sure, it can be said even in the midst of institutionalized life: 'In the world of machines and "cultural values", of great alleviations, life slips away like water between the fingers that would hold it because it is the highest of goods. From out of unfathomable depths it is called in question.' Yet this questionableness is experienced only in the free realm of subjectivity, and no longer in terms of the uncertainty and the historic character of the outside world.

This tendency towards the institutionalization of public life, together with the fact that the arts and sciences have become so abstract that only caricatures of them can now find ideological application, has had the result that the Christian religion is left alone and unopposed on the field of ideologies and world views in the highly industrialized countries. Darwinism in its day was bitterly contested by the Christian confessions. Modern genetics, however, whose technical consequences are beyond our range of vision, does not disturb them, because this is a science of boundless complexity and cannot turn into a speculative opponent. Christian theology accordingly finds itself in a position of being able to assert a neo-dogmatism and say things which can neither be proved nor contested on the ground of real experience, and which can therefore acquire for modern man a binding character which he hardly even disputes any more. On the contrary, he is prepared to delegate to the

Church as an institution the problems regarding his own believing decision, and to leave the detailed questions to theological specialists. If, however, the vital decisions are delegated to the Church as an institution, which is then regarded as an institute for relieving us of them, then the result is the religious attitude of an institutionalized non-committal outlook. 'Christianity' becomes a social axiom and is relegated to one's environment. Matters of theological dispute are regarded as 'confessional witch-hunting' and banished from public life. On the other hand, the ecclesiastical institution of religious modes of conduct acquires a new social significance. For indeed even the modern, institutionalized consciousness retains somewhere on the margin an inkling of the horrors of history. It does not find articulate expression in normal times. Yet this subliminal consciousness of crisis results in a general, if also non-committal, recognition of the religious institutions as the guarantors of life's security in general. The institution of the churches then has the effect of being an ultimate institution overshadowing the institutional security of life, and one from which security is expected against the ultimate fears of existence. In this respect, too, Christianity has a certain social significance for modern society. Yet it is the significance of an institutionalized non-committal outlook. This, too, is religious movement within the limits of a social standstill. It is Christianity as prescribed by the social milieu.

This brief sketch of the new social roles of religion, of the Church and of the Christian faith has made it plain that these roles – 'religion as the cult of subjectivity', 'religion as the cult of co-humanity' and 'religion as the cult of the institution' – are not the result of the good-will or illwill of individual men, nor can they be laid to the charge of theologies determined by the history of ideas, but arise from that which, difficult as it is to grasp, must be called the socially 'axiomatic'. The theological 'self-understanding' (*Selbstverständnis*) of the Christian faith always stands in a relation to the socially 'axiomatic' (*Selbstver-ständliche*). Only where we become critically aware of this connection can the symbiosis be resolved and the peculiar character of the Christian faith come to expression in conflict with the things that are socially axiomatic. If Christianity, according to the will of him in whom it believes and in whom it hopes, is to be different and to serve a different purpose, then it must address itself to no less a task than that of breaking out of these its socially fixed roles. It must then display a kind of conduct which is not in accordance with these. That is the conflict which is imposed on every Christian and every Christian minister. If the God who called them to life should expect of them something other than what modern industrial society expects and requires of them, then Christians must venture an exodus and regard their social roles as a new Babylonian exile. Only where they appear in society as a group which is not wholly adaptable and in the case of which the modern integration of everything with everything else fails to succeed, do they enter into a conflict-laden, but fruitful partnership with this society. Only where their resistance shows them to be a group that is incapable of being assimilated or of 'making the grade', can they communicate their own hope to this society. They will then be led in this society to a constant unrest which nothing can allay or bring to accommodation and rest. Here the task of Christianity today is not so much to oppose the ideological glorification of things, but rather to resist the institutional stabilizing of things, and by 'raising the question of meaning' to make things uncertain and keep them moving and elastic in the process of history. This aim – here formulated to begin with in very general terms – is not achieved simply by stirring up 'historicality', vitality and mobility in the realms which are socially unburdened but have been brought socially to general stagnation. It is achieved precisely by breaking through this social stagnation. Hope alone keeps life – including public, social life – flowing and free.

Source: Jürgen Moltmann, Theology of Hope, SCM Press, 1967,
pp. 19–22, 321–4.

Further reading

A good background can be found in Tillich's *Perspectives on Nineteenth and Twentieth Century Protestant Theology* and Stackhouse's *Creeds, Society and Human Rights*. For a Lutheran perspective, see Moltmann, *On Human Dignity: Political Theology and Ethics* and for a Calvinist point of view, Dooyeweerd, *Roots of Western Culture*. There are general expositions in Part 3 of Wogaman's *Christian Perspectives on Politics* and in Part 1 of Mott's *A Christian Perspective on Political Thought*. See also De Gruchy, *Liberating Reformed Theology* and, concentrating on the United States, Everett's *God's Federal Republic*.

PART TWO

Political Christianity in the Contemporary World

Chapter Seven

THE UNITED STATES

Introduction

The separation of Church and State is one of the cardinal principles of the United States Constitution with its prominent declaration, in the First Amendment, that 'Congress shall make no law respecting an establishment of religion'. But the same Amendment also declares that Congress shall not prohibit the free exercise of religion. And on these two principles religion flourishes in the United States as in few other advanced industrial countries. This is partly because the ways in which the First Amendment can be interpreted are so various as to give rise to continuous controversy. More importantly, religious groups in the United States are treated as voluntary associations with no legal privileges or disabilities and thus left with considerable freedom of manoeuvre which many have exploited to the full in what is essentially a society whose prime motor is the activities of pressure groups. And the strong tie between religious affiliation and ethnic identity has served to enhance the strength of these religious pressure groups.

Alongside this religious diversity, there emerged the 'civil religion' described by Bellah in the extract below – a kind of lowest common denominator which afforded a sacred character to national ceremonies and civic obligations. This civil religion is seen as a functional necessity to a stable democracy, a set of transcendent beliefs which bind together an otherwise excessively individualistic society. A more explicit version of this is given by Michael Novak:

> The Trinity becomes a vision of the importance of individualism over against the constraints of community; the Incarnation becomes a reality principle that warns us against the utopian hopes of socialism; the value of many biblical narratives is that they 'envisage human life

as a contest'; the doctrine of Original Sin serves mainly to convince us that no economic system can ever be free of some evil; the doctrine of the Two Kingdoms becomes an argument for laissez-faire; and the principle of love in the Judaeo-Christian tradition mainly suggests that we should respect the freedom of the individual.

Christianity, in other words, serves to endorse the establishment values of competition, this-worldly individual enterprise, social adjustment, etc. On this view, religion can provide an over-arching sacred canopy which serves to integrate diverse beliefs under the rubric of 'religion of democracy'.

At the same time, the consensual and conservative nature of American civil religion is inevitably challenged by more specific and articulate forms of Christianity. The US Catholic Bishops, for example, in their pastoral letter of 1986 on economic justice maintained the dignity of the human person was supreme and that therefore all economic decisions should be judged 'in the light of what they do for the poor, what they do to the poor and what they enable the poor to do for themselves'. More strikingly, the rise of the New Christian Right in the 1980s injected a note of strong fundamentalism into United States politics. Using all the powerful means available to interest groups, such organizations as the Moral Majority and the Christian Coalition have used evangelical Protestantism to campaign against the way in which, as they see it, the permissive society has eroded the moral standards set by Christianity.

(a) Bellah: Civil Religion in America

The words and acts of the founding fathers, especially the first few presidents, shaped the form and tone of the civil religion as it has been maintained ever since. Though much is selectively derived from Christianity, this religion is clearly not itself Christianity. For one thing, neither Washington nor Adams nor Jefferson mentions Christ in his inaugural address; nor do any of the subsequent presidents, although not one of them fails to mention God. The God of the civil religion is not only rather 'unitarian', he is also on the austere side; much more related to order, law, and right than to salvation and love. Even though he is somewhat deist in cast, he is by no means simply a watchmaker God. He is actively interested and involved in history, with a special concern for America. Here the analogy has much less to do with natural law than with ancient Israel; the equation of America with Israel in the idea of the 'American Israel' is not infrequent. What was implicit in the words of Washington becomes explicit in Jefferson's second inaugural when he said: 'I shall need, too, the favor of that Being in whose hands we are, who led our fathers, as Israel of old, from their native land and planted them in a country flowing with all the necessaries and comforts of life.' Europe is Egypt; America, the promised land. God has led his people to establish a new sort of social order that shall be a light unto all the nations.

This theme, too, has been a continuous one in the civil religion. We have already alluded to it in the case of the Kennedy inaugural. We find it again in President Johnson's inaugural address:

> They came here – the exile and the stranger, brave but frightened – to find a place where a man could be his own man. They made a covenant with this land. Conceived in justice, written in liberty, bound in union, it was meant one day to inspire the hopes of all mankind; and it binds us still. If we keep its terms, we shall flourish.

What we have, then, from the earliest years of the republic is a collection of beliefs, symbols, and rituals with respect to sacred things and institutionalized in a collectivity. This religion – there seems no other word for it – while not antithetical to and indeed sharing much in common with Christianity, was neither sectarian nor in any specific sense Christian. At a time when the society was overwhelmingly Christian, it seems unlikely that this lack of Christian reference was meant to spare the feelings of the tiny non-Christian minority. Rather, the civil religion expressed what those who set the precedents felt was appropriate under the circumstances. It reflected their private as well as public views. Nor was the civil religion simply 'religion in general'. While generality was undoubtedly seen as a virtue by some . . . the civil religion was specific enough when it came to the topic of America. Precisely because of this specificity, the civil religion was saved from empty formalism and served as a genuine vehicle of national religious self-understanding.

But the civil religion was not, in the minds of Franklin, Washington, Jefferson, or other leaders, with the exception of a few radicals like Tom Paine, ever felt to be a substitute for Christianity. There was an implicit but quite clear division of function between the civil religion and Christianity. Under the doctrine of religious liberty, an exceptionally wide sphere of personal piety and voluntary social action was left to the churches. But the churches were neither to control the state nor to be controlled by it. The national magistrate, whatever his private religious views, operates under the rubrics of the civil religion as long as he is in his official capacity. This accommodation was undoubtedly the product of a particular historical moment and of a cultural background dominated by Protestantism of several varieties and by the

Enlightenment, but it has survived despite subsequent changes in the cultural and religious climate.

In reifying and giving a name to something that, though pervasive enough when you look at it, has gone on only semiconsciously, there is risk of severely distorting the data. But the reification and the naming have already begun. The religious critics of 'religion in general', or of the 'religion of the "American Way of Life"', or of 'American Shinto' have really been talking about the civil religion. As usual in religious polemic, they take as criteria the best in their own religious tradition and as typical the worst in the tradition of the civil religion. Against these critics, I would argue that the civil religion at its best is a genuine apprehension of universal and transcendent religious reality as seen in or, one could almost say, as revealed through the experience of the American people. Like all religions, it has suffered various deformations and demonic distortions. At its best, it has neither been so general that it has lacked incisive relevance to the American scene nor so particular that it has placed American society above universal human values. I am not at all convinced that the leaders of the churches have consistently represented a higher level of religious insight than the spokesmen of the civil religion. Reinhold Niebuhr has this to say of Lincoln, who never joined a church and who certainly represents civil religion at its best:

> An analysis of the religion of Abraham Lincoln in the context of the traditional religion of his time and place and of its polemical use on the slavery issue, which corrupted religious life in the days before and during the Civil War, must lead to the conclusion that Lincoln's religious convictions were superior in depth and purity to those, not only of the political leaders of his day, but of the religious leaders of the era.

Perhaps the real animus of the religious critics has been not so much against the civil religion in itself but against its pervasive and dominating influence within the sphere of church religion. As S. M. Lipset has recently shown, American religion at least since the early nineteenth century has been predominantly activist, moralistic, and social rather than contemplative, theological, or innerly spiritual. De Tocqueville spoke of American church religion as 'a political institution which powerfully contributes to the maintenance of a democratic republic among the Americans' by supplying a strong moral consensus amidst continuous political change. Henry Bargy in 1902 spoke of American church religion as 'la poésie du civisme'.

It is certainly true that the relation between religion and politics in

America has been singularly smooth. This is in large part due to the dominant tradition. As de Tocqueville wrote:

> The greatest part of British America was peopled by men who, after having shaken off the authority of the Pope, acknowledged no other religious supremacy: they brought with them into the New World a form of Christianity which I cannot better describe than by styling it a democratic and republican religion.

The churches opposed neither the Revolution nor the establishment of democratic institutions. Even when some of them opposed the full institutionalization of religious liberty, they accepted the final outcome with good grace and without nostalgia for an *ancien régime*. The American civil religion was never anticlerical or militantly secular. On the contrary, it borrowed selectively from the religious tradition in such a way that the average American saw no conflict between the two. In this way, the civil religion was able to build up without any bitter struggle with the church powerful symbols of national solidarity and to mobilize deep levels of personal motivation for the attainment of national goals.

Such an achievement is by no means to be taken for granted. It would seem that the problem of a civil religion is quite general in modern societies and that the way it is solved or not solved will have repercussions in many spheres. One needs only to think of France to see how differently things can go. The French Revolution was anticlerical to the core and attempted to set up an anti-Christian civil religion. Throughout modern French history, the chasm between traditional Catholic symbols and the symbolism of 1789 has been immense.

American civil religion is still very much alive. Just three years ago we participated in a vivid re-enactment of the sacrifice theme in connection with the funeral of our assassinated president. The American Israel theme is clearly behind both Kennedy's New Frontier and Johnson's Great Society. Let me give just one recent illustration of how the civil religion serves to mobilize support for the attainment of national goals. On 15 March 1965 President Johnson went before Congress to ask for a strong voting-rights bill. Early in the speech he said:

> Rarely are we met with the challenge, not to our growth or abundance, or our welfare or our security – but rather to the values and the purposes and the meaning of our beloved nation.
>
> The issue of equal rights for American Negroes is such an issue. And should we defeat every enemy, and should we double our wealth and conquer the stars and still be unequal to this issue, then we will have failed as a people and as a nation.

For with a country as with a person, 'What is a man profited, if he shall gain the whole world, and lose his own soul?'

And in conclusion he said:

Above the pyramid on the great seal of the United States it says in Latin, 'God has favored our undertaking.'

God will not favor everything that we do. It is rather our duty to divine his will. I cannot help but believe that He truly understands and that He really favors the undertaking that we begin here tonight.

The civil religion has not always been invoked in favor of worthy causes. On the domestic scene, an American-Legion type of ideology that fuses God, country and flag has been used to attack non-conformist and liberal ideas and groups of all kinds. Still, it has been difficult to use the words of Jefferson and Lincoln to support special interests and undermine personal freedom. The defenders of slavery before the Civil War came to reject the thinking of the Declaration of Independence. Some of the most consistent of them turned against not only Jeffersonian democracy but Reformation religion; they dreamed of a South dominated by medieval chivalry and divine-right monarchy. For all the overt religiosity of the radical right today, their relation to the civil religious consensus is tenuous, as when the John Birch Society attacks the central American symbol of Democracy itself.

With respect to America's role in the world, the dangers of distortion are greater and the built-in safeguards of the tradition weaker. The theme of the American Israel was used, almost from the beginning, as a justification for the shameful treatment of the Indians so characteristic of our history. It can be overtly or implicitly linked to the idea of manifest destiny which has been used to legitimate several adventures in imperialism since the early nineteenth century. Never has the danger been greater than today. The issue is not so much one of imperial expansion, of which we are accused, as of the tendency to assimilate all governments or parties in the world which support our immediate policies or call upon our help by invoking the notion of free institutions and democratic values. Those nations that are for the moment 'on our side' become 'the free world'. A repressive and unstable military dictatorship in South Viet-Nam becomes 'the free people of South Viet-Nam and their government'. It is then part of the role of America as the New Jerusalem and 'the last hope of earth' to defend such governments with treasure and eventually with blood. When our soldiers are actually dying, it becomes possible to consecrate the struggle further by invoking the great theme of sacrifice. For the majority of the American people who are unable to judge whether the people in South Viet-Nam (or

wherever) are 'free like us', such arguments are convincing. Fortunately President Johnson has been less ready to assert that 'God has
favored our undertaking' in the case of Viet-Nam than with respect to
civil rights. But others are not so hesitant. The civil religion has exercised long-term pressure for the humane solution of our greatest
domestic problem, the treatment of the Negro American. It remains to
be seen how relevant it can become for our role in the world at large,
and whether we can effectually stand for 'the revolutionary beliefs for
which our forebears fought', in John F. Kennedy's words.

The civil religion is obviously involved in the most pressing moral
and political issues of the day. But it is also caught in another kind of
crisis, theoretical and theological, of which it is at the moment largely
unaware. 'God' has clearly been a central symbol in the civil religion
from the beginning and remains so today. This symbol is just as central
to the civil religion as it is to Judaism or Christianity. In the late eighteenth century this posed no problem; even Tom Paine, contrary to his
detractors, was not an atheist. From left to right and regardless of
church or sect, all could accept the idea of God. But today, as even
Time has recognized, the meaning of the word *God* is by no means so
clear or so obvious. There is no formal creed in the civil religion. We
have had a Catholic president; it is conceivable that we could have a
Jewish one. But could we have an agnostic president? Could a man
with conscientious scruples about using the word *God* the way
Kennedy and Johnson have used it be elected chief magistrate of our
country? If the whole God symbolism requires reformulation, there
will be obvious consequences for the civil religion, consequences perhaps of liberal alienation and of fundamentalist ossification that have
not so far been prominent in this realm. The civil religion has been a
point of articulation between the profoundest commitments of the
Western religious and philosophical tradition and the common beliefs
of ordinary Americans. It is not too soon to consider how the deepening
theological crisis may affect the future of this articulation.

In conclusion it may be worthwhile to relate the civil religion to the
most serious situation that we as Americans now face, what I call the
third time of trial. The first time of trial had to do with the question of
independence, whether we should or could run our own affairs in our
own way. The second time of trial was over the issue of slavery, which
in turn was only the most salient aspect of the more general problem
of the full institutionalization of democracy within our country. This
second problem we are still far from solving though we have some
notable successes to our credit. But we have been overtaken by a third
great problem which has led to a third great crisis, in the midst of which
we stand. This is the problem of responsible action in a revolutionary

world, a world seeking to attain many of the things, material and spiritual, that we have already attained. Americans have, from the beginning, been aware of the responsibility and the significance our republican experiment has for the whole world. The first internal political polarization in the new nation had to do with our attitude towards the French Revolution. But we were small and weak then, and 'foreign entanglements' seemed to threaten our very survival. During the last century, our relevance for the world was not forgotten, but our role was seen as purely exemplary. Our democratic republic rebuked tyranny by merely existing. Just after World War I we were on the brink of taking a different role in the world, but once again we turned our back.

Since World War II the old pattern has become impossible. Every president since Roosevelt has been groping toward a new pattern of action in the world, one that would be consonant with our power and our responsibilities. For Truman and for the period dominated by John Foster Dulles that pattern was seen to be the great Manichaean confrontation of East and West, the confrontation of democracy and 'the false philosophy of Communism' that provided the structure of Truman's inaugural address. But with the last years of Eisenhower and with the successive two presidents, the pattern began to shift. The great problems came to be seen as caused not solely by the evil intent of any one group of men, but as stemming from much more complex and multiple sources. For Kennedy, it was not so much a struggle against particular men as against 'the common enemies of man: tyranny, poverty, disease and war itself'.

But in the midst of this trend toward a less primitive conception of ourselves and our world, we have somehow, without anyone really intending it, stumbled into a military confrontation where we have come to feel that our honor is at stake. We have in a moment of uncertainty been tempted to rely on our overwhelming physical power rather than on our intelligence, and we have, in part, succumbed to this temptation. Bewildered and unnerved when our terrible power fails to bring immediate success, we are at the edge of a chasm the depth of which no man knows.

I cannot help but think of Robinson Jeffers, whose poetry seems more apt now than when it was written, when he said:

> Unhappy country, what wings you have! . . .
> Weep (it is frequent in human affairs), weep for
>   the terrible magnificence of the means,
> The ridiculous incompetence of the reasons, the
>   bloody and shabby
> Pathos of the result.

But as so often before in similar times, we have a man of prophetic stature [Nixon], without the bitterness or misanthropy of Jeffers, who, as Lincoln before him, calls this nation to its judgment:

> When a nation is very powerful but lacking in self-confidence, it is likely to behave in a manner that is dangerous both to itself and to others.
>
> Gradually but unmistakably, America is succumbing to that arrogance of power which has afflicted, weakened and in some cases destroyed great nations in the past.
>
> If the war goes on and expands, if that fatal process continues to accelerate until America becomes what it is not now and never has been, a seeker after unlimited power and empire, then Vietnam will have had a mighty and tragic fallout indeed.
>
> I do not believe that will happen. I am very apprehensive but I still remain hopeful, and even confident, that America, with its humane and democratic traditions, will find the wisdom to match its power.

Without an awareness that our nation stands under higher judgment, the tradition of the civil religion would be dangerous indeed. Fortunately, the prophetic voices have never been lacking. Our present situation brings to mind the Mexican-American war that Lincoln, among so many others, opposed. The spirit of civil disobedience that is alive today in the civil rights movement and the opposition to the Viet-Nam war was already clearly outlined by Henry David Thoreau when he wrote, 'If the law is of such a nature that it requires you to be an agent of injustice to another, then I say, break the law.' Thoreau's words, 'I would remind my countrymen that they are men first, and Americans at a late and convenient hour,' provide an essential standard for any adequate thought and action in our third time of trial. As Americans, we have been well favored in the world, but it is as men that we will be judged.

Out of the first and second times of trial have come, as we have seen, the major symbols of the American civil religion. There seems little doubt that a successful negotiation of this third time of trial – the attainment of some kind of viable and coherent world order – would precipitate a major new set of symbolic forms. So far the flickering flame of the United Nations burns too low to be the focus of a cult, but the emergence of a genuine trans-national sovereignty would certainly change this. It would necessitate the incorporation of vital international symbolism into our civil religion, or, perhaps a better way of putting it, it would result in American civil religion becoming simply one part of a new civil religion of the world. It is useless to speculate on the form such a civil religion might taken though it obviously would draw on religious traditions beyond the sphere of biblical religion alone. Fortunately, since the American civil religion is not the worship of the American nation but an understanding of the American experience in the light of ultimate and universal reality, the reorganization entailed by such a new situation need not disrupt the American civil religion's continuity. A world civil religion could be accepted as a fulfillment and not a denial of American civil religion. Indeed, such an outcome has been the eschatological hope of American civil religion from the beginning. To deny such an outcome would be to deny the meaning of America itself.

Behind the civil religion at every point lie biblical archetypes: Exodus, Chosen People, Promised Land, New Jerusalem, Sacrificial Death and Rebirth. But it is also genuinely American and genuinely new. It has its own prophets and its own martyrs, its own sacred events and sacred places, its own solemn rituals and symbols. It is concerned that America be a society as perfectly in accord with the will of God as men can make it, and a light to all the nations.

It has often been used and is being used today as a cloak for petty interests and ugly passions. It is in need – as is any living faith – of continual reformation, of being measured by universal standards. But it is not evident that it is incapable of growth and new insight.

It does not make any decision for us. It does not remove us from moral ambiguity, from being, in Lincoln's fine phrase, an 'almost chosen people'. But it is a heritage of moral and religious experience from which we still have much to learn as we formulate the decisions that lie ahead.

Source: R. Bellah, 'Civil Religion in America', *Daedalus*, vol. 96 no. 1, Winter 1967, pp. 7–8, 12–19.

(b) *Bruce:* The New Christian Right

Supporters of the NCR (New Christian Right) see the rejection of their religious beliefs and their commitment to a moral orthodoxy as the work of secular humanists. Certainly secular humanists believe in the removal of religion from the public arena, in the tolerance of alternative life-styles, and in the extension of choice but the sociologist of modernity sees the secular humanist position as being little more than the intellectual endorsement of what has already come to pass. While some of the changes which the NCR lump under the secular humanist label have been hastened by liberal moral entrepreneurs, most are the *unintended* consequences of modernity. When even those who are conservative on economic and foreign policy matters wish to retain the right to pursue their own life-styles, the only circumstance under which the NCR could succeed is a return to cultural homogencity. Nothing visible to the student of the empirical social world suggests that the internal cultural fragmentation of modern societies is about to be reversed. In his analysis of the present, the sociologist thus becomes a curious bedfellow of the Bob Jones University fundamentalist; the necessary pre-condition for the success of the NCR is a massive religious revival. Where I differ from Bob Jones III is that I see no reason to suppose such a revival likely.

Were the grievances of American fundamentalists the result of the actions of secular humanists, they could be removed by the power of fundamentalist numbers expressed through the ballot box. After all, conservative Protestants remain one of the largest cultural minorities in America, and America is, generally speaking, a democracy. But at least part of what bothers fundamentalists is the apparent tension between items of modern scientific and technical knowledge and parts of the conservative Protestant world-view. To concentrate on evolution, it may well be that a modern industrial economy can permit the survival of pre-scientific ideas in certain limited spheres. The ability to make missiles, launch space rockets, exploit natural resources, and competitively produce cars may not be threatened by the belief that the world is less than a million years old and was made by God in six days. However, despite the willingness of Justices Rehnquist and Scalia to leave the matter of the origins of species to the vote of state legislatures, it seems clear that the general tendency of modern societies to accord priority in debates about matters of scientific interest to those with good credentials represents some sort of functional imperative, something that could not be different without posing a major threat to the knowledge base of the society. If that is the case, fundamentalists are not going to win their arguments with scientists and technologists, despite the occasional minor victory.

Something similar could be said of other areas of concern to the NCR. While there has been increasing hostility to the power of the professions, it still remains the case that in all advanced industrial societies, professionally accredited occupational groups dominate particular spheres of activity. Even on matters such as education, or the civil rights of the unborn or the terminally ill, where technical considerations are obviously informed by moral judgements, the opinions of professionals carry far more weight than those of lay people, largely because it is in the very nature of the modern society to translate moral and ethical matters into technical considerations. The basic assumptions that inform modern industrial production – that all complex objects and procedures can be reduced to repeatable acts and replaceable components; that nothing is more than the sum of its parts; that everything can be measured and calculated; that nothing is sacred and that everything can be improved; that increased efficiency is the main imperative – cannot be confined to the world of work. The formal rationality which dominates that sphere gradually invades all other areas of social action. There is not the space here to present this argument in sufficient detail to convince the sceptical but it is accepted by most sociologists (of varying ideological positions) that it is characteristic of the modern world to subordinate the moral to the technical and the lay to the professional.

My point is that the authority of professionals (especially natural scientists) is such that fundamentalists are unlikely to establish the principle that arguments such as that over the origins of the species should be settled by votes rather than by the consensus of accredited experts. Even in matters that are more commonly seen as moral and ethical rather than technical and professional, the tendency is to defer to the professionals.

But even if one does not accept these claims about the scientific and technical consequences of modernity, one cannot think away the consequence of pluralism. And, if, as I suggest, secular humanism is simply a convenient blanket term for the necessary consequences of pluralism, then clearly fundamentalists have no hope of attaining their goals because what offends them is nothing more or less than modernity itself.

The awkward position of the NCR can now be fully described by bringing the above observations about the universalizing tendencies of modern societies together with the earlier discussion of the NCR's fall-back position of presenting itself as a disadvantaged minority.

Blacks, women, and homosexuals have built their claims by pointing to the failure of parts of the economy, the polity, and the social structure to live up to the rhetoric of universalism. Far from challenging modernity, they have appealed to its core values by identifying areas in which universal principles regarding economic and political rights have not been rigorously pursued. They have presented themselves as discriminated against by the failure of the state to prevent the continuation of particularistic practices in employment, political representation, and social valuation. The demands of these minorities are thus, in theory, demands which can be met by a modern industrial society simply giving more effort to its existing dynamics. The outlawing of racism and sexism can be seen as merely giving more substance to the universalizing tendency. Racist and sexist language, for example, can be eradicated by stripping the culture of certain particularistic features; by making it more bland.

The NCR's claims to the status of a legitimate minority seem quite different. The supporters of the NCR are not disadvantaged in terms of socio-economic status (or at least, in so far as they are, it is because of their class, region, levels of education, and other characteristics not specifically related to their shared religious culture). Where they are disadvantaged is in the status which the state is willing to accord their culture. This disadvantage cannot be remedied by an extension of the twin principles of universalism in the public sphere and the relegation of particularism to the private world. It is precisely these two principles which have produced most of the changes which offend supporters of the new Christian right. Thus although the shift from (a) aiming to re-Christianize America to (b) claiming only that their values, beliefs, and symbols be accorded due status in the public arena is a sensible change in strategy for new Christian rightists, an understanding of the most abstract features of modernity gives every reason to suppose that it is a strategy doomed to fail.

There is a tendency to see the NCR as a reactionary movement, an outburst of resurgent traditionalism. Certainly its proponents are fond of describing it in terms such as those of the title of one manifesto: *Back to Basics*. In part this characterization is appropriate but it is important also to stress the extent to which the movement has itself accommodated to modernity. This accommodation is not just a matter of adjusting rhetoric so that the religion of creationism becomes creation science and the virtues of fundamentalism are presented, not as divine injunctions, but as socially functional arrangements. It is also a matter of conceding crucial ground to the pluralism of the modern world by accepting the need to separate religious values and socio-moral positions so that alliances can be formed with advocates of competing religious values. Leaders of the NCR insist that they have not accepted the denominational attitude (in which truth is relativized so a number of apparently and previously competing visions can all be seen as being in some sense equally valid) but they have accepted another crucial element of modernity; they compartmentalize. They operate in a world of social action that has been divided into separate spheres with different values. In church, with their own people, in prayer meetings, they remain fundamentalist Protestants. But when pursuing the public agenda of socio-moral issues they operate with a quite different set of criteria. That is, they have conceded a major part of what the modern pluralistic society demands of religion: its restriction to the private home world.

Although their behaviour in the public sphere is still informed by religious considerations, it is not dominated by them, and they have been diluted in order to attract maximum support from people who do not share the values and beliefs of conservative Protestantism.

The alternative to denominationalism is sectarianism: the continued insistence that what one has is *the* truth and that those who differ are simply wrong. To present the situation of religion in a modern society in the starkest possible terms, the choice is between sectarianism and denominationalism. Modernity constantly increases the costs of sectarianism. Those people who wish to maintain orthodox religious beliefs find themselves having to retreat further and further into either regional or socially constructed laagers. The NCR has tried to reduce the costs, both by seeking public support for its positions and by resisting the encroachments of the central secular state. But in trying to do those things, it has been forced to accept the denominational attitude. One can see this clearly in conservative Protestant reasoning about the possibility of a third party. Where religion exists in its 'church' form, it does not need to be represented by a political party because its presence is so all pervading; Catholicism in the Republic of Ireland is a case in point. Where it exists in a sectarian form, it produces a coherent confessional party; the Calvinist Anti-revolutionary party in nineteenth-century Holland is an example. American conservative Protestants realize a confessional party is not a possibility. Those who talk about a religious party at all recognize that it would have to be at least a Christian or even a Judaeo-Christian party. But most of them realize that even a Judaeo-Christian party would not work; any viable third party would have to be a secular party informed by traditional (i.e. religious) values. That is denominationalism and it is a long way down the road to the point where religion is hardly a factor at all, where religiosity appears only through political attitudes which reflect general class and status interests. The situation becomes one where the second words in the phrases 'conservative Protestant', 'conservative Catholic', and 'conservative Jew' become redundant.

Modernity does not challenge religion. Instead it subtly undermines it and corrodes it. Fundamentalists tacitly recognize this when they refuse to be impressed or comforted by the state's willingness to permit – to *tolerate* – Mormons, Witnesses, Christian Scientists, Rastafarians, Scientologists, Moonies, and any number of more exotic religions. Although few fundamentalists say it openly, some of them recognize that it is better to be persecuted than to be tolerated as (in the language of American forms) a 'religion of your preference'.

Twenty or so years ago many of the sociologists who endorsed the above picture of modernity supposed that secularization – the decline

110

of religion – was an irreversible characteristic of modern societies. Recently the sociological orthodoxy seems to have been running in the opposite direction. Although I remain committed to a version of the secularization thesis, I do not expect religion to disappear completely or quickly. And in so far as it is the broad liberal denominations which are losing support fastest, one would expect traditional supernaturalist Protestantism to become relatively more popular and influential. There is thus nothing surprising about the appearance of the New Christian Right. So long as there are sizeable numbers of conservative Protestants in America, there will be movement organizations which campaign and lobby on their behalf. There will continue to be skirmishes and boundary disputes. Precisely because the conflict is not between two groups of believers, but between the adherents to a coherent belief-system and modernity, it will always be difficult to judge accurately the outcome of any battle.

> Source: S. Bruce, *The Rise and Fall of the New Christian Right:*
> *Conservative Protestant Politics in America 1978–1987,*
> Clarendon Press, 1988, pp. 187–92.

Further reading

For good introductions see Wald's *Religion and Politics in the United States* and his article in Moyser's *Politics and Religion in the Modern World*. Also the articles in Witte's *Christianity and Democracy in Global Context*. The religious origins of American politics are well covered in Bailyn's *The Ideological Origins of the American Revolution*, Everett's *God's Federal Republic*, and Hatch's *The Democratization of American Christianity*. For the alleged decline of civil religion, see Bellah's *The Broken Covenant*. For a thorough account of recent developments see Wuthnow's *The Restructuring of American Religion* and the racy survey of Wills, *Under God: Religion and American Politics*. The influence of fundamentalism is traced in Bruce, *The Rise and Fall of the New Christian Right*.

Chapter Eight

SOUTH AMERICA AND SOUTH AFRICA

Introduction

Living in an exploited and dependent continent where the violence implicit in much of the domination is sanctioned, and often practised, by the established order, Latin American liberation theologians are more radical than even the most 'progressive' theologies produced in the West. For they reject the secularizing theology which accepts the autonomy of the secular as little more than an uncritical acquiescence in what, seen from Latin America, is an essentially oppressive system. Even the political theology emanating from Germany is criticized for being too abstract and, in effect, reformist as it refuses to opt for socialism on the grounds that an eschatological perspective necessarily relativizes all political options.

In its origin in the early 1960s, liberation theology was mainly a clerical movement of younger theologians whose studies in Europe had led them to abandon traditional Thomism in favour of biblical and patristic sources and the 'salvation history' contained therein. They were also influenced, on their own continent, by such works as *Pedagogy of the Oppressed* by the Brazilian educator Paolo Freire and the various polemics of Ivan Illich from the Intercultural Centre for Documentation at Cuernavaca in Mexico. The countries who have made the biggest contribution to liberation theology are Argentina, Uruguay, Chile, Peru and Brazil – which has more Catholics than any other country in the world. And it will come as no surprise that, in such a continent-wide movement, there are very diverse currents. Liberation theology is supported by a significant – though definitely minoritarian – part of the episcopate, including such notable figures as Helder Camara,

Archbishop of Recife in Brazil from 1964 to 1984. Its theologians vary from the Columbian Camillo Torres, who felt he could best fulfil his priestly vocation by joining the guerillas, was killed by the security forces, and has become something of a martyr of the Left, to the decidedly more nuanced writings of the Peruvian Jesuit Gustavo Gutiérrez whose *Theology of Liberation*, from which the excerpt below is taken, is the best selling of liberation theology books.

The politically radical nature of the early liberation theology writings, with their strong admixture of Marxism, has been somewhat modified by the return to civilian government and formal democracy in much of the continent.

This radical mixture of Christianity and politics has met with disapproval in Rome. What worried the Vatican was the emergence of basic Christian communities which threatened the hierarchical nature of the Church, encouraged the social and political involvement of the poor to whose insights priority was accorded, and seemed to relativize the doctrines of the Church.

Finally, the extract from the Kairos document illustrates the thinking behind the role played by the Christian Church in the downfall of the apartheid regime in South Africa. It is an impressive vision of the part Christian communities could play in the liberation and reconstruction of a nation.

(a) *Gutiérrez:* A Theology of Liberation

The options which Christians in Latin America are taking have brought a fundamental question to the fore: What is the *meaning of the faith* in a life committed to the struggle against injustice and alienation? How do we relate the work of building a just society to the absolute value of the Kingdom? For many the participation in the process of liberation causes a wearying, anguished, long, and unbearable dichotomy between their life of faith and their revolutionary commitment. What is called for is not to accuse them of confusing the Kingdom with revolution, only because they take the latter seriously and because they believe that the Kingdom is incompatible with the present unjust situation and that in Latin America the coming of the Kingdom presupposes the breaking up of this state of affairs; these accusations often come from those who are comfortably established in a very safe 'religious' life. Rather, what is called for is to search out theological responses to the problems which arise in the life of a Christian who has chosen for the oppressed and against the oppressors. Moreover, the close collaboration with people of different spiritual outlooks which this option provides

113

leads one to ponder the contribution proper to the faith. This question must be carefully considered in order to avoid the petty ambition of 'having more'.

The problem, however, is not only to find a new theological framework. The *personal and community prayer* of many Christians committed to the process of liberation is undergoing a serious crisis. This could purify prayer life of childish attitudes, routines, and escapes. But it will not do this if new paths are not broken and new spiritual experiences are not lived. For example, without 'contemplative life', to use a traditional term, there is no authentic Christian life; yet what this contemplative life will be is still unknown. There is great need for a spirituality of liberation; yet in Latin America those who have opted to participate in the process of liberation as we have outlined it above, comprise, in a manner of speaking, a first Christian generation. In many areas of their life they are without a theological and spiritual tradition. They are creating their own.

The Latin American reality, *the historical moment* which Latin America is experiencing, is *deeply conflictual*. One of Medellín's great merits is to have been rooted in this reality and to have expressed it in terms surprisingly clear and accessible for an ecclesiastical document. Medellín marks the beginning of a new relationship between theological and pastoral language on the one hand and the social sciences which seek to interpret this reality on the other. This relationship gives rise to statements which are to a large extent contingent and provisional; this is the price one must pay for being incisive and contemporary and for expressing the Word *today* in our everyday words. But this language is only a reflection of a deeper process, a new awareness. The commitments and statements referred to in the two preceding chapters are placing us face to face with a new social experience of Latin Americans and with new directions that the Christian community is beginning to take. It is important to be aware of the newness of this phenomenon. It implies a different, very concrete way of looking at the historical process, that is, of perceiving the presence of the Lord in history, who encourages us to be artisans of this process. Moreover, because of close contact with those who see historical development from a Marxist viewpoint, we are led to review and revitalize the eschatological values of Christianity, which stress not only the provisional nature of historical accomplishments, but above all their openness towards the total communion of all men with God. We Christians, however, are not used to thinking in conflictual and historical terms. We prefer peaceful conciliation to antagonism and an evasive eternity to a provisional arrangement. We must learn to live and think of peace in conflict and of what is definitive in what is historical. Very important in this regard are collaboration and dialogue with those who from different vantage points are also struggling for the liberation of oppressed peoples. At stake is the meaning of Christians' participation in this liberation.

The Latin American Church is sharply *divided* with regard to the process of liberation. Living in a capitalist society in which one class confronts another, the Church, in the measure that its presence increases, cannot escape – nor try to ignore any longer – the profound division among its members. Active participation in the liberation process is far from being a uniform position of the Latin American Christian community. The majority of the Church continues to be linked in many different ways to the established order. And what is worse, among Latin American Christians there are not only different political options within a framework of free interplay of ideas; the polarization of these options and the extreme seriousness of the situation have even placed some Christians among the oppressed and persecuted and others among the oppressors and persecutors, some among the tortured and others among the torturers or those who condone torture. This gives rise to a serious and radical confrontation between Christians who suffer from injustice and exploitation and those who benefit from the established order. Under such circumstances, life in the contemporary Christian community becomes particularly difficult and conflictual. Participation in the Eucharist, for example, as it is celebrated today, appears to many to be an action which, for want of the support of an authentic community, becomes an exercise in make-believe.

From now on it is impossible not to face the problems which arise from this division between Christians, which has reached such dramatic proportions. Clarion calls to Christian unity which do not take into account the deep causes of present conditions and the real prerequisites for building a just society are merely escapist. We are moving towards a new idea of unity and communion in the Church. Unity is not an event accomplished once and for all, but something which is always in the process of becoming, something which is achieved with courage and freedom of spirit, sometimes at the price of painful, heart-rending decisions. Latin America must brace itself for such experiences.

In Latin America, the Church must place itself squarely within the process of revolution, amid the violence which is present in different ways. The Church's *mission* is defined practically and theoretically, pastorally and theologically in relation to this revolutionary process. That is, its mission is defined more by the political context than by intraecclesiastical problems. Its greatest 'o-mission' would be to turn in upon itself. Because of the options which, with the qualifications we have indicated, the Christian community is making, it is faced ever more clearly with the dilemma now confronting the whole continent: to be for or against the system, or more subtly, to be for reform or revolution. Many Christians have resolutely decided for the difficult path which leads to the latter. Confronted with this polarization, can ecclesiastical authority remain on the level of general statements? On the other hand, can it go beyond them and still remain within what is traditionally considered to be its specific mission?

For the Latin American Church, it is becoming increasingly clearer that to be in the world without being of the world means concretely to be in the system without being of the system. It is evident that only a break with the unjust order and a frank commitment to a new society can make the message of love which the Christian community bears credible to Latin Americans. These demands should lead the Church to a profound revision of its manner of preaching the Word and of living and celebrating its faith.

Closely connected with this problem is another very controversial question: Should *the Church put its social weight* behind social transformation in Latin America? Some are worried that it would be a mistake for the Church to attempt to achieve the necessary and urgent changes. The fear is that the Church will become linked to the future established order, albeit a more just one. There is also a fear that an effort in this direction will end in a noisy failure: the Latin American bishops are not all of one mind and do not have the necessary means at their disposal to orientate Christians as a whole toward social progress.

The relevance of these fears cannot be denied. There is indeed great risk. But the social influence of the Church is a fact. Not to exercise this influence in favor of the oppressed of Latin America is really to exercise it against them, and it is difficult to determine beforehand the consequences of this action. Not to speak is in fact to become another kind of Church of silence, silence in the face of the despoliation and exploitation of the weak by the powerful. On the other hand, would not the best way for the Church to break its links with the existing order – and in the process lose its ambiguous social prestige – be precisely to denounce the fundamental injustice upon which this order is based? Often the Church alone is in a position publicly to raise its voice and its protest. When some churches have attempted to do this, they have been harassed by the dominant groups and repressed by the political power. In order to reflect on what action the Latin American Church should take and to act accordingly, it is necessary to consider its historical and social coordinates, its here and now. To neglect doing this is to remain on an abstract and ahistorical theological level; or, perhaps more subtly, it is to remain on the level of a theology more concerned with avoiding past errors than with discovering the originality of the present situation and committing itself to tomorrow.

The Latin American Christian community lives on a poor continent, but the image it projects is not, as a whole, that of a *poor Church*. The *Conclusions* of Medellín accurately acknowledge this fact, which can be verified by anyone who takes the time to get to know the impressions of the average Latin American. Prejudices and generalizations undoubtedly distort the image, but no one can deny its fundamental validity. The majority of the Church has covertly or openly been an accomplice of the external and internal dependency of our peoples. It has sided with the dominant groups, and in the name of 'efficacy' has dedicated its best efforts to them. It has identified with these sectors and adopted their style of life. We often confuse the possession of basic necessities with a comfortable position in the world, freedom to preach the Gospel with protection by powerful groups, instruments of service with the means of power. It is nevertheless important to clarify exactly what the witness of poverty involves.

Despite the hopes aroused by the options we have mentioned, many Christians in Latin America regard them very skeptically. They think that these choices have opened up too late and that real changes in the Church will result only from the social transformations which the whole continent is undergoing. Many even fear – as do many non-Christians – that the efforts of the Latin American Church will only make it the Latin American version of di Lampedusa's 'Leopard'.

This danger is real and we must be aware of it. In any case, by confronting the problems facing it – with all their peculiar characteristics – the Latin American Church ought to be gradually asserting its *own personality*. The situation of dependency which pervades the continent is also present in the ecclesiastical realm. The Latin American Church was born dependent and still remains in circumstances which have prevented it from developing its peculiar gifts. Like on the socio-economic and political levels, this dependency is not only an external factor; it molds the structures, life and thought of the Latin American Church, which has been more a Church-reflection than a Church-source.

This is another of the constant complaints of laymen, priests, religious, and bishops in Latin America. Overcoming the colonial mentality is one of the important tasks of the Christian community. In this way, it will be able to make a genuine contribution to the enrichment of the universal Church; it will be able to face its real problems and to sink deep roots into a continent in revolution.

[. . .]

Material poverty is a scandalous condition. Spiritual poverty is an attitude of openness to God and spiritual childhood. Having clarified these two meanings of the term *poverty* we have cleared the path and can now move forward towards a better understanding of the Christian witness of poverty. We turn now to a third meaning of the term: poverty as a commitment of solidarity and protest.

We have laid aside the first two meanings. The first is subtly deceptive; the second partial and insufficient. In the first place, if *material poverty* is something to be rejected, as the Bible vigorously insists, then a witness of poverty cannot make of it a Christian ideal. This would be to aspire to a condition which is recognized as degrading to man. It would be, moreover, to move against the current of history. It would be to oppose any idea of the domination of nature by man and the consequent and progressive creation of better conditions of life. And finally, but not least seriously, it would be to justify, even if involuntarily, the injustice and exploitation which is the cause of poverty.

On the other hand, our analysis of the Biblical texts concerning *spiritual poverty* has helped us to see that it is not directly or in the first instance an interior detachment from the goods of this world, a spiritual attitude which becomes authentic by incarnating itself in material poverty. Spiritual poverty is something more complete and profound. It is above all total availability to the Lord. Its relationship to the use or ownership of economic goods is inescapable, but secondary and partial. Spiritual childhood – an ability to receive, not a passive acceptance – defines the total posture of human existence before God, men, and things.

How are we therefore to understand the evangelical meaning of the witness of a real, material, concrete poverty? *Lumen gentium* invites us to look for the deepest meaning of Christian poverty *in Christ*:

> Just as Christ carried out the work of redemption in poverty and under oppression, so the Church is called to follow the same path in communicating to men the fruits of salvation. Christ Jesus, though He was by nature God . . . emptied himself, taking the nature of a slave (Phil. 2.6), and being rich, he became poor (2 Cor. 8.9) for our sakes. Thus, although the Church needs human resources to carry out her mission, she is not set up to seek earthly glory, but to proclaim humility and self-sacrifice, even by her own example. (no. 8)

The Incarnation is an act of love. Christ became man, died, and rose from the dead to set us free so that we might enjoy freedom (Gal. 5.1). To die and to rise again with Christ is to vanquish death and to enter into a new life (cf. Rom. 6.1–11). The cross and the resurrection are the seal of our liberty.

The taking on of the servile and sinful condition of man, as foretold in Second Isaiah, is presented by Paul as an act of voluntary impoverishment: 'For you know how generous our Lord Jesus Christ has been: He was rich, yet for your sake he became poor, so that through his poverty you might become rich' (2 Cor. 8.9). This is the humiliation of Christ, his *kenosis* (Phil. 2.6–11). But he does not take on man's sinful condition and its consequences to idealize it. It is rather because of love for and solidarity with men who suffer in it. It is to redeem them from their sin and to enrich them with his poverty. It is to struggle against human selfishness and everything that divides men and enables there to be rich and poor, possessors and dispossessed, oppressors and oppressed.

Poverty is an act of love and liberation. It has a redemptive value. If the ultimate cause of man's exploitation and alienation is selfishness, the deepest reason for voluntary poverty is love of neighbor. Christian poverty has meaning only as a commitment of solidarity with the poor, with those who suffer misery and injustice. The commitment is to witness to the evil which has resulted from sin and is a breach of communion. It is not a question of idealizing poverty, but rather of taking it on as it is – an evil – to protest against it and to struggle to abolish it. As Ricoeur says, you cannot really be with the poor unless you are struggling against poverty. Because of this solidarity – which must manifest itself in specific action, a style of life, a break with one's social class – one can also help the poor and exploited to become aware of their exploitation and seek liberation from it. Christian poverty, an expression of love, is solidarity *with the poor* and is a protest *against poverty*. This is the concrete, contemporary meaning of the witness of poverty. It is a poverty lived not for its own sake, but rather as an authentic imitation of Christ; it is a poverty which means taking on the sinful condition of man to liberate him from sin and all its consequences.

Luke presents the community of goods in the early Church as an ideal. 'All whose faith had drawn them together held everything in common' (Acts 2.44); 'not a man of them claimed any of his possessions as his own, but everything was held in common' (Acts 4.33). They did this with a profound unity, one 'in heart and soul' (*ibid.*). But as J. Dupont correctly points out, this was not a question of erecting poverty as an ideal, but rather of seeing to it that there were no poor: 'They had never a needy person among them, because all who had property in land or houses sold it, brought the proceeds of the sale, and laid the money at the feet of the apostles; it was then distributed to any who stood in need' (Acts 4.34–5). The meaning of the community of goods is clear: to eliminate poverty because of love of the poor person. Dupont rightly concludes, 'If goods are held in common, it is not therefore in order to become poor for love of an ideal of poverty; rather it is so that there will be no poor. The ideal pursued is, once again, charity, a true love for the poor.'

We must pay special attention to the words we use. The term *poor* might seem not only vague and churchy, but also somewhat sentimental and aseptic. The 'poor' person today is the oppressed one, the one marginated from society, the member of the proletariat struggling for his most basic rights; he is the exploited and plundered social class, the country struggling for its liberation. In today's world the solidarity and protest of which we are speaking have an evident and inevitable 'political' character insofar as they imply liberation. To be with the oppressed is to be against the oppressor. In our times and on our continent to be in solidarity with the 'poor', understood in this way, means to run personal risks – even to put one's life in danger. Many Christians – and non-Christians – who are committed to the Latin American revolutionary process are running these risks. And so there are emerging new ways of living poverty which are different from the classic 'renunciation of the goods of this world'.

Only by rejecting poverty and by making itself poor in order to protest against it can the Church preach something that is uniquely its own: 'spiritual poverty', that is, the openness of man and history to the future promised by God. Only in this way will the Church be able to fulfill authentically – and with any possibility of being listened to – its prophetic function of denouncing every injustice to man. And only in this way will it be able to preach the word which liberates, the word of genuine brotherhood.

Only authentic solidarity with the poor and a real protest against the poverty of our time can provide the concrete, vital context necessary for a theological discussion of poverty. The absence of a sufficient commitment to the poor, the marginated, and the exploited is perhaps the fundamental reason why we have no solid contemporary reflection on the witness of poverty.

For the Latin American Church especially, this witness is an inescapable and much-needed sign of the authenticity of its mission.

Source: G. Gutiérrez, *A Theology of Liberation*, SCM Press, 1974, pp. 299–302, 134–40.

(b) The Kairos Document

The Bible, of course, does not only *describe* oppression, tyranny and suffering. The message of the Bible is that oppression is sinful and wicked, an offence against God. The oppressors are godless sinners and the oppressed are suffering because of the sins of their oppressors.

But there is *hope* because Yahweh, the God of the Bible, will *liberate* the oppressed from their suffering and misery. 'He will redeem their lives from exploitation and outrage' (Ps. 74.14). 'I have seen the miserable state of my people in Egypt. I have heard their appeal to be free of their slave-drivers. I mean to deliver them out of the hands of the Egyptians' (Exod. 3.7).

Throughout the Bible God appears as the liberator of the oppressed: 'For the plundered poor, for the needy who groan, now I will act, says Yahweh' (Ps. 12.5). God is not neutral. He does not attempt to reconcile Moses and Pharaoh, to reconcile the Hebrew slaves with their Egyptian oppressors or to reconcile the Jewish people with any of their later oppressors. 'You have upheld the justice of my cause . . . judging in favour of the orphans and exploited so that earthborn man (human beings) may strike fear no more. My enemies are in retreat, stumbling, perishing as you confront them. Trouble is coming to the rebellious, the defiled, the tyrannical city' (Ps. 9.4; 10.18; 9.3; Zeph. 3.1). Oppression is a crime and it cannot be compromised with, it must be done away with. 'They (the rulers of Israel) will cry out to God. But he will not answer them. He will hide his face at that time because of all the crimes they have committed' (Mic. 3.4). 'God, who does what is right, is always on the side of the oppressed' (Ps. 103.6).

There can be no doubt that Jesus, the Son of God, also takes up the cause of the poor and the oppressed and identifies himself with their interests. When he stood up in the synagogue at Nazareth to announce his mission he made use of the words of Isaiah.

> The Spirit of the Lord has been given to me.
> For he has anointed me.
> He has sent me to bring the good news to the poor,
> to proclaim liberty to captives
> and to the blind new sight,
> to set the downtrodden free
> to proclaim the Lord's year of favour
>
> (Luke 4.18–19)

Not that Jesus is unconcerned about the rich and the oppressed. These he calls to repentance. At the very heart of the gospel of Jesus Christ and at the very centre of all true prophecy is a message of hope. Jesus has taught us to speak of this hope as the coming of God's Kingdom. We believe that God is at work in our world turning hopeless and evil situations to good so that God's Kingdom may come and God's Will may be done on earth as it is in heaven. We believe that goodness and justice and love will triumph in the end and that tyranny and oppression cannot last forever. One day 'all tears will be wiped away' (Rev. 7.17;

12.4) and 'the lamb will lie down with the lion' (Isa. 11.6). True peace and true reconciliation are not only desirable, they are assured and guaranteed. This is our faith and our hope. We believe in and hope for the resurrection.

Nothing could be more relevant and more necessary at this moment of crisis in South Africa than the Christian message of hope. As the crisis deepens day by day, what both the oppressor and the oppressed can legitimately demand of the Churches is a message of hope. Most of the oppressed people in South Africa today and especially the youth do have hope. They are acting courageously and fearlessly because they have a sure hope that liberation will come. Often enough their bodies are broken but, nothing can now break their spirit. But hope needs to be confirmed. Hope needs to be maintained and strengthened. Hope needs to be spread. The people need to hear it said again and again that God is with them and that 'the hope of the poor is never brought to nothing' (Ps. 9.18).

On the other hand the oppressor and those who believe the propaganda of the oppressor are desperately fearful. They must be made aware of the diabolical evils of the present system and they must be called to repentance. 'By what right do you crush my people and grind the face of the poor' (Isa. 3.15). But they must also be given something to hope for. At present they have false hopes. They hope to maintain the status quo and their special privileges with perhaps some adjustments and they fear any real alternative. But there is much more than that to hope for and nothing to fear. Can the Christian message of hope not help them in this matter?

A prophetic theology for our times will focus our attention on the future. What kind of future do the oppressed people of South Africa want? What kind of future do the political organizations of the people want? What kind of future does God want? And how, with God's help are we going to secure that future for ourselves? We must begin to plan the future now but above all we must heed God's call to action to secure God's future for ourselves in South Africa.

There is hope. There is hope for all of us. But the road to that hope is going to be very hard and very painful. The conflict and the struggle will intensify in the months and years ahead. That is now inevitable – because of the intransigence of the oppressor. But God is with us. We can only learn to become the instruments of his peace even unto death. We must participate in the cross of Christ if we are to have the hope of participating in his resurrection.

Why is it that this powerful message of hope has not been highlighted in 'Church Theology', in the statements and pronouncements of Church leaders? Is it because they have been addressing themselves to the

122

oppressor rather than to the oppressed? Is it because they do not want to encourage the oppressed to be too hopeful for too much?

Now is the time to act – to act hopefully, to act with full confidence and trust in God.

To say that the Church must now take sides unequivocally and consistently with the poor and the oppressed is to overlook the fact that the majority of Christians in South Africa have already done so. By far the greater part of the Church in South Africa is poor and oppressed. Of course it cannot be taken for granted that everyone who is oppressed has taken up their own cause and is struggling for their own liberation. Nor can it be assumed that all oppressed Christians are fully aware of the fact that their cause is God's cause. Nevertheless it remains true that the Church is already on the side of the oppressed because that is where the majority of its members are to be found. This fact needs to be appropriated and confirmed by the Church as a whole.

At the beginning of this document it was pointed out that the present crisis has highlighted the divisions in the Church. We are a divided Church precisely because not all the members of our Churches have taken sides against oppression. In other words not all Christians have united themselves with God 'who is always on the side of the oppressed' (Ps. 103.6). As far as the present crisis is concerned, there is only one way forward to Church unity and that is for those Christians who find themselves on the side of the oppressor or sitting on the fence, to cross over to the other side to be united in faith and action with those who are oppressed. Unity and reconciliation within the Church itself is only possible around God and Jesus Christ who are to be found on the side of the poor and the oppressed.

If this is what the Church must become, if this is what the Church as a whole must have as its project, how then are we to translate it into concrete and effective action?

Christians, if they are not doing so already, must quite simply participate in the struggle for liberation and for a just society. The campaigns of the people, from consumer boycotts to stayaways, need to be supported and encouraged by the Church. Criticism will sometimes be necessary but encouragement and support will also be necessary. In other words the present crisis challenges the whole Church to move beyond a mere 'ambulance ministry' to a ministry of involvement and participation.

The Church has its own specific activities: Sunday services, communion services, baptisms, Sunday school, funerals and so forth. It also has its specific way of expressing its faith and its commitment, that is, in the form of confessions of faith. All of these activities must be reshaped to be more fully consistent with a prophetic faith related to the KAIROS that God is offering us today. The evil forces we speak of in baptism must be named. We know what these evil forces are in South Africa today. The unity and sharing we profess in our communion services or Masses must be named. It is the solidarity of the people inviting all to join in the struggle for God's peace in South Africa. The repentance we preach must be named. It is repentance for our share of the guilt for the suffering and oppression in our country.

Much of what we do in our Church services has lost its relevance to the poor and the oppressed. Our services and sacraments have been appropriated to serve the need of the individual for comfort and security. Now these same Church activities must be reappropriated to serve the real religious needs of all the people and to further the liberating mission of God and the Church in the world.

Over and above its regular activities the Church would need to have special programmes, projects and campaigns because of the special needs of the struggle for liberation in South Africa today. But there is a very important caution here. The Church must avoid becoming a 'Third Force', a force between the oppressor and the oppressed. The Church's programmes and campaigns must not duplicate what the people's organizations are already doing and, even more seriously, the Church must not confuse the issue by having programmes that run counter to the struggles of those political organizations that truly represent the grievances and demands of the people. Consultation, co-ordination and co-operation will be needed. We all have the same goals even when we differ about the final significance of what we are struggling for.

Once it is established that the present regime has no moral legitimacy and is in fact a tyrannical regime certain things follow for the Church and its activities. In the first place *the Church cannot collaborate with tyranny*. It cannot or should not do anything that appears to give legitimacy to a morally illegitimate regime. Secondly, the Church should not only pray for a change of government, it should also mobilize its members in every parish to begin to think and work and plan for a change of government in South Africa. We must begin to look ahead and begin working now with firm hope and faith for a better future. And finally the moral illegitimacy of the apartheid regime means that the Church will have to be involved at times in *civil disobedience*. A Church that takes its responsibilities seriously in these circumstances will sometimes have to confront and to disobey the State in order to obey God.

The people look to the Church, especially in the midst of our present crisis, for moral guidance. In order to provide this the Church must first make its stand absolutely clear and never tire of explaining and dialoguing about it. It must then help people to understand their rights and their duties. There must be no misunderstanding about the *moral duty* of all who are oppressed to resist oppression and to struggle for liberation and justice. The Church will also find that at times it does need to curb excesses and to appeal to the consciences of those who act thoughtlessly and wildly.

But the Church of Jesus Christ is not called to be a bastion of caution and moderation. The Church should challenge, inspire and motivate people. It has a message of the cross that inspires us to make sacrifices for justice and liberation. It has a message of hope that challenges us to wake up and to act with hope and confidence. The Church must preach this message not only in words and sermons and statements but also through its actions, programmes, campaigns and divine services.

Source: *The Kairos Document*, Eerdmans, 1986, pp. 25–30.

Further reading

There are good short introductions in the chapters by Chopp in Ford's collection *The Modern Theologians*, by Medhurst in Moyser's *Politics and Religions in the Modern World* and by McGrath and Sigmund in Witte, *Christianity and Democracy in Global Context*. See also Wogaman's *Christian Perspectives on Politics*, Chapter 4. The best short book is Berryman's *Liberation Theology*. There is a useful collection in Hennelley's *Liberation Theology: A Documentary History*. On Christian base communities, see Boff's *Ecclesiogenesis* and on the question of violence, Bonino's *Towards a Christian Political Ethics*. For criticism from a more conservative standpoint, see Sigmund's *Liberation Theology at the Crossroads*. Also the more Marxist criticisms in the books by Kee, *Marx and the Failure of Liberation Theology* and Scott, *Theology, Ideology and Liberation*.

The main works by leading liberation theologians such as Boff, Gutiérrez, Bonino, Segundo and Sobrino are listed in the Bibliography.

Chapter Nine

EUROPE

Introduction

The end of the Second World War saw the transformation of the confessional political parties, which had been created fifty years earlier, into Christian Democratic parties. These pursued in general a fairly centrist line with reformist and even anti-capitalist policies which could appeal to the moderate left. Although undoubtedly more conservative in the last two decades, the Christian (and more specifically Catholic) background has given the drive for European integration a distinct 'social' dimension. This Catholic tradition has dwelt on the social character of the human person and emphasized social human rights – as brought out in the pieces by Huber and Papini below. Indeed, the European Union's whole approach to what might be called 'social capitalism' is rooted in the doctrines of the Catholic Church and the Commission's approach is permeated with Catholic terminology and assumptions. Jacques Delors is but the most evident example of a politician/bureaucrat who considers his attitudes to stem from this sort of Catholic social teaching. In the past, the Church has had a powerful instinct to advocate the authoritative allocation of goods on a monarchic model derived from the Old Testament: a sort of command economy where concepts of just wage and just price figure as part of a divine plan.

Given current electoral volatility and the decline in the political cohesiveness of religious groups, it is likely that the impact of Christian democracy will be more diffuse in the future. Nevertheless, the attitude of John Paul II with his nostalgia for the restoration of the Christendom model in which the Church guides and shapes society contains obvious dangers – as explained in the extract from Forrester below. A Christianity which learnt lessons from the past would be less triumphalist and more interested in the challenges of developing a pluralist vision.

Finally, the role of Christianity in the 'velvet revolutions' of 1989 was important. In many cases, the churches fostered the development of an oppositional democratic politics in the face of increasingly bankrupt authoritarian governments. The most striking example is that of the Lutheran Church in Germany described in the extract from De Gruchy below.

(a) Papini:
The Christian Democratic Movement

The main task of Christian Democracy must be to persuade political and social forces, European governments, and the European Community to work out a global policy towards the East that will take account of cultural and spiritual factors. Otherwise they will only be risking new disappointments. Nor can the United States afford to stand aside. It must necessarily play a leading role in this mutual effort, redeploying the enormous resources that were previously tied up in maintaining a balance of military power with the Soviet Union.

A second challenge to democracy in Europe is presented by the millions of non-European Community citizens who have emigrated from the South of the world and whose presence is a real threat to the stability of many European countries – a problem that will become even graver if more millions arrive from Eastern Europe. If a multi-racial, multi-cultural integrated society is the ideal, at the moment the countries of Western Europe are up against mounting and apparently insoluble problems. Mediterranean Islam, and the Shiite area in particular, presents a problem that our pluralist democracies do not find easy to solve. How can Islam's unitary conception of religion and politics and the relationship between Muslims and non-Muslims (the latter being the 'infidels' or at best, like Christians and Jews, the 'protected') be reconciled with our concept of the lay society?

The Church, which has struggled so hard to reach the shores of democracy, can do much to present the face of a Christianity that is conciliar, not triumphalistic, and the virtues of a democracy that does not automatically mean Westernization and secularization. Who is best fitted to renew the spiritual values of the world if not the great religious traditions, provided that in mutual dialogue they are capable of accepting modernity without committing suicide?

The problem, however, is also political, and the Christian Democrat parties must do their utmost to create a Community policy that will combine respect for human rights with the conditions essential for a change of course that will inevitably upset Europe's present cultural balances. That said, there is no getting away from the fact that the only long-term solution to this problem is the true development of the South, and now the East as well.

Lastly, there is the challenge of development. Closely linked to environmental issues, this is one of humanity's greatest challenges, after the victory over Communism and hence over the threat of nuclear war. In the West, the quality of development is increasingly seen as the main goal, and this issue is very closely connected to the first in an interdependent global economy. Hence arises the problem of how those who will be affected are to participate in the making of decisions involving development strategies and policies, decisions that most people feel should not be left to interested economic groups that are not subject to democratic controls. And hence arises the question of extending social and economic rights, on which so much insistence is placed today, a question connected to the current debate on ethics and economy and the search for rules that will provide ethical guidelines for the market. This problem underlies economic democracy in the sense of a balanced relationship between market and democracy, which is by now central in the evolution of our society. It is a burning question that can only be touched on here. After reflecting on the Church's long contention with political liberalism, it is at least worth remembering its equally long contention with economic liberalism, especially now that socialism, the other protagonist in this triangular conflict of modern times, has admitted its own failure.

A restrictive view of democracy tends to prevail in the West today, seeing it as a sort of free political market in which, as in the economic market, social demand and political offer have free play. Economic ultra-liberalism cannot satisfy the needs of social integration, for these are inseparable from democracy; it can only aggravate the imbalances between the North and the South of the world and, inside the Western societies, the gap between rich and poor.

In the wake of *Mater et Magistra*, *Gaudium et Spes* offers a basic ethical criterion: starting from the centrality of the human person and the principle that property is intended for the benefit of the whole of humanity, not just a privileged few, justice dictates that the greatest possible number of interested persons should participate as freely as possible in decisions of an economic nature. Although it fully recognizes the functionality of the market, the encyclical *Centesimus Annus* is not afraid to recall the public powers to the need for it to be regulated juridically, so that human economic rights will be safeguarded and interested persons guaranteed the right to share in the making of economic decisions.

At the end of a long and eventful journey, the Church has thus discovered economic rights, after social and then political rights, coupled with a growing awareness that the preservation of each one of these is dependent on the existence of the others. The Church's long dispute with economic liberalism has affected the evolution of Christian Democratic thinking and the practice of the parties to which it applies. The Christian Democratic idea, like the social Christian idea, although opening up new horizons for political democracy and social organization, has always found it difficult to work out its own economic models. Since 1945 the Christian Democrat parties have tended instead to borrow from economic liberalism or the Labour movement, depending on the country, and then adapting it. Helped by the evolution of capitalism – or, rather, capitalisms, for now the term must be used in the plural – they have managed to create models that have combined economic with social policy. Perhaps the two outstanding examples are the social market economy of West Germany and Italy's policy of state intervention.

Economic democracy has often been proposed as a means for improving industrial relations, or even for their joint management. But, for a series of reasons, including sometimes union opposition, the idea has remained in the shadows in many European countries. This is a pity, for it would be a natural vexillum for parties which, since their birth, see themselves as democratic and social.

The evolution of the Church towards a more community-oriented conception of itself – a process in which the development of the democratic societies has certainly exercised some influence – has also enriched democracy. For, during this evolution, the action of the Church has in some way been purified, so that today it tends to propose values that nourish democratic societies and direct them towards a greater democratic ideal.

On the other hand, the conflict and the reciprocal differentiation between Christianity and society, with the birth of a secular conscience, have also been a feature of modernization in the West, offset, however, by the progressive mutual penetration of the two spheres. And there can be no doubt that if the Western industrial societies today incorporate the Christian values of equity and solidarity, this is, at least in part, thanks to the evolution of the Church.

The Church's new understanding of its role in history is the reason for its greater involvement in its dialogue with, and service to, mankind

129

and society. This involvement is not based solely on doctrinal positions but also on moral choices. And it is significant here that the Church's social doctrine is no longer presented as a 'third way' but as a part of moral theology. The result is that the Church, which is displaying great ethical and social dynamism all over the world today, is recognized as a moral reference point.

Democracy, too, is going through a phase of worldwide extension and self-examination. With the steady collapse of the authoritarian regimes, be they of the left or the right, the idea of democracy is replacing that of revolution, while the explosion of national awareness is once more calling into question the traditional concept of the state as centralizer, to a greater or lesser degree. Certainly there are risks of violence connected with the resurgence of nationalism and religious fundamentalism in this phase of decolonization, following the end of the political and ideological blocks. The world is experiencing a profound shakedown in which democracy and solidarity will have a major role to play.

History, of course, does not finish with the end of Communism. The end of the Communist regimes is a liberating event but at the same time one that creates new responsibilities. Despite the 'victory' of their great antagonist, capitalism, the demand for freedom and social liberation that Communism could not satisfy persists.

Does this mean the end of the quest for forms of society that are more compatible with human dignity? Will capitalism be capable of reforming itself in a truly democratic way? What hopes can be held out to the oppressed and the poor of the world? Much is said about the new world order, but what concrete form will it take, and what will be its response to these poor and oppressed people?

What will Europe's role be in this new order? The steady shift of the world's centre of gravity from the Atlantic to the Pacific has often been perceived on the other side of the Atlantic as a question mark over Europe's identity and planning capacity, sometimes with the sensation that it will revert to being no more than a small promontory of Asia. There is also, however, an awareness that Europe today is a spiritual frontier, especially in the way it is tackling the problems of modernity and post-modernity, a frontier in which more than the fate of Europe is at stake. The end of the historical conflict between Church and democracy does not yet mean the end to tensions between the Church and modernity, a fact that democracy cannot afford to ignore. Here, the Church can provide a great reservoir of critical energy and a driving force towards renewing democracy and making it respond better to the needs of humanity.

In examining the origins of our democracy, in Europe and in the United States of America, democracy in which Christianity has played such an important part, we shall discover why this new world order should be the true expression of democracy and collaboration between peoples.

Source: R. Papini, 'The Christian Democratic Movement', in
Christianity and Democracy in Global Context,
ed. J. Witte, Westview, 1993, pp. 42–6.

(b) *Huber:* Christianity and Democracy

We live in a period of new challenges for the democratic culture in Europe. Four processes intensify these challenges.

First, there is the so-called European, in reality until now Western-European, economic integration with the completion of an internal market of 340 million 'consumers' by 31 December 1992. The question is whether there will be an effective democratic framework for this concentration of economic, and that means also political, power.

Second, there is the end of authoritarian one-party systems and centrally planned economies in Middle and Eastern Europe and the opening of those regions for the process of democratization. The question is whether this process leads to new impulses for a more appropriate form of democracy under the conditions of the late twentieth century. We are witnesses of a civil war on ethnic grounds in Yugoslavia, of the dissociation of the Soviet Union on the basis of the demand for national self-determination, of a struggle over the unity of Czechoslovakia, and so on. It is a critical question whether federal forms of democracy offer a helpful model between the Scylla of bureaucratic centralism and the Charybdis of nationalistic and ethnic fragmentation.

Third, there is the growing gap between the three rich and powerful economic regions of the world – North America, Western Europe, and Japan – and the other parts of the globe as well as the growing mass of poor and starving people in the world. The question is whether our democratic structures can help us to develop a new kind of responsibility towards the poorest parts of the world population.

Finally, there is the dramatic decline of the ecological conditions of life within one generation, which consequently demands an ecological transformation of our highly industrialized countries. Once again the question is how effective our democratic attitudes and procedures will be with respect to this unparalleled challenge.

Looking at the problem of Christianity and democracy in Europe in terms of these challenges I want to emphasize the following results of the previous reflection.

First, on the one hand, the history of Europe affords no reason for a Christian triumphalism. The formula of a 'Christian Europe' is characterized by a lack of honesty with regard to the past and by a lack of convincing strength with regard to the future. The identification of Christianity with Europe was meaningful only during the Middle Ages. By the beginning of the modern era, America was opened for Christianity and Europe for secularity. Since then it is impossible to identify Europe with Christianity. The integralistic concept of Europe is an atavism.

On the other hand, it would be irresponsible to deprecate the possible contribution of Christian political ethics to the development of the necessary world ethics of today. It is not fair to accept the global expansion of the European-American industrial civilization including its instruments of violence but at the same time to declare that democracy and human rights are a European-American peculiarity which cannot be transferred to other cultures. In Europe I observe from time to time a new kind of cultural imperialism. It says that our political culture is based on important assumptions of Christian anthropology centered around the idea of the equal dignity of all humans. Regions with another religious and cultural background have no access to these assumptions, so they are not capable of understanding human rights and realizing democracy in the full sense of the word. The idea of universal human rights is meaningless for such a kind of cultural imperialism. Instead, human rights are bound to the European-American cultural circle.

It seems to me to take a special kind of arrogance to confront the other regions of the world with the beneficent as well as the disastrous consequences of technology and industrialization but, at the same time, to declare them incapable of a proper understanding of democracy and human rights. It is simply arrogant when Europeans deny to Buddhists or the adherents of African religions the capability of developing their own concept and understanding of human dignity. And even the often-used example of the alleged imperviousness of Islamic fundamentalism to democracy would only be convincing if we could say the same of Christian fundamentalism and its difficulties with religious tolerance, acceptance of the stranger, and democracy. Only on the basis of a self-critical attitude will we begin to be open for the contribution of others to the political culture of tomorrow.

If we look on this debate from the perspective of the victims we can see that there is at least a universal understanding of the violation of human rights and democracy. Wherever people are tortured or starving, wherever people have neither shelter nor work, wherever people are excluded from political participation and lack even 'the right to have rights', it is obvious that we need a global understanding of human dignity. But this dignity as well as a really embracing concept of human rights and democracy needs openness to differing foundations. It has to be acknowledged that access to them can be found from different traditions and cultures. The ideas of human rights and democratic participation are characterized by a relative universalism. They were developed in the context of Christianity and the Enlightenment, but they can be linked to other interpretations and are open to changes by them. Openness of human rights and democracy to various foundations is one of the elements of political culture for which Europeans have a special responsibility.

It has to be added that there is no exclusive linkage between Christianity and one political party. The Gospel itself can never be claimed by one political party alone. The existence of 'Christian Democratic' parties should not obscure the fact that Christians are, for good reasons, active in other political associations. In Europe, for instance, there is a strong and important Christian wing in the Social Democratic Parties emphasizing the equal dignity and freedom of all, a preferential awareness for the dependent, and a new responsibility for non-human nature. For those Christians who work in a Social Democratic party the basic values of this political movement – freedom, justice, and solidarity – are characterized by a specific affinity to fundamental Christian convictions. But comparable reflections can be found when Christians decide to be actively involved in a liberal or a green party. As far as Germany is concerned it cannot be said that the German constitution of 1949 has to be interpreted as the expression of a Christian-Democratic concept of the state as opposed to a Social-Democratic or Liberal concept. The constitution is founded in the respect for human dignity and human rights but is open for different political explications and applications of this basic consensus.

Second, the debate on the political culture of Europe concentrates today on the polarities of plurality and identity, of multiculturality and integralism. The tradition of Christian Democracy tends toward an integralistic view of the European political culture. In this framework we can even observe in some quarters a tendency toward a certain kind of reconfessionalization of European politics. I see one example in the rather integralistic interpretation of the relationship between Christianity and democracy by Pope John Paul II, as explained during his last travel to Poland as well as on other occasions. Another is the rather strange and only partly intended fact that today most of the high officials in German politics named by CDU or CSU are Catholics – to an extent which is without parallel since the early days of the Federal Republic of Germany

In opposition to the tendencies towards a new kind of integralism it has to be emphasized that a European identity to come necessarily includes the equal freedom of the diverse. The dramatic migration movements of our time are a test case for this understanding of European identity. The different European countries need a clear concept of integration of immigrants and of procedures for handling the different kinds of refugees. Obviously Germany has a special problem because Article 16, 2 of its constitution incorporated a very generous formulation on the right of individuals to obtain asylum. In addition, two-thirds of all immigrants and refugees who now arrive in Western Europe from the East or from the South end up in Germany. So it is necessary to find practical solutions to the emerging problems. But all attacks on the right of refugees 'to have rights' and also all kinds of aggressive hostility towards foreigners and refugees endanger the political culture of Europe itself. The coexistence of different cultures forms an inseparable part of European history and therefore also a part of its identity. An integralistic or even more a fundamentalistic negation of the plural reality in Europe is a political regression and an offense against the history as well as the future tasks of the continent.

Third, the most important contribution of the Catholic tradition to the European political culture is its explanation of the social character of the human person and as a consequence its emphasis on solidarity and social human rights. From this perspective the situation in Europe is still characterized by a remarkable deficit. The Western European understanding of human rights still gives a prerogative to individual liberties over social rights. Even countries like Germany who signed and ratified the United Nations Covenant on Social and Economic rights did not yet incorporate those rights into their own constitution. The reason has partly to be found in the confidence in the market economy newly justified by the disaster of all centrally planned economies in Eastern Europe. But the social imbalances which result from the market system are obvious. They have a regional dimension mainly in the relatively high degree of unemployment and a global dimension in the continuous deepening of the gulf between the rich and the poor parts of the world. The Evangelical Church in Germany emphasized these imbalances as a major challenge to Christian responsibility in a new memorandum on economic questions, published in October 1991. Looking at these imbalances I am not convinced that 'development' is any longer the key word for the solution of those problems. After 30 years of development, it seems that a higher degree of self-criticism on the part of the industrialized countries is needed. In a situation in which the industrial civilization experiences its own crisis – in terms of the ecological crisis as well as in terms of social imbalances – the solution cannot be to export the Western model of industrialization under the heading of 'development'. Our contribution is to offer the accessible means of technology, communication, and organization to partners in other parts of the world but to let them define for themselves their future and their destiny. If justice as fairness gives to others the same right to define their objectives as I claim for myself, then not 'development' but 'justice' should be the key word for the relations between the rich and the poor parts of our globe.

It seems to me that of all the problems democracy is facing in Europe the following three are really crucial: (1) the situation of the post-Communist countries; (2) the surge of migration to the European Community countries from the South of the world, and now increasingly from the East; and (3) development and economic rights.

John Paul II dedicated his latest encyclical, *Centesimus Annus*, to the problem of the post-Communist countries. The Pope's aim is to minimize the traumas in the arduous transition to a political democracy and a market economy based on Western models, which reflect a culture that is utilitarian when it is not nihilistic. The democratic institutions that have been set up in countries where, among other things, the great majority of the population has no experience of Western democracy, need the support of a structured society, but they lack, in every sector, an entreprencurial culture that can stimulate its growth. Faced with an extraordinary vacuum of faith, moral apathy and generalized fragmentation of society – Communism's worst legacy – only a new culture of hope, the Pope would say a new solidarity, can provide the basis for a democracy capable of withstanding the risks of disintegration and social violence, the resurgence of old and new nationalisms (it has already happened in Yugoslavia), and economic chaos.

The European Community and the West in general are guilty of short-sightedness if they believe that economic aid – which, incidentally, might otherwise have been given to the Third World – is the panacea for all the ills of these countries. Even if the flow of aid will be an important factor in consolidating their young democracies, what is needed above all is increased educational and cultural cooperation, to help democracy put down firm roots in the consciousness of the people. In some countries in particular, the Church can do a great deal to encourage a spirit of solidarity, by reminding the people of their common roots in European Christendom, although it must avoid the temptation to reassert its claim to temporal power.

Source: W. Huber, 'Christianity and Democracy', in *Christianity and Democracy in Global Context*, ed. J. Witte, Westview, 1993, pp. 42–6.

(c) Forrester: Christianity in Europe

We still live every day in Europe in the aftermath of the Enlightenment project. In some ways religion has been marginalized and effectively confined to the private realm. Europe is, and will continue to be, a plural and secular society. But religion in general, and Christianity in particular, have been shown by recent events to be far more powerful and resilient than many people had suspected. So we have to ask about the place and contribution of Christianity to the new Europe that is in the process of emerging today, in the aftermath of the Cold War, with old wounds and alignments re-emerging, old bitternesses coming out into the open, and the European community seeking simultaneously economic prosperity and the healing of ancient animosities which led to two world wars and incalculable suffering.

There are, it seems to me, two broad options for Christianity in the New Europe. It can either seek a restoration of Christendom, a Christian Europe once more, with the church at its heart. Or it can seek to act as a creative, questioning and serving minority, accepting pluralism as a given and the new position of the church as an opportunity rather than a weakness.

The Christendom option has again and again re-asserted itself in modern times. In the aftermath of the first world war, Hilaire Belloc in his polemical little book *Europe and the Faith* in rather crude and polemical form called for the restoration of a Christian Europe as the heart of Christendom. The catholic faith as embodied in the Catholic Church, he said, remains 'the soul of our Western civilization', and without this faith and its essential institutional expression Europe would disintegrate and cease to be. Europe has been nurtured by Christianity and must continue to be shaped by Christianity: 'Europe must return to the faith or Europe will perish.' Indeed, the relationship between the faith and Europe is so close that neither is conceivable without the other: 'Europe is the faith and the faith is Europe.' The restoration of a Christian Europe as the heart of Christendom is for Belloc the only possibility for the survival of Europe. Otherwise Europe will fragment and destroy itself, and a new Dark Ages will be upon us. *The only way forward is to go back.*

The Belloc revivalist view is alive and well today. Long before he became Pope, Karol Wojtyla confidently predicted the collapse of communism and saw this as leaving behind a vacuum which only Christianity could fill. From this emerged his project of a unified and re-Christianized Europe stretching from the Atlantic to the Urals, which could be in a real sense the heart of the Christian world. This project was fully articulated first in the Pope's 'Declaration to Europe' which he delivered in Compostela on 9 November 1982. The place was significant. Compostela was the most important pilgrimage centre in Europe, the pilgrim ways linking together the various nations of Europe and the pilgrimage itself giving some sense of European identity, even when Europe was politically fragmented. What he did not emphasize was that St James, the patron of Compostela, was also understood as the harrier and destroyer of Muslims. So the pilgrimage celebrated a unity of Europe involving the ejection and destruction of the alien and those of other faiths. But the Pope proclaimed:

> It can be said that the European identity is not understandable without Christianity and it is precisely in Christianity that are found those common roots by which the continent has seen its civilization mature: its culture, its dynamism, its activity, its capacity for *constructive expansion in other continents* as well: in a word all that makes up its glory. And truly still, the soul of Europe remains united because, beyond its common origin, it has similar Christian and human values, such as those of the dignity of the human person, a deep sense of justice and of liberty, of industry and a spirit of initiative, of love for the family, of respect for life, of tolerance with the desire for co-operation and peace, which are notes which characterize it.

But Europe has been troubled and divided by secularized, atheistic and materialistic ideologies. Hence the Pope calls Europe to:

> *Find yourself again. Be yourself.* Discover your origins, revive your roots. Return to those authentic values which made your history a glorious one and your present so beneficial . . . You can still be the guiding light of civilization and the stimulus of progress for the world.

Similar notes have been sounded with clarity and urgency since the collapse of the communist regimes in eastern Europe in the *Declaration of the Special Assembly for Europe of the Synod of Bishops,* 1991, in some of the recent calls for the re-evangelization of Europe, and in the Pope's Encyclical *Centesimus Annus* (1991).

All this discourse, and the ecclesiastical policies to which it gives birth, I find disturbing. The proper place of the church, it is affirmed, is at the heart of things, controlling and guiding power and shaping society. It has only temporarily been displaced and forced to the margins by the interludes of Marxism, secularism and materialism. By implication too, religious pluralism is an aberration. The Pope – and Belloc – tell only part of the story of Europe. Europe, in their view, has brought enlightenment, culture, virtue and faith to the rest of the world. There is no mention of the slave trade, of genocide, of ruthless exploitation, of cultural and religious arrogance on the part of Christian Europe. [The year] 1992 is a time to celebrate 'the evangelization of the Americas'. Nor is attention given to the extent to which Christianity has been, and continues to be, a perennial major factor in

European disunity – witness Croatia, Serbia, Bosnia and Northern Ireland. A similar one-sidedness is shown in the understanding of the church and its role. The church – and it is the Roman Catholic Church that is meant – can guide, animate, heal and unite Europe. It has nothing to repent of, no lessons to be learnt. It speaks to Europe from strength, not weakness. It claims its proper place at the centre of things, at the heart of Europe, which is itself the heart of Christendom. The overall message is unambiguous – and radically flawed: the church, having consistently stood for justice, liberty, solidarity and human dignity, is now ready to resume its role, guiding and directing Europe.

In this Christian vision of Europe there appears to be no place for pluralism. At the heart of a pluralistic society there is believed to be a vacuum only Christianity can fill. Secularism, and indeed enlightenment, are to be rolled back, so that Christendom may be restored. And here the church once again has the dual task of legitimating and moderating the power structures of society. We are pointed back to the Constantinian settlement as some kind of ideal. But the Christendom experience of the past should teach us that alongside massive and impressive achievement there were dangerous distortions of the nature and mandate and responsibilities of the church, and also of the gospel message.

What alternative, then, might there be to the Christendom model? I would suggest that a church can see in numeric decline and in marginalization possibilities of a recovery of authenticity and opportunities to perform a truly Christian service to Europe, as the salt of the earth and the leaven of the lump. This possibility can only be embraced by churches which resolutely eschew triumphalism, face up honestly to the profound ambiguity in the history of Christian Europe and of Christendom, and express penitence for much that has been done in Europe in the name of Christ.

A rejection of the Christendom model also involves the abandonment of any Bellocian assumption that European and Christian values are one and the same, the adoption of a stance of constructive dissidence, and the conviction that a commitment to truth is not the same thing as constantly shoring up the system. The church, if it is to serve a diverse and dynamic Europe effectively must learn, or relearn, what it is to be a creative, but non-privileged minority. As Karl Barth put it after the second world war:

> The Church will have to learn afresh to walk towards its Lord as Peter did, not along smooth paths and up fine staircases with handsome balustrades, but on the water. It will have to learn to live on the edge of a precipice, as it did of necessity in its beginning. It must

learn again how to fulfil its duty nonetheless – simply in the impetus and magnetism of its own beginning and its own aim.

Vaclav Havel, in his remarkable collection of essays, *Living in Truth*, suggests that those who endeavour to live within the truth inevitably become dissidents in societies whose dominant operative values and priorities are inhumane and materialist. Dissent arises simply from the fact that endeavouring to live within the truth is in itself a challenge to the system of lies. It involves a deep commitment to the priority of people over systems, truth over ideologies and lies. The task is dissent, resistance:

> It seems to me that all of us, East and West, face one fundamental task from which all else should follow. That task is one of resisting vigilantly, thoughtfully and attentively, but at the same time, with total dedication, at every step and everywhere, the irrational momentum of anonymous, impersonal and inhuman power – the power of ideologies, systems, *apparat*, bureaucracy, artificial languages and political slogans. We must resist their complex and wholly alienating pressure, whether it takes the form of consumption, advertising, repression, technology or cliche all of which are blood brothers of fanaticism and the wellspring of totalitarian thought.

The dissidents who endeavour to live in truth do so not as individuals or in isolation, but in solidarity. Thus there is rediscovered what it means to be the church. The community of dissidents by the way it structures its life and its relations becomes a demonstration that fellowship is possible. Just as the congregations in the late Roman Empire offered in a fragmented society the possibility of fellowship and belonging, so the Christian churches in Europe today are challenged not just to talk about community, but to demonstrate that community is possible, community that is not introverted, partial, *incurvatus in se*, but open, joyful and responsible for and to the world.

The fatal temptation is that of the ghetto. Living in truth is inescapably concerned with the welfare of others, and holds out a model of community to the European Community which stresses justice, responsibility and hope in Europe's relation to the rest of the world, and particularly to the poor countries of the South and to the poor in Europe. As in the Church, so in the European Community in its global setting – rich and poor, strong and weak should be responsible for one another and to one another. The collapse of centrally imposed utopianism does not deprive us of the need for a grounded hope. Disillusion with the command economy should not lead us to make an idol of the market. The failure of communism to deliver social justice does not free us from the obligation to strive for it.

And so a church which overcomes its wistfulness for the past, for the time when Europe was in one sense Christian (and in other senses not Christian at all), for a place at the top table and a position of power and influence, is capable of being a constructively dissident minority community which constantly reminds Europe of the need for true community, of the priority of justice for the weakest, of the need to empower the powerless (the true meaning of subsidiarity) and of the necessity of freedom and of truthfulness. That should be the project of a penitent and hopeful Christianity in the Europe of today and tomorrow.

Source: D. Forrester, 'Christianity in Europe', in *Religion in Europe*, ed. U. King et al., Kok Pharos, 1995, pp. 40–4.

(d) Chadwick: Christianity in Eastern Europe

Throughout Eastern Europe the difficulties were fourfold. Firstly, change of government was no automatic recipe for prosperity. Communism as a system failed the people by its heavy hand of bureaucracy. But if Communist leaders disappeared the people were still poor.

Secondly, to survive and be effective, to keep sacraments among their people and churches in being, Christian leaders from Moscow to Prague and Belgrade had played along with their dictatorial politburos. They had not all gone so far in adulation as the patriarchs Justin and Teoctist of Romania, who had had to endure a dictator with megalomania, but they had had to say things and do things of which it was not easy afterwards to be proud. When the Communists fell, everyone who had worked with them was in trouble. There was a potential source of conflict, even of schism, between the legitimate Church authorities and their clergy and people, some of whom thought that their superiors had lost all credibility. This was not true of a few – Cardinal Tomašek in Prague, because he went on so long without being corrupted, and most of the Church leaders in Poland and Yugoslavia.

Thirdly, for forty-five years the schoolchildren of Eastern Europe had been taught scientific materialism at school. We have seen that nevertheless a majority of undergraduates in Slovenia went to church. And everyone is agreed that children do not listen to what they are taught in school. Nevertheless this long process of education which was partly, but only partly, miseducation must have consequences which no one can yet foresee. If Churches were going to be important again in the States because nationalism was again a force and they were a shrine of the history of the nation – if Churches were going to be important in the State because the people wanted freedom and for forty years Churches were identified with the ideals of freedom and human rights – then the Churches were going to need to be adaptable in the face of a population which had been schooled in Marxism even when it had not listened. And they were bound to continue to meet the contemptuous dismissal of faith, which was less common in the West where those who dismissed religion as obsolete usually did so with respect for it and sometimes with regret.

This dismissal of religion was likely to be especially flat in countries where previous experience led some of the people to an anticlerical or antireligious outlook – East Germany, which was Nazi for twelve years before the Communists; Bohemia, with its tradition of anti-Habsburg atheism; Kosovo in southern Yugoslavia, where there looked to be little future in Islam and yet all the Christian peoples seemed to be enemies; and above all Russia, because of its reverence for Lenin – Marx was sick, but Lenin lived on.

Fourthly, though persecution strengthens Church people in their fervour, it also makes them more conservative as they cling to what they have inherited which is now under attack. That had made dialogue difficult in the Communist states. After 1990 dialogue was possible. But, so far as the dialogue meant Christians opening their minds to their critics, it must at first be more difficult because of the immediate past of repression.

To what extent was the persistence of Christianity responsible for the toppling of the regimes in most of Eastern Europe during 1989–90?

Hardly at all. All the East European states had had Communist governments forced upon them. The people would put up with them only so long as they brought work and good wages or, if they failed in that duty, so long as force was backed by the threat of Russian tanks. When Communism failed to achieve what it intended and was little but a heavy-handed bureaucracy, and when the Soviet economy ran into such trouble that the menace of invasion receded, the satellite states need no longer be satellites. The revolutions did not need the Churches.

And yet the East German revolution began in Leipzig, where demonstrators met in churches and then went out to the squares to confront armed police. The Romanian revolution began when the Hungarian Reformed pastor Tökes at Timişoara refused to be evicted and was backed by his congregation and then by the people. In Poland the party which attained power to overthrow the Communists was a Catholic party: the elections were often organized by the local priest, and the committee met in his church hall. In Latvia the Lutheran pastor Modris Plate, whose group had overthrown a complaisant archbishop, was one of the leaders of the party for the independence of Latvia, the Latvian Popular Front. In Slovakia the Catholic Church, or rather its 'dissenting' elements who refused to toe an official prelatical line, was the focus of opposition to the government in Prague.

To account for these, and other incidents like them, this much can be said:

1 Christianity was the only 'official' opposition which the Marxist states allowed. They deplored religion but recognized that it existed and tried to neutralize it by keeping it inside church walls and by controlling its leaders. For a while they largely succeeded. But still, it was an opposition in being. And as such it started to draw in others, who were not particularly religious but cared passionately about freedom and human rights.

Western Europe knew several world-views. Because it was permitted no other, Eastern Europe knew only two outlooks on the world, the Marxist and the religious, and the first despised the second and the second regretted the first. The real clash was not about doctrine – 'no sane person can believe in miracles' versus 'no sane person can believe in the dictatorship of the proletariat' – but about morality. Do ethical values ultimately rise from the community and its temporary needs or do they also come from outside and above the community? This juxtaposition of only two world-views made the Christians into the quiet and unofficial critics in the realm of ideas. To those who rejected Marxism, they were the only home that beckoned.

2 None of the Communist governments was 'legitimate': without exception they had been installed by coup. Former Western leaders of coups from King Pepin to Napoleon and Hitler and Mussolini, and even contemporary Western leaders of coups like General Franco and the Greek colonels, had tried to gain the legitimacy which they lacked with the aid of religion, by coronations or by bestowing privileges upon the Churches. This option was not usually open to the Marxist governments. In Romania the dictator Ceauşescu succeeded with Patriarch Justin, who (as near as made no difference) crowned him, but this hardly had any effect upon the people. Only in East Germany, with its tradition of Christian Socialism among the Lutherans and the high Lutheran doctrine of the State, could religion be a help to a relatively less inhuman Marxist government.

Therefore the governments' doctrinaire attitude to their religions had in the long run to be a weakness in their claims upon the loyalty of their peoples.

3 Churches were part of the history of the nations. They helped to frame the language, and raised the most historic buildings, and

shared in all the great events of the centuries. The Communists said that the unity of mankind was a unity by class – workers or not – and not a unity by tribe or clan, which was obsolete and could lead to war between the peoples. But since the heart of humanity was its family and, wider, its clan and, wider, its nation, Communism pretended that what was inherent need not exist. The peoples needed their past. But there was a danger: that nationality, barely tolerated, would take its revenge in nationalism, and that the East European Churches might find themselves caught again, as already in Kosovo and the Ukraine and Ireland, in a strife where they were expected to be assistants in a struggle between rival nationalisms.

The future of Europe was unknown. It was at a turning-point. The Churches found it difficult enough to cope with a free Western world: how would they manage with a newly free Eastern world, if it was yet free? It remained to be seen how the two big differences between Eastern Europe and Western Europe over forty-five years would react on each other: in the one, nearly all the children taught religion, though often badly; in the other, all the children taught irreligion, though often badly; in the one, the easy sense that freedom and human rights are independent of religions; in the other, the painfully gained experience that the religious conscience is an ultimate safeguard of human freedom.

Source: O. Chadwick, *The Christian Church in the Cold War*, Allen Lane, 1992, pp. 205–9.

Further reading

See in general the collection edited by King, *Religion in Europe*. Also the articles by Huber and Papini in Witte's *Christianity and Democracy in Global Context* and that by Madeley in Moyser's *Politics and Religion in the Modern World*. For Eastern Europe and the Soviet Union, see the article by Ramet in the Moyser collection and by Berman in that by Witte. Also the book by Michel, *Politics and Religion in Eastern Europe*. On Western Europe see, Fogarty, *Christian Democracy in Western Europe 1820–1953*, McManners, *Church and State in France 1870–1914*, and Edwards, *Christians in a New Europe*.

Chapter Ten

THE UNITED KINGDOM

Introduction

At first sight, the United Kingdom seems to be a peculiarly secular society. However important in the past may have been the role of the established Anglican Church as 'the Tory party at prayer' or of the dissenting Churches as supportive of Liberal and then socialist opposition, their social bases and political influence have been eroded in late industrial Britain.

The same is not, however, true of Northern Ireland where the conflicts appear to be firmly based on religious adherence. The role of religion here is debatable, as the extract below demonstrates. Some claim that religion here is a cloak for a conflict which is more accurately seen as based on class or colonialism. But it is at least arguable that the perpetuation of the conflict is due to irreducibly religious attitudes.

Even in mainland Britain, the erosion of what are seen as Christian values by the increasing marketization of society has led to a growing tension between Church and State. There is growing frustration in Church circles at being called upon by those in political authority to put back into society the moral and spiritual backbone which is being simultaneously eaten away by current political and economic initiations proposed by the same authorities. At the same time, the integrated structure of the British State is seen by many as a cause of Britain's decline, a reversal of which would involve a radical reformation of the role of the monarchy and the disestablishment of the Church. Such problems are highlighted by the increasingly pluralist nature of the British religious scene: while the membership of traditional Churches is in decline, the growth areas are Islam and the charismatic evangelical and pentecostal Churches, particularly in the Black community, seen both as an assertion of racial identity and as the heart of a heartless world.

(a) *Thatcher:* Address to the Scottish Kirk

May I also say a few words about my personal belief in the relevance of Christianity to public policy – to the things that are Caesar's?

The Old Testament lays down in Exodus the Ten Commandments as given to Moses, the injunction in Leviticus to love our neighbour as ourselves and generally the importance of observing a strict code of law. The New Testament is a record of the Incarnation, the teachings of Christ and the establishment of the Kingdom of God. Again we have the emphasis on loving our neighbour as ourselves and to 'Do-as-you-would-be-done-by'.

I believe that by taking together these key elements from the Old and New Testaments, we gain:

a view of the universe,
a proper attitude to work,
and principles to shape economic and social life.

We are told we must work and use our talents to create wealth. 'If a man will not work he shall not eat' wrote St Paul to the Thessalonians. Indeed, abundance rather than poverty has a legitimacy which derives from the very nature of Creation.

Nevertheless, the Tenth Commandment – Thou shalt not covet – recognises that making money and owning things could become selfish activities. But it is not the creation of wealth that is wrong but love of money for its own sake. The spiritual dimension comes in deciding what one does with the wealth. How could we respond to the many calls for help, or invest for the future, or support the wonderful artists and craftsmen whose work also glorifies God, unless we had first worked hard and used our talents to create the necessary wealth? And remember the woman with the alabaster jar of ointment.

I confess that I always had difficulty with interpreting the Biblical precept to love our neighbours 'as ourselves' until I read some of the words of C. S. Lewis. He pointed out that we don't exactly love *ourselves* when we fall below the standards and beliefs we have accepted. Indeed we might even *hate* ourselves for some unworthy deed.

None of this, of course, tells us exactly what kind of political and social institutions we should have. On this point, Christians will very often genuinely disagree, though it is a mark of Christian manners that they will do so with courtesy and mutual respect. What is certain, however, is that any set of social and economic arrangements which is not founded on the acceptance of individual responsibility will do nothing but harm. We are all responsible for our own actions. We cannot blame society if we disobey the law. We simply cannot delegate the exercise of mercy and generosity to others. The politicians and other secular powers should strive by their measures to bring out the good in people and to fight down the bad: but they can't create the one or abolish the other. They can only see that the laws encourage the *best* instincts and convictions of the people, instincts and convictions which I am convinced are far more deeply rooted than is often supposed.

Nowhere is this more evident than the basic ties of the family which are at the heart of our society and are the very nursery of civic virtue.

It is on the family that we in government build our own policies for welfare, education and care.

You recall that Timothy was warned by St Paul that anyone who neglects to provide for his own house (meaning his own family) has disowned the faith and is 'worse than an infidel'.

We must recognise that modern society is infinitely more complex than that of Biblical times and of course new occasions teach new duties. In our generation, the only way we can ensure that no-one is left without sustenance, help or opportunity, is to have laws to provide for health and education, pensions for the elderly, succour for the sick and disabled.

But intervention by the State must never become so great that it effectively removes personal responsibility. The same applies to taxation for while you and I would work extremely hard whatever the circumstances, there are undoubtedly some who would not unless the incentive was there. And we need *their* efforts too.

Moderator, recently there have been great debates about religious education. I believe strongly that politicians must see that religious education has a proper place in the school curriculum.

In Scotland as in England there is an historic connection expressed in our laws between Church and State. The two connections are of a somewhat different kind, but the arrangements in both countries are designed to give symbolic expression to the same crucial truth – that the Christian religion – which, of course, embodies many of the great spiritual and moral truths of Judaism – is a fundamental part of our national heritage. I believe it is the wish of the overwhelming majority of people that this heritage should be preserved and fostered. For centuries it has been our very life blood. Indeed we are a nation whose ideals are founded on the Bible.

Also, it is quite impossible to understand our history or literature

146

without grasping this fact. *That* is the strong practical case for ensuring that children at school are given adequate instruction in the part which the Judaic–Christian tradition has played in moulding our laws, manners and institutions. How can you make sense of Shakespeare and Sir Walter Scott, or of the constitutional conflicts of the 17th century in both Scotland and England, without some such fundamental knowledge?

But I go further than this. The truths of the Judaic–Christian tradition are infinitely precious, not only, as I believe, because they are true, but also because they provide the moral impulse which alone can lead to that peace, in the true meaning of the word, for which we all long.

To assert absolute moral values is not to claim perfection for ourselves. No true Christian could do that. What is more, one of the great principles of our Judaic–Christian inheritance is tolerance.

People with other faiths and cultures have always been welcomed in our land, assured of equality under the law, of proper respect and of open friendship.

There is absolutely nothing incompatible between this and our desire to maintain the essence of our own identity. There is no place for racial or religious intolerance in our creed.

When Abraham Lincoln spoke in his famous Gettysburg speech of 1863 of 'government of the people, by the people, and for the people', he gave the world a neat definition of democracy which has since been widely and enthusiastically adopted. But what he enunciated as a form of government was not in itself especially Christian, for nowhere in the Bible is the word democracy mentioned. Ideally, when Christians meet, as Christians, to take counsel together their purpose is not (or should not be) to ascertain what is the mind of the majority but what is the mind of the Holy Spirit – something which may be quite different.

Nevertheless I am an enthusiast for democracy. And I take that position, not because I believe majority opinion is inevitably right or true, indeed no majority can take away God-given human rights. But because I believe it most effectively safeguards the value of the individual, and, more than any other system, restrains the abuse of power by the few. And that *is* a Christian concept.

But there is little hope for democracy if the hearts of men and women in democratic societies cannot be touched by a call to something greater than themselves. Political structures, state institutions, collective ideals are not enough. *We* Parliamentarians can legislate for the rule of *law*. *You* the Church can teach the life of faith.

For, when all is said and done, a politician's role is a humble one. I always think that the whole debate about the Church and the State has never yielded anything comparable in insight to that beautiful hymn 'I vow to thee my country'. It begins with a triumphant assertion of what might be described as secular patriotism, a noble thing indeed in a country like ours:

> I vow to thee my country all earthly things above;
> entire, and whole and perfect the service of my love.

It goes on to speak of 'another country I heard of long ago' whose King cannot be seen and whose armies cannot be counted, but 'soul by soul and silently her shining bounds increase'. Not group by group or party by party or even church by church – but soul by soul and each one counts.

That, members of the Assembly, is the country which you chiefly serve. You fight your cause under the banner of an historic church. Your success matters greatly – as much to the temporal as to the spiritual welfare of the nation.

> Source: M. Thatcher, 'Address to the Scottish Kirk', in J. Raban, *God, Man and Mrs. Thatcher*, Chatto & Windus, 1989, pp. 11–20.

(b) Medhurst and Moyser:
Church and Politics in a Secular Age

The Church's political witness has been motivated by more than the modish pursuit of secular fashions but it has also been characterized by a certain pragmatism of an often reactive kind. There has been a tendency to tackle issues as they arise and on the basis of relatively discrete bodies of experience, expertise, or theological insight. They have not been tackled in the light of a clearly articulated view of the place of politics within the Church's overall purposes, and they have been dealt with inside a largely unquestioned framework of Church–State relationships. Successive reports on these relationships have largely been concerned with the piecemeal adjustment of existing arrangements rather than the subjection of these to radical scrutiny. However, the extent of twentieth-century theological, cultural, social, and political change might seem to warrant just such a scrutiny. Changes in the Church's self-understanding and in its environment now present such novel challenges or opportunities that a more comprehensive, theologically critical, and institutionally self-conscious review of inherited arrangements might seem appropriate.

The promotion of such self-consciousness, it may be suggested, is not the sole preserve of moral theologians nor even of official clerical leaders. They have an important part to play in stimulating and guiding discussion, but within the context of a wide-ranging debate to which clergy and laity throughout the ecclesiastical system might contribute. Such a debate is, in some measure, already proceeding. What is perhaps needed is to give greater impetus to established tendencies.

Partly this is a matter of intensifying dialogue between differing theological traditions in order to identify or widen areas of common ground. It is also a question of critically evaluating secular political options with a particular view to establishing more clearly what, in the Church's own positions, is the product of secular ideology and what has more obviously theological roots. Ultimately, the process might be expected to express itself in considered strategies that allow for such questions as with whom, and on what terms, the Church should ally itself in pursuit of its own more clearly defined objectives.

It is recognized that, in the medium term, extensive debate might fuel controversy outside the Church and exacerbate tensions within it. It is acknowledged too that any quest for complete consensus would be illusory. But it is suggested that the mobilization of large bodies of theologically informed political opinion does presuppose such an exercise.

In pointing to such a task we reject that view of English society which sees Church and State as two expressions of one underlying religio-political reality. The emergence of an ideologically pluralistic society, and the erosion of a Christian-based moral consensus, seem to render that 'Christendom' model anachronistic. But we also reject the notion of a wholly secularized society in which the Church must eschew public controversy. There are several reasons for regarding this as an unrealistic position. First, theological and institutional legacies point to a continuing sense of Christian concern for the public realm that cannot readily be discounted. It also seems unrealistic to suppose that ecclesiastical leaders will hold their peace in the midst of a society which, albeit in attenuated form, still bears the imprint of Christian influences. Not least, there are areas of moral concern which humanists may regard as purely private matters but which are perceived by Church leaders and others to have implications for society's general health. Within such a context, Christian spokesmen are likely to regard contributions to debate as appropriate acts of service to the wider community. Certainly, the appropriate model for the Church seems to be that of society's servant rather than the triumphalist one which has often characterized the Christendom approach.

Such service may be discharged at different levels and in a number of complementary fashions. At arguably the deepest level, the Church through its routine witness may, in conjunction with others, help to preserve or replenish society's reserves of moral wisdom and so, at least indirectly, affect the temper and terms of public debate. Certainly, social commentators sometimes underestimate the extent to which

149

Church members help to keep society's fabric in tolerable repair. Our evidence confirms a general impression that active Church members are more likely than most to join in public and voluntary group activity – activity whose cumulative effect on the quality of public life may be overlooked.

Secondly, such activity, pursued in more self-conscious or theologically informed ways, could conceivably assist in the quest for a refashioned moral consensus. Tolerable levels of stability within pluralistic societies may presuppose some minimal areas of shared moral insight and some filling of that moral vacuum which sometimes seems to characterize modern industrial states. Given our culture's history, the Churches may still have creative functions to fulfil on this front. The extent to which values of Christian provenance remain diffused in English society, and the reserves of goodwill upon which avowedly Christian institutions can still draw, point to a role that may yet be played, alongside others, in defining and articulating a more widely shared system of values – a system with implications for the conduct of political debate.

More concretely, the Church perhaps has a modest part to play in writing the nation's political agenda. This is partly a matter of facilitating that prophetic ministry which discerns the underlying import of existing trends and so puts on the agenda issues, of a long-term significance, that hard-pressed politicians may overlook. It could also be a question of seeking to reallocate priorities on already established agendas. In conjunction with others, the Church can so orchestrate discussion as to push low-priority matters higher up the nation's agenda.

Still more concretely, the Church may modestly contribute to the resolution of specific policy questions. In this area, there is the danger of platitudinous moralizing or of technically ill-informed judgements. But this has to be set against the danger of too readily abdicating responsibility in favour of narrowly based technical specialists. The Church perhaps has a distinctive part to play in placing ostensibly technical issues within the relevant moral frameworks. Not least, the credibility of its own political witness partly depends on contributing positive and well-informed policy proposals. A merely negative denunciatory role will not, in the long run, enable the Church to be heard in the public arena.

Finally, the Church through public pressure and/or private lobbying may seek to promote very specific causes. In such cases, the aim may be to influence or change specific governmental policies and even particular decisions. Within a limited number of areas, the Church may engage in such activities on the assumption that it will automatically receive a hearing. This may be true, for example, of legal questions obviously affecting the family. Elsewhere, however, it may have to earn the right to be heard. Elsewhere, however, it may have to earn the right to be heard. This is partly a matter of demonstrating its own competence. It is also a question of speaking for obviously significant bodies of informed opinion, which clearly puts a premium on mobilizing and educating Church members. It also points to a reinforcement of ecumenical links. Ecclesiastical leaders who can claim to speak authoritatively for Christians at large seem more likely to command attention than those speaking from a narrower base. The Church of England's established status once impeded the development of such alliances. Currently, however, this is not a major issue. Not only is there little pressure for disestablishment from within the Church of England itself, there is also considerable support from Nonconformists for a continuing State link. Such a link is commonly perceived as a visible reminder of England's officially Christian past and the creative role that the Churches could consequently continue to play in national life. Thus, for the immediate future, radical changes seem most unlikely. What might fall within the realm of practical politics is consideration of some further loosening of the State link. The model of the Church of Scotland is one that could offer a basis for discussion.

A redefinition of the State link could significantly affect the Church's own institutional life and, partly as a consequence of this, the institution's relationship with the surrounding society. Not least, questions arise concerning synodical government. At present, the General Synod functions in accordance with a parliamentary model whose general *modus operandi* is largely shaped by influences of secular political rather than strictly theological origin. The whole synodical system is operated by small groups who, at least in the laity's case, seem in significant measure to be elected on the basis of conventional social criteria. Though arguments can be deployed in defence of this situation, it does present difficulties for a National Church which seeks to minister to all social sectors and which is in the process of reconsidering its political commitments. In particular, there is the question of whether governmental models of at least partially secular provenance, and especially congenial to middle-class professionals, are necessarily the most appropriate instruments for wrestling with the contemporary Church's dilemmas.

Answers to these problems may partly lie in modifying attitudes at the synodical system's base. Within parishes and deaneries, attention could be paid to developing less stereotyped models of lay leadership. There may for example be room for experimentation with sub-parochial entities, analogous to South American 'base communities', which might enable the Church to penetrate areas of society now largely beyond its

151

reach and, consequently, to nurture new styles of leadership. Perhaps Bishop David Jenkins had such entities in mind when he proposed 'communities of endurance' capable of sustaining locally rooted Christians in the midst of contemporary conflicts in England. Similarly, one could envisage a network of training institutions, similar to the Academies supported by German Churches, geared to the training of appropriate leaders. At present, St George's, Windsor, plays a valuable role in providing 'in-house' training for senior clergy and in promoting dialogue between churchmen and national élites. There seems room for similar but more localized institutions. Such initiatives could form part of more general strategies for engaging with sectors in which the Church has traditionally been weak. Ultimately, they could also have an impact on patterns of representation within the institution.

There may also be scope for greater experimentation with non-territorial structures. The Church already has networks of specialized chaplains working in industry, education, hospitals, prisons, and even local government. One strategy for more effectively penetrating and mobilizing support within such settings might be to divert more human and material resources into this work. Representation within the General Synod might be organized on a more functional or non-territorial basis than is currently the case. Already limited provision is made for this in the shape of Synodical members representing university theologians, service chaplains, and religious communities. A similar but much extended segment of Synodical opinion, representing Christians in industry or other important branches of national life, might be cause and effect of a process whereby the Church becomes more attuned to the problems of groups lying largely beyond its influence. The result could be a more pastorally effective Church. It could also be a Church better equipped for witness within the political domain.

Such developments presuppose bold leadership and a controversial reordering of institutional priorities. They would signal some loosening of the Church's traditional ties with English society and a fresh understanding of what it means to be a National Church. But they might also signal a greater determination to associate the Church with society's most stressful points. The result could be a more faithful expression of that 'Bias to the Poor' which can be seen as one of the major contemporary Christian rediscoveries. Ultimately, the carving out of a new identity could mean renewed relevance amidst this ostensibly secular age.

Source: K. Medhurst and G. Moyser, eds., *Church and Politics in a Secular Age*, Clarendon Press, 1988, pp. 362–7.

(c) Badham: The Contribution of Religion to the Conflict in Northern Ireland

What has to be asked is not why people of two cultural and ethnic traditions came to co-exist in a small province, but why they have never merged and today remain as apart as ever. No one can question that there are two communities in Northern Ireland, one self-consciously British, the other self-consciously Irish, each with its own perception of history, each with its own culture, each associating almost exclusively with other members of the same group. The factors that keep this separate identity alive are that the Catholic and Protestant populations of Northern Ireland go to different schools with a fundamentally different ethos; they participate in different cultural activities and sports; they support different political parties; and in a culture where Church-going and Church-related social events remain of great importance they attend different places of worship; they associate only with each other and have a very strong prejudice against intermarriage. Since religious conviction is the reason for the separate school system, the reason for the separate political parties, and the reason for the prejudice against intermarriage, the contribution of religion to the continuation of the divisions in Northern Ireland would appear to be very considerable. If we then take note of the part played by explicitly sectarian political leaders to frustrate the cautious attempts made by more liberal leaders to lessen the cultural apartheid of Northern Ireland we can see that religion is a major factor in the current troubles. Let us therefore look in more detail at each of these points.

The greatest error we can make regarding Ulster is to look at its problems in the ways we are accustomed to look at our own. In the rest of Britain religion is not a central concern. Churchgoing is very much a minority taste, and both in the Churches and in the wider life of society a pluralist, ecumenical, toleration is taken for granted by almost everyone. This is just not true of Northern Ireland where we face a culture with one of the highest rates of religious commitment in the world and where no aspect of life is immune from its influence. According to the 1985/86 UK Christian Handbook 13 per cent of the people of England are Church members contrasted with 80 per cent of the people of Northern Ireland. If we turn to Church attendance we find that among Ulster Catholics 90 per cent attend mass each Sunday, while among Ulster Protestants 39 per cent attend weekly, 20 per cent more than once a month, and 30 per cent attend occasionally. Such figures represent a level of commitment higher than anywhere else in Europe except perhaps the Irish Republic. Hence it is not surprising that in such a

153

context religious identification and commitment has far greater implications in the life of society than in more secular societies.

The tragedy of Ulster is that it remains imprisoned by its past. Its two rival communities are weighed down by the sad history of centuries of communal strife, and in this context religion has done little but strengthen the barriers between the other two communities. In almost all other countries of the world an ecumenical spirit of goodwill and brotherhood has transformed the relationship between Christian communities. In Northern Ireland where such a spirit might do the greatest good it has been the most lacking. This presents a real challenge to the leaders and religious thinkers of the main Christian Churches in Northern Ireland to overcome the theological conservatism and narrowness of outlook which still characterize their Churches, and help to bring the good news of a Gospel of Reconciliation to a people who profess profound belief in its reality and yet have so far failed to translate their belief into the reality of their human experience.

Source: P. Badham, *The Contribution of Religion to the Conflict in Northern Ireland,* Centre for the Study of Religion and Society, Canterbury, 1987, pp. 6–7, 10, 17–19.

Further reading

On the religious dimension to the troubles in Northern Ireland, in addition to the book from which the above extract is taken, see Rose's *Northern Ireland* and Bruce's *God Save Ulster!* On Margaret Thatcher's approach, see Raban's caustic *God, Man and Mrs. Thatcher.* There is a scholarly discussion of the Church of England in Medhurst and Moyser's *Church and Politics in a Secular Age* and good collections in Badham's *Religion, State and Society in Modern Britain.* For some views by the protagonists themselves, see Habgood's emphasis on the integrative role of the Church in his *Church and Nation in a Secular Age.* See also Cohn-Sherbok and McLellan's *Religion in Public Life.*

PART THREE

Politics and Christianity

Chapter Eleven

CONSERVATISM

Introduction

At least since the Constantinian settlement, there has always been a strong conservative element in Christianity. This has been almost necessarily true of the established churches since the very bulk of large institutions makes them slow to change and, in any case, they usually have had a lot of power to conserve. Thus it is not surprising that both Church and State have generated similarly conservative ideas.

In the tradition of conservative political thought, the following six interlinked elements stand out. First, an emphasis on the importance of custom, tradition itself, the inherited wisdom of previous generations, and the reliability of experience. Second, while there is recognition that change and adaptation are necessary, there is approval for the slow, incremental, organic nature of this change as opposed to abstract blueprints for radical reformation. Both these aspects of conservative thought are prominent in Burke with whom modern consciously conservative political thought begins and who rejected the principles of the French Revolution in the name of a providential order and divinely sanctioned natural justice. Third, conservatism wishes to stress the value of private property the possession and use of which is both a defence against too much state power and a useful school of practical experience for those engaged in public affairs. From this follows, fourth, a sense of hierarchical order in society since individuals are very differentially equipped in the culture necessary for governance. These two aspects are evident in the writings of Coleridge, who elaborated on the benefits of a National Church as guardian of culture and moral aspirations, and in Eliot's stress on class and order which he saw as essential to defend beliefs and customs being destroyed by the advance of a mechanical civilization. Fifth, conservatives typically wish to anchor their political thought in the transcendant, the work of God of which human laws can only be an imperfect manifestation. This is clear in Simone Weil with her insistence that duties, as opposed to rights, are founded in the realm of what is eternal and only to be met in societies firmly rooted in values elaborated and treasured over generations. Lastly, there is a pessimism about human nature which fits well with the Christian doctrine of original sin: corrupt human nature needs the force of tradition and hierarchy to prevent its running out of control.

More generally, conservative thought emphasizes the importance of ideas and values, unlike approaches which prefer to anchor themselves in individual rights or more worldly notions of economic and social justice. In this perspective it is similar to much of mainstream Christianity which has stressed the importance of belief and inner piety often at the expense of more secular engagement.

(a) Burke:
An Appeal from the New to the Old Whigs

I cannot too often recommend it to the serious consideration of all men who think civil society to be within the province of moral jurisdiction, that, if we owe to it any duty, it is not subject to our will. Duties are not voluntary. Duty and will are even contradictory terms. Now, though civil society might be at first a voluntary act, (which in many cases it undoubtedly was), its continuance is under a permanent standing covenant, coexisting with the society; and it attaches upon every individual of that society, without any formal act of his own. This is warranted by the general practice, arising out of the general sense of mankind. Men without their choice derive benefits from that association; without their choice they are subjected to duties in consequence of these benefits; and without their choice they enter into a virtual obligation as binding as any that is actual. Look through the whole of life and the whole system of duties. Much the strongest moral obligations are such as were never the results of our option. I allow, that, if no Supreme Ruler exists, wise to form, and potent to enforce, the moral law, there is no sanction to any contract, virtual or even actual, against the will of prevalent power. On that hypothesis, let any set of men be strong enough to set their duties at defiance, and they cease to be duties any longer. We have but this one appeal against irresistible power,

> Si genus humanum et mortalia temnitis arma,
> At sperate Deos memores fandi atque nefandi.

Taking it for granted that I do not write to the disciples of the Parisian philosophy, I may assume that the awful Author of our being is the Author of our place in the order of existence, and that, having disposed and marshalled us by a divine tactic, not according to our will, but according to his, he has in and by that disposition virtually subjected us to act the part which belongs to the place assigned us. We have obligations to mankind at large, which are not in consequence of any special voluntary pact. They arise from the relation of man to man, and the relation of man to God, which relations are not matters of choice. On the contrary, the force of all the pacts which we enter into with any particular person or number of persons amongst mankind depends upon those prior obligations. In some cases the subordinate relations are voluntary, in others they are necessary – but the duties are all compulsive. When we marry, the choice is voluntary, but the duties are not matter of choice: they are dictated by the nature of the situation. Dark and inscrutable are the ways by which we come into the world. The instincts which give rise to this mysterious process of Nature are not of our making. But out of physical causes, unknown to us, perhaps unknowable, arise moral duties, which, as we are able perfectly to comprehend, we are bound indispensably to perform. Parents may not be consenting to their moral relation; but, consenting or not, they are bound to a long train of burdensome duties towards those with whom they have never made a convention of any sort. Children are not consenting to their relation; but their relation, without their actual consent, binds them to its duties – or rather it implies their consent, because the presumed consent of every rational creature is in unison with the predisposed order of things. Men come in that manner into a community with the social state of their parents, endowed with all the benefits, loaded with all the duties of their situation. If the social ties and ligaments, spun out of those physical relations which are the elements of the commonwealth, in most cases begin, and always continue, independently of our will, so, without any stipulation on our own part, are we bound by that relation called our country, which comprehends (as it has been well said) 'all the charities of all'. Nor are we left without powerful instincts to make this duty as dear and grateful to us as it is awful and coercive. Our country is not a thing of mere physical locality. It consists, in a great measure, in the ancient order into which we are born. We may have the same geographical situation, but another country; as we may have the same country in another soil. The place that determines our duty to our country is a social, civil relation.

Source: E. Burke, 'An Appeal from the New to the Old Whigs', *The Works of Edmund Burke*, Nimmo, 1899, vol. 4, pp. 164–7.

(b) Coleridge: Church and State

The mercantile and commercial class, in which I here comprise all the four classes that I have put in antithesis to the Landed Order, the guardian, and depository of the *Permanence* of the Realm, as more characteristically conspiring to the interests of its progression, the improvement and general freedom of the country – this class did as I have already remarked, in the earlier states of the constitution, exist but as in the bud. But during all this period of potential existence, or what we may call the minority of the burgess order, the National Church was the substitute for the most important national benefits resulting from the same. The National Church presented the only breathing hole of hope. The Church alone relaxed the iron fate by which feudal dependency, primogeniture, and entail would otherwise have predestined every native of the realm to be lord or vassal. To the Church alone could the nation look for the benefits of existing knowledge, and for the means of future civilization. Lastly, let it never be forgotten, that under the fostering wing of the Church, the class of free citizens and burgers were reared. To the feudal system we owe the *forms,* to the Church the *substance,* of our liberty. We mention only two of many facts that would form the proof and comment of the above; first, the origin of towns and cities, in the privileges attached to the vicinity of churches and monasteries, and which preparing an asylum for the fugitive Vassal and oppressed Franklin, thus laid the first foundation of a class of freemen detached from the land. Secondly, the holy war, which the national clergy, in this instance faithful to their national duties, waged against slavery and villenage, and with such success, that in the reign of Charles II, the law which declared every native of the realm free by birth, had merely to sanction an *opus jam consummatum* [work already completed]. Our Maker has distinguished man from the brute that perishes, by making hope first an instinct of his nature; and secondly, an indispensable condition of his moral and intellectual progression:

> For every gift of noble origin
> Is breathed upon by Hope's perpetual breath.
> WORDSWORTH

But a natural instinct constitutes a right, as far as its gratification is compatible with the equal rights of others. And this principle we may expand, and apply to the idea of the National Church.

Among the primary ends of a State (in that highest sense of the word, in which it is equivalent to the nation, considered as one body politic, and therefore includes the National Church), there are two, of which the National Church (according to its idea), is the especial and constitutional organ and means. The one is, to secure to the subjects of the realm generally, the hope, the chance, of bettering their own or their children's condition. And though during the last three or four centuries, the National Church has found a most powerful surrogate and ally for the effectuation of this great purpose in her former wards and foster-children, i.e. in trade, commerce, free industry, and the arts – yet still the nationalty, under all defalcations, continues to feed the higher ranks by drawing up whatever is worthiest from below, and thus maintains the principle of Hope in the humblest families, while it secures the possessions of the rich and noble. This is one of the two ends.

The other is, to develop, in every native of the country, those faculties, and to provide for every native that knowledge and those attainments, which are necessary to qualify him for a member of the state, the free subject of a civilized realm. We do not mean those degrees of moral and intellectual cultivation which distinguish man from man in the same civilized society, much less those that separate the Christian from the this-worldian; but those only that constitute the civilized man in contra-distinction from the barbarian, the savage, and the animal.

I have now brought together all that seemed requisite to put the intelligent reader in full possession of (what I believe to be) the right Idea of the National Clergy, as an estate of the realm. But I cannot think my task finished without an attempt to rectify the too frequent false feeling on this subject, and to remove certain vulgar errors, errors, alas! not confined to those whom the world call the vulgar. *Ma nel mondo non è se non volgo* [But in the world there are only the vulgar], says Machiavel. I shall make no apology therefore, for interposing between the preceding statements, and the practical conclusion from them, the following paragraph, extracted from a work long out of print, and of such very limited circulation that I might have stolen from myself with little risk of detection, had it not been my wish to shew that the convictions expressed in the preceding pages, are not the offspring of the moment, brought forth for the present occasion; but an expansion of sentiments and principles publicly avowed in the year 1817.

Among the numerous blessings of the English Constitution, the introduction of an established Church makes an especial claim on the gratitude of scholars and philosophers; in England, at least, where the principles of Protestantism have conspired with the freedom of the government to double all its salutary powers by the removal of its abuses.

That the maxims of a pure morality, and those sublime truths of the divine unity and attributes, which a Plato found hard to learn, and more difficult to reveal; that these should have become the almost hereditary property of childhood and poverty, of the hovel and the workshop; that even to the unlettered they sound as *common place*; this is a phenomenon which must withhold all but minds of the most vulgar cast from undervaluing the services even of the pulpit and the reading desk. Yet he who should *confine* the efficiency of an Established Church to these, can hardly be placed in a much higher rank of intellect. That to every parish throughout the kingdom there is transplanted a germ of civilization; that in the remotest villages there is a nucleus, round which the capabilities of the place may crystallize and brighten; a model sufficiently superior to excite, yet sufficiently near to encourage and facilitate, imitation; *this* unobtrusive, continuous agency of a Protestant Church Establishment, *this* it is, which the patriot, and the philanthropist, who would fain unite the love of peace with the faith in the progressive amelioration of mankind, cannot estimate at too high a price – 'It cannot be valued with the gold of Ophir, with the precious onyx, or the sapphire. No mention shall be made of coral or of pearls: for the price of wisdom is above rubies.' The clergyman is with his parishioners and among them; he is neither in the cloistered cell, nor in the wilderness, but a neighbour and family-man, whose education and rank admit him to the mansion of the rich landholder, while his duties make him the frequent visitor of the farmhouse and the cottage. He is, or he may become, connected with the families of his parish or its vicinity by marriage. And among the instances of the blindness or at best of the short-sightedness, which it is the nature of cupidity to inflict, I know few more striking, than the clamours of the farmers against church property. Whatever was not paid to the clergymen would inevitably at the next lease be paid to the landholder, while, as the case at present stands, the revenues of the Church are in some sort the reversionary property of every family that may have a member educated for the Church, or a daughter that may marry a clergyman.

Source: S. Coleridge, 'Church and State' (1829): *On Politics and Society*, ed. J. Morrow, Princeton University Press, 1991, pp. 189–92.

(c) Eliot: The Idea of a Christian Society

I conceive then of the Christian State as of the Christian Society under the aspect of legislation, public administration, legal tradition, and form. Observe that at this point I am not approaching the problem of Church and State except with the question: with what kind of State can the Church have a relation? By this I mean a relation of the kind which has hitherto obtained in England; which is neither merely reciprocal tolerance, nor a Concordat. The latter seems to me merely a kind of compromise, of doubtful durability, resting on a dubious division of authority, and often a popular division of loyalty; a compromise which implies perhaps a hope on the part of the rulers of the State that their

rule will outlast Christianity, and a faith on the part of the Church that it will survive any particular form of secular organisation. A relation between Church and State such as is, I think, implied in our use of the term, implies that the State is in some sense Christian. It must be clear that I do not mean by a Christian State one in which the rulers are chosen because of their qualifications, still less their eminence, as Christians. A regiment of Saints is apt to be too uncomfortable to last. I do not deny that some advantages may accrue from persons in authority, in a Christian State, being Christians. Even in the present conditions, that sometimes happens; but even if, in the present conditions, *all* persons in positions of the highest authority were devout and orthodox Christians, we should not expect to see very much difference in the conduct of affairs. The Christian and the unbeliever do not, and cannot, behave very differently in the exercise of office; for it is the general ethos of the people they have to govern, not their own piety, that determines the behaviour of politicians. One may even accept F. S. Oliver's affirmation – following Buelow, following Disraeli – that real statesmen are inspired by nothing else than their instinct for power and their love of country. It is not primarily the Christianity of the statesmen that matters, but their being confined, by the temper and traditions of the people which they rule, to a Christian framework within which to realise their ambitions and advance the prosperity and prestige of their country. They may frequently perform un-Christian acts; they must never attempt to defend their actions on un-Christian principles.
[. . .]

I confine myself therefore to the assertion, which I think few will dispute, that a great deal of the machinery of modern life is merely a sanction for un-Christian aims, that it is not only hostile to the conscious pursuit of the Christian life in the world by the few, but to the maintenance of any Christian society *of* the world. We must abandon the notion that the Christian should be content with freedom of cultus, and with suffering no worldly disabilities on account of his faith. However bigoted the announcement may sound, the Christian can be satisfied with nothing less than a Christian organisation of society – which is not the same thing as a society consisting exclusively of devout Christians. It would be a society in which the natural end of man – virtue and well-being in community – is acknowledged for all, and the supernatural end – beatitude – for those who have the eyes to see it.

I do not wish, however, to abandon my previous point, that a Christian community is one in which there is a unified religious-social code of behaviour. It should not be necessary for the ordinary individual to be wholly conscious of what elements are distinctly religious and Christian, and what are merely social and identified with his religion by no logical implication. I am not requiring that the community should contain more 'good Christians' than one would expect to find under favourable conditions. The religious life of the people would be largely a matter of behaviour and conformity; social customs would take on religious sanctions; there would no doubt be many irrelevant accretions and local emphases and observances – which, if they went too far in eccentricity or superstition, it would be the business of the Church to correct, but which otherwise could make for social tenacity and coherence. The traditional way of life of the community would not be imposed by law, would have no sense of outward constraint, and would not be the result merely of the sum of individual belief and understanding.

The rulers, I have said, will, *qua* rulers, accept Christianity not simply as their own faith to guide their actions, but as the system under which they are to govern. The people will accept it as a matter of behaviour and habit. In the abstraction which I have erected, it is obvious that the tendency of the State is toward expediency that may become cynical manipulation, the tendency of the people toward intellectual lethargy and superstition. We need therefore what I have called 'the Community of Christians', by which I mean, not local groups, and not the Church in any one of its senses, unless we call it 'the Church within the Church'. These will be the consciously and thoughtfully practising Christians, especially those of intellectual and spiritual superiority. It will be remarked at once that this category bears some resemblance to what Coleridge has called 'the clerisy' – a term recently revived, and given a somewhat different application, by Mr Middleton Murry. I think that my 'Community of Christians' is somewhat different from either use of the term 'clerisy'. The content which Coleridge gave to the term, certainly, has been somewhat voided by time. You will remember that Coleridge included in the extension of meaning three classes: the universities and great schools of learning, the parochial pastorate, and the local schoolmasters. Coleridge's conception of the clerical function, and of its relation to education was formed in a world that has since been strangely altered: his insistence that clergy should be 'in the rule married men and heads of families' and his dark references to a foreign ecclesiastical power, now sound merely quaint; and he quite failed to recognise the enormous value which monastic orders can and should have in the community. The term which I use is meant to be at once wider and more restricted. In the field of education it is obvious that the conformity to Christian belief and the possession of Christian knowledge, can no longer be taken for granted; nor can the supremacy of the theologian be either expected or imposed in the same way. In any future Christian society that I can conceive, the educational system will be formed according to Christian presuppositions of what education – as distinct from mere instruction – is for; but the personnel will inevitably be mixed: one may even hope that the mixture may be a benefit to its intellectual vitality. The mixture will include persons of exceptional ability who may be indifferent or disbelieving; there will be room for a proportion of other persons professing other faiths than Christianity. The limitations imposed upon such persons would be similar to those imposed by social necessity upon the politician who, without being able to believe the Christian faith, yet has abilities to offer in the public service, with which his country could ill dispense.

It would be still more rash of me to embark upon a criticism of the contemporary ideals of education, than it is for me to venture to criticise politics; but it is not impertinent to remark upon the close relationship of educational theory and political theory. One would indeed be surprised to find the educational system and the political system of any country in complete disaccord; and what I have said about the negative character of our political philosophy should suggest a parallel criticism of our education, not as it is found in practice here or there, but in the assumptions about the nature and purpose of education which tend to affect practice throughout the country. And I do not need to remind you that a pagan totalitarian government is hardly likely to leave education to look after itself, or to refrain from interfering with the traditional methods of the oldest institutions: of some of the results abroad of such interference on the most irrelevant grounds we are quite well aware. There is likely to be, everywhere, more and more pressure of circumstance towards adapting educational ideals to political ideals, and in the one as in the other sphere, we have only to choose between a higher and a lower rationalisation. In a Christian Society education must be religious, not in the sense that it will be administered by ecclesiastics, still less in the sense that it will exercise pressure, or attempt to instruct everyone in theology, but in the sense that its aims will be directed by a Christian philosophy of life. It will no longer be merely a term comprehending a variety of unrelated subjects undertaken for special purposes or for none at all.

Source: T. S. Eliot, *The Idea of a Christian Society*, Faber & Faber, 1939, pp. 26–7, 33–7.

(d) *Weil:* The Need for Roots

The notion of obligations comes before that of rights, which is subordinate and relative to the former. A right is not effectual by itself, but only in relation to the obligation to which it corresponds, the effective exercise of a right springing not from the individual who possesses it, but from other men who consider themselves as being under a certain obligation towards him. Recognition of an obligation makes it effectual. An obligation which goes unrecognized by anybody loses none of the full force of its existence. A right which goes unrecognized by anybody is not worth very much.

It makes nonsense to say that men have, on the one hand, rights, and on the other hand, obligations. Such words only express differences in point of view. The actual relationship between the two is as between object and subject. A man, considered in isolation, only has duties, amongst which are certain duties towards himself. Other men, seen from his point of view, only have rights. He, in his turn, has rights, when seen from the point of view of other men, who recognize that they have obligations towards him. A man left alone in the universe would have no rights whatever, but he would have obligations.

The notion of rights, being of an objective order, is inseparable from the notions of existence and reality. This becomes apparent when the obligation descends to the realm of fact; consequently, it always involves to a certain extent the taking into account of actual given states and particular situations. Rights are always found to be related to certain conditions. Obligations alone remain independent of conditions. They belong to a realm situated above all conditions, because it is situated above this world.

The men of 1789 did not recognize the existence of such a realm. All they recognized was the one on the human plane. That is why they started off with the idea of rights. But at the same time they wanted to postulate absolute principles. This contradiction caused them to tumble into a confusion of language and ideals which is largely responsible for the present political and social confusion. The realm of what is eternal, universal, unconditioned is other than the one conditioned by facts, and different ideas hold sway there, ones which are related to the most secret recesses of the human soul.

Obligations are only binding on human beings. There are no obligations for collectivities, as such. But they exist for all human beings who constitute, serve, command or represent a collectivity, in that part of their existence which is related to the collectivity as in that part which is independent of it.

All human beings are bound by identical obligations, although these are performed in different ways according to particular circumstances. No human being, whoever he may be, under whatever circumstances, can escape them without being guilty of crime; save where there are two genuine obligations which are in fact incompatible, and a man is forced to sacrifice one of them.

The imperfections of a social order can be measured by the number of situations of this kind it harbours within itself.

But even in such a case, a crime is committed if the obligation so sacrificed is not merely sacrificed in fact, but its existence denied into the bargain.

The object of any obligation, in the realm of human affairs, is always the human being as such. There exists an obligation towards every human being for the sole reason that he or she *is* a human being, without any other condition requiring to be fulfilled, and even without any recognition of such obligation on the part of the individual concerned.

This obligation is not based upon any *de facto* situation, nor upon jurisprudence, customs, social structure, relative state of forces, historical heritage, or presumed historical orientation; for no *de facto* situation is able to create an obligation.

This obligation is not based upon any convention; for all conventions are liable to be modified according to the wishes of the contracting parties, whereas in this case no change in the mind and will of Man can modify anything whatsoever.

This obligation is an eternal one. It is coextensive with the eternal destiny of human beings. Only human beings have an eternal destiny. Human collectivities have not got one. Nor are there, in regard to the latter, any direct obligations of an eternal nature. Duty towards the human being as such – that alone is eternal.

This obligation is an unconditional one. If it is founded on something, that something, whatever it is, does not form part of our world. In our world, it is not founded on anything at all. It is the one and only obligation in connexion with human affairs that is not subject to any condition.

This obligation has no foundation, but only a verification in the common consent accorded by the universal conscience. It finds expression in some of the oldest written texts which have come down to us. It is recognized by everybody without exception in every single case where it is not attacked as a result of interest or passion. And it is in relation to it that we measure our progress.

The recognition of this obligation is expressed in a confused and imperfect form, that is, more or less imperfect according to the particular case, by what are called positive rights. To the extent to which positive rights are in contradiction with it, to that precise extent is their origin an illegitimate one.

Although this eternal obligation is coextensive with the eternal destiny of the human being, this destiny is not its direct motive. A human being's eternal destiny cannot be the motive of any obligation, for it is not subordinate to external actions.

The fact that a human being possesses an eternal destiny imposes only one obligation: respect. The obligation is only performed if the respect is effectively expressed in a real, not a fictitious, way; and this can only be done through the medium of Man's earthly needs.

On this point, the human conscience has never varied. Thousands of years ago, the Egyptians believed that no soul could justify itself after death unless it could say: 'I have never let any one suffer from hunger.' All Christians know they are liable to hear Christ himself say to them one day: 'I was an hungered, and ye gave me no meat.' Every one looks on progress as being, in the first place, a transition to a state of human society in which people will not suffer from hunger. To no matter whom the question may be put in general terms, nobody is of the opinion that any man is innocent if, possessing food himself in abundance and finding some one on his door-step three parts dead from hunger, he brushes past without giving him anything.

So it is an eternal obligation towards the human being not to let him suffer from hunger when one has the chance of coming to his assistance. This obligation being the most obvious of all, it can serve as a model on which to draw up the list of eternal duties towards each human being.

Source: S. Weil, *The Need for Roots*,
Routledge & Kegan Paul, 1952, pp. 3–6.

(e) *Kirk:* The Conservative Mind

The twentieth-century conservative is concerned, first of all, for the regeneration of spirit and character – with the perennial problem of the inner order of the soul, the restoration of the ethical understanding and the religious sanction upon which any life worth living is founded. This is conservatism at its highest; but it cannot be accomplished as a deliberate program of social reform, 'political Christianity'. As Christopher Dawson observes, 'There is a tendency, especially among the English-speaking Protestant peoples, to treat religion as a kind of social tonic in order to extract a further degree of moral effort from the people.' If the conservatives' effort comes to no more than this, it will not succeed. Recovery of moral understanding cannot be merely a means to social restoration: it must be its own end, though it will produce social consequences. In the words of T. S. Eliot, 'If you will not have God (and he is a jealous God) you should pay your respects to Hitler or Stalin.'

The conservative is concerned with the problem of leadership, which has two aspects: the preservation of some measure of reverence, discipline, order, and class; and the purgation of our system of education, so that learning once more may become liberal in the root sense of that word. Only just leadership can redeem society from the mastery of the ignoble elite.

The conservative is concerned with the phenomenon of the proletariat – which word does not signify the poor only. The mass of modern men must find status and hope within society: true family, links with the past, expectations for the future, duty as well as right, resources that matter more than the mass-amusement and mass-vices with which the modern proletarian (who may be affluent) seeks to forget his loss of an object. The degeneration of the family to mere common house-tenancy menaces the essence of recognizable human character; and the plague of social boredom, spreading in ever-widening circles to almost every level of civilized existence, may bring a future more dreary than the round of life in the decaying Roman system. To restore purpose to labor and domestic existence, to give men back old hopes and long views and thought of posterity, will require bold imagination.

The conservative is concerned with resistance to the armed doctrine, the clutch of ideology. He endeavors to restore the right reason of true political philosophy; he insists that although we cannot create the Terrestrial Paradise, we can make our own Terrestrial Hell through infatuation with ideology. And he declares that while this recovery of political normality is in process, we must hold the line – often by hard diplomatic and military decisions – against the adversaries of order and justice and freedom.

The conservative is concerned with the recovery of true community, local energies and co-operation; with what Orestes Brownson called 'territorial democracy', voluntary endeavor, a social order distinguished by multiplicity and diversity. Free community is the alternative to compulsive collectivism. It is from the decay of community, particularly at the level of the 'little platoon', that crime and violence shoot up. In this realm, misguided 'liberal' measures have worked mischief that may not be undone for decades or generations, especially in the United States. Miscalled 'urban renewal' (actually the creation, often, of urban deserts and jungles), undertaken out of mixed humanitarian and profiteering motives, has uprooted in most American cities whole classes and local communities, under dubious cover of federal statute; inordinate building of highways has had the same consequence. Urban rioting, the swift increase of major crimes, and the boredom that encourages addiction to narcotics are products of such foolish programs. In the phrase of Hannah Arendt, 'the rootless are always violent'. So it is that the conservative talks of the need for roots in community, not of more measures of 'mass welfare'.

And of course the conservative is concerned with a number of other primary questions, and with a vaster array of prudential questions, to which the answers must vary with the circumstances and the time. With Burckhardt, the twentieth-century conservative separates himself from the 'terrible simplifiers'. As H. Stuart Hughes remarks very truly, 'Conservatism is the negation of ideology.' There exists no simple set of formulas by which all the ills to which flesh is heir may be swept away. Yet there do exist general principles of morals and of politics to which thinking men may turn.

'And the more thoroughly we understand our own political tradition, the more readily its whole resources are available to us, the less likely we shall be to embrace the illusions which wait for the ignorant and the unwary.' So said a learned disciple of Burke, Michael Oakeshott, in his inaugural lecture upon assuming the professorial chair at the London School of Economics and Political Science, which previously had been occupied by radical scholars, Graham Wallas and Harold Laski. These fallacies, he continued, are 'the illusion that in politics we can get on without a tradition of behaviour, the illusion that the abridgement of a tradition is itself a sufficient guide, and the illusion that in politics there is anywhere a safe harbour, a destination to be reached or even a detectable strand of progress. The world is the best of all possible worlds, and everything in it is a necessary evil.'

This is a world away from the mentality of the total planner. 'As a negative impulse, conservatism is based on a certain distrust of human nature, believing that the immediate impulses of the heart and visions of the brain are likely to be misleading guides.' So wrote Paul Elmer More, in 1915. 'But with this distrust of human nature is closely connected another and more positive factor of conservatism – its trust in the controlling power of the imagination.' In this same essay on Disraeli, More observed that 'Conservatism is in general the intuition of genius, whereas liberalism is the efficiency of talent.' By the 1980s, conservatives were exercising once more those powers of imagination and intuition. The New Elite might find it necessary to reckon with the Resurrected Philosophers.

Source: R. Kirk, *The Conservative Mind from Burke to Eliot*,
Regency, 1986, pp. 472–5.

Further reading

Introductory material can be found in Mott's *Christian Perspectives on Political Thought*, Chapter 8 and Wogaman's *Christian Perspectives on Politics*, Chapter 5. The classic commentary on the authors excerpted above is Kirk's *The Conservative Mind*. For the United States, see Rossiter's *Conservatism in America* and, for a theological point of view, Neuhaus's *The Naked Public Square*. The Anglican classic here is Hooker's *Ecclesiastical Polity* and, by contrast, see Simone Weil's scintillating discussion of French history in *The Need for Roots*. A good general introduction to conservative thought is Nisbet's *Conservatism: Dream and Reality*.

Chapter Twelve

LIBERALISM

Introduction

Liberal ideology is based on a concept of freedom of the individual which has two main sources. The first is the Protestant Reformation with its opposition to traditional Catholic notions of hierarchy and its emphasis on dissent and freedom of conscience; the second, and later, is the secular Enlightenment which advocated government by consent, the idea of social contract and the use of calculative reason in politics. In the latter, particularly, an analogy was drawn between the emergence of market relationships and the growth of modern liberal democracy.

The Puritan ethic undoubtedly provided a basis for economic freedom and expansion by encouraging a life-style which combined asceticism with a provident calculating approach to economic affairs. And it is difficult to underestimate the influence of the Puritan idea of religious associations as a covenant in which individuals pledged themselves to create a society which embodied their religious values. The Puritan covenant in turn supported the idea of individual rights and government by consent. This idea of the basic legal equality of all citizens stemming from the designs of God for humankind can be seen in Locke. There is a strong emphasis here on natural law which is not seen (as, for example, in Aquinas) as aiming at some common good, with associated duties, but as facilitating the desires of individuals with their associative rights.

In time, however, as Weber remarked: 'the pursuit of wealth, stripped of its religious and ethical meaning, tends to become associated with purely mundane passion'. The strong separation between Church and State advocated by liberalism turns religious belief into a private affair. It is argued that the influence of religion is inappropriate in a liberal democracy where the grounds of decision-making should have an interpersonal validity which extends to all members of society. Any religion in such a society would have to be the kind of civil religion described by Rousseau – an anaemic lowest common denominator. This can lead to a justification of the view that society is necessarily a jungle in which the survival of the fittest is the only law. It is obviously difficult to reconcile this with a Christian outlook. The idea that religious belief is a private matter is at variance with all the Christian tradition; reward according to economic ability accords ill with biblical conceptions of a just society where people's needs are predominant; and, more generally, a permissive, consumerist, competitive, market-orientated liberalism seems to undermine central Christian ideas of solidarity and community.

(a) *Locke:* Two Treatises on Government

It having been shown in the foregoing discourse,

(1) That Adam had not either by natural right of fatherhood, or by positive donation from God, any such authority over his children, or dominion over the world as is pretended.

(2) That if he had, his heirs, yet, had no right to it.

(3) That if his heirs had, there being no law of nature nor positive law of God that determines, which is the right heir in all cases that may arise, the right of succession, and consequently of bearing rule, could not have been certainly determined.

(4) That if even that had been determined, yet the knowledge of which is the eldest line of Adam's posterity, being so long since utterly lost, that in the races of mankind and families of the world, there remains not to one above another, the least pretence to be the eldest house, and to have the right of inheritance.

All these premises having, as I think, been clearly made out, it is impossible that the rulers now on earth, should make any benefit, or derive any the least shadow of authority from that, which is held to be the fountain of all power, Adam's private dominion and paternal jurisdiction, so that, he that will not give just occasion, to think that all government in the world is the product only of force and violence, and that men live together by no other rules but that of beasts, where the strongest carries it, and so lay a foundation for perpetual disorder and mischief, tumult, sedition and rebellion, (things that the followers of that hypothesis so loudly cry out against) must of necessity find out another rise of government, another original of political power, and another way of designing and knowing the persons that have it, than what Sir Robert Filmer hath taught us.

[. . .]

To understand political power right, and derive it from its original, we must consider what state all men are naturally in, and that is, a state of perfect freedom to order their actions, and dispose of their possessions, and persons as they think fit, within the bounds of the law of nature, without asking leave, or depending upon the will of any other man.

A state also of equality, wherein all the power and jurisdiction is reciprocal, no one having more than another: there being nothing more evident, than that creatures of the same species and rank promiscuously born to all the same advantages of nature, and the use of the same faculties, should also be equal one amongst another without subordination or subjection, unless the lord and master of them all, should by any manifest declaration of his will set one above another, and confer on him by an evident and clear appointment an undoubted right to dominion and sovereignty.

[. . .]

But though this be a state of liberty, yet it is not a state of licence, though man in that state have an uncontrollable liberty, to dispose of his person or possessions, yet he has not liberty to destroy himself, or so much as any creature in his possession, but where some nobler use, than its bare preservation calls for it. The state of nature has a law of nature to govern it, which obliges everyone: and reason, which is that law, reaches all mankind, who will but consult it, that being all equal and independent, no one ought to harm another in his life, health, liberty, or possessions. For men being all the workmanship of one omnipotent, and infinitely wise Maker, all the servants of one sovereign master, sent into the world by his order and about his business, they are his property, whose workmanship they are, made to last during his, not one another's pleasure. And being furnished with like faculties, sharing all in one community of nature, there cannot be supposed any such subordination among us, that may authorize us to destroy one another, as if we were made for one another's uses, as the inferior ranks of creatures are for ours. Everyone as he is bound to preserve himself, and not to quit his station wilfully; so by the like reason when his own preservation comes not in competition, ought he, as much as he can, to preserve the rest of mankind, and may not unless it be to do justice on an offender, take away, or impair the life, or what tends to the preservation of the life, the liberty, health, limb or goods of another.

And that all men may be restrained from invading others' rights, and from doing hurt to one another, and the law of nature be observed, which willeth the peace and preservation of all mankind, the execution of the law of nature is in that state, put into every man's hands, whereby everyone has a right to punish the transgressors of that law to such a degree, as may hinder its violation. For the law of nature would, as all other laws that concern men in this world, be in vain, if there were nobody that in the state of nature, had a power to execute that law, and thereby preserve the innocent and restrain offenders, and if anyone in the state of nature may punish another, for any evil he has done, everyone may do so. For in that state of perfect equality, where naturally there is no superiority or jurisdiction of one, over another, what any may do in prosecution of that law, everyone must needs have a right to do.

And thus in the state of nature, one man comes by a power over another; but yet no absolute or arbitrary power, to use a criminal when he has got him in his hands, according to the passionate heats, or boundless extravagancy of his own will, but only to retribute to him, so far as calm reason and conscience dictates, what is proportionate to his transgression, which is so much as may serve for reparation and restraint. For these two are the only reasons, why one man may lawfully do harm to another, which is what we call punishment. In transgressing the law of nature, the offender declares himself to live by another rule, than that of reason and common equity, which is that measure God has set to the actions of men, for their mutual security: and so he becomes dangerous to mankind, the tie, which is to secure them from injury and violence, being slighted and broken by him. Which being a trespass against the whole species, and the peace and safety of it, provided for by the law of nature, every man upon this score, by the right he hath to preserve mankind in general, may restrain, or where it is necessary, destroy things noxious to them, and so may bring such evil on anyone, who hath transgressed that law, as may make him repent the doing of it, and thereby deter him, and by his example others, from doing the like mischief. And in this case, and upon this ground, every man hath a right to punish the offender, and be executioner of the law of nature. [. . .]

To this strange doctrine, *viz.* that in the state of nature, everyone has the executive power of the law of nature, I doubt not but it will be objected, that it is unreasonable for men to be judges in their own cases, that self-love will make men partial to themselves and their friends. And on the other side, that ill nature, passion and revenge will carry them too far in punishing others. And hence nothing but confusion and disorder will follow, and that therefore God hath certainly appointed government to restrain the partiality and violence of men [Romans 13.4]. I easily grant, that civil government is the proper remedy for the inconveniences of the state of nature, which must certainly be great, where men may be judges in their own case, since 'tis easily to be imagined, that he who was so unjust as to do his brother an injury, will

174

scarce be so just as to condemn himself for it: but I shall desire those who make this objection, to remember that absolute monarchs are but men, and if government is to be the remedy of those evils, which necessarily follow from men's being judges in their own cases, and the state of nature is therefore not [to] be endured, I desire to know what kind of government that is, and how much better it is than the state of nature, where one man commanding a multitude, has the liberty to be judge in his own case, and may do to all his subjects whatever he pleases, without the least liberty to anyone to question or control those who execute his pleasure? And in whatsoever he doth, whether led by reason, mistake or passion, must be submitted to? Much better it is in the state of nature wherein men are not bound to submit to the unjust will of another: and if he that judges, judges amiss in his own, or any other case, he is answerable for it to the rest of mankind.

'Tis often asked as a mighty objection, where are, or ever were, there any men in such a state of nature? To which it may suffice as an answer at present; that since all princes and rulers of independent governments all through the world, are in a state of nature, 'tis plain the world never was, nor ever will be, without numbers of men in that state. I have named all governors of independent communities, whether they are, or are not, in league with others: for 'tis not every compact that puts an end to the state of nature between men, but only this one of agreeing together mutually to enter into one community, and make one body politic; other promises and compacts, men may make one with another, and yet still be in the state of nature. The promises and bargains for truck, etc. between the two men in the desert island, mentioned by Garcilaso de la Vega, in his history of Peru, or between a Swiss and an Indian, in the woods of America, are binding to them, though they are perfectly in a state of nature, in reference to one another. For truth and keeping of faith belongs to men, as men, and not as members of society.

Source: J. Locke, *Two Treatises of Government*, Dent, 1993, pp. 115, 116, 117–18, 121–2.

(b) *Rousseau:* The Social Contract

Christianity as a religion is entirely spiritual, occupied solely with heavenly things; the country of the Christian is not of this world. He does his duty, indeed, but does it with profound indifference to the good or ill success of his cares. Provided he has nothing to reproach himself with, it matters little to him whether things go well or ill here on earth. If the State is prosperous, he hardly dares to share in the public happiness, for fear he may grow proud of his country's glory; if the State is languishing, he blesses the hand of God that is hard upon His people.

For the State to be peaceable and for harmony to be maintained, all the citizens without exception would have to be good Christians; if by ill hap there should be a single self-seeker or hypocrite, a Catiline or a Cromwell, for instance, he would certainly get the better of his pious compatriots. Christian charity does not readily allow a man to think hardly of his neighbours. As soon as, by some trick, he has discovered the art of imposing on them and getting hold of a share in the public authority, you have a man established in dignity; it is the will of God that he be respected: very soon you have a power; it is God's will that it be obeyed: and if the power is abused by him who wields it, it is the scourge wherewith God punishes his children. There would be scruples about driving out the usurper: public tranquillity would have to be disturbed, violence would have to be employed, and blood spilt; all this accords ill with Christian meekness; and after all, in this vale of sorrows, what does it matter whether we are free men or serfs? The essential thing is to get to heaven, and resignation is only an additional means of doing so.

[. . .]

The right which the social compact gives the Sovereign over the subjects does not, we have seen, exceed the limits of public expediency. The subjects then owe the Sovereign an account of their opinions only to such an extent as they matter to the community. Now, it matters very much to the community that each citizen should have a religion. That will make him love his duty; but the dogmas of that religion concern the State and its members only so far as they have reference to morality and to the duties which he who professes them is bound to do to others. Each man may have, over and above, what opinions he pleases, without its being the Sovereign's business to take cognizance of them; for, as the Sovereign has no authority in the other world, whatever the lot of its subjects may be in the life to come, that is not its business, provided they are good citizens in this life.

There is therefore a purely civil profession of faith of which the Sovereign should fix the articles, not exactly as religious dogmas, but as social sentiments without which a man cannot be a good citizen or a faithful subject. While it can compel no one to believe them, it can banish from the State whoever does not believe them – it can banish him, not for impiety, but as an anti-social being, incapable of truly loving the laws and justice, and of sacrificing, at need, his life to his duty. If any one, after publicly recognizing these dogmas, behaves as if he does not believe them, let him be punished by death: he has committed the worst of all crimes, that of lying before the law.

The dogmas of civil religion ought to be few, simple, and exactly worded, without explanation or commentary. The existence of a mighty,

intelligent, and beneficent Divinity, possessed of foresight and providence, the life to come, the happiness of the just, the punishment of the
wicked, the sanctity of the social contract and the laws: these are its
positive dogmas. Its negative dogmas I confine to one, intolerance,
which is a part of the cults we have rejected.

Source: J. J. Rousseau: *The Social Contract*, trans. Cole,
Dent, 1913, pp. 304–8.

(c) De Tocqueville: Democracy in America

The greatest part of British America was peopled by men who, after
having shaken off the authority of the Pope, acknowledged no other
religious supremacy: they brought with them into the New World a
form of Christianity which I cannot better describe than by styling it a
democratic and republican religion. This contributed powerfully to the
establishment of a republic and a democracy in public affairs; and from
the beginning, politics and religion contracted an alliance which has
never been dissolved.

[. . .]

In the United States the influence of religion is not confined to the
manners, but it extends to the intelligence of the people. Among the
Anglo-Americans some profess the doctrines of Christianity from a
sincere belief in them, and others do the same because they fear to be
suspected of unbelief. Christianity, therefore, reigns without obstacle,
by universal consent; the consequence is, as I have before observed,
that every principle of the moral world is fixed and determinate,
although the political world is abandoned to the debates and the experiments of men. Thus the human mind is never left to wander over a
boundless field; and whatever may be its pretensions, it is checked from
time to time by barriers that it cannot surmount. Before it can innovate,
certain primary principles are laid down, and the boldest conceptions
are subjected to certain forms which retard and stop their completion.

The imagination of the Americans, even in its greatest flights, is
circumspect and undecided; its impulses are checked and its works
unfinished. These habits of restraint recur in political society and are
singularly favorable both to the tranquility of the people and to the
durability of the institutions they have established. Nature and circumstances have made the inhabitants of the United States bold, as is
sufficiently attested by the enterprising spirit with which they seek for
fortune. If the mind of the Americans were free from all hindrances,
they would shortly become the most daring innovators and the most
persistent disputants in the world. But the revolutionists of America are

obliged to profess an ostensible respect for Christian morality and equity, which does not permit them to violate wantonly the laws that oppose their designs; nor would they find it easy to surmount the scruples of their partisans even if they were able to get over their own. Hitherto no one in the United States has dared to advance the maxim that everything is permissible for the interests of society, an impious adage which seems to have been invented in an age of freedom to shelter all future tyrants. Thus, while the law permits the Americans to do what they please, religion prevents them from conceiving, and forbids them to commit, what is rash or unjust.

Religion in America takes no direct part in the government of society, but it must be regarded as the first of their political institutions; for if it does not impart a taste for freedom, it facilitates the use of it. Indeed, it is in this same point of view that the inhabitants of the United States themselves look upon religious belief. I do not know whether all Americans have a sincere faith in their religion – for who can search the human heart? – but I am certain that they hold it to be indispensable to the maintenance of republican institutions. This opinion is not peculiar to a class of citizens or to a party, but it belongs to the whole nation and to every rank of society.

In the United States, if a politician attacks a sect, this may not prevent the partisans of that very sect from supporting him; but if he attacks all the sects together, everyone abandons him, and he remains alone.

[. . .]

The philosophers of the eighteenth century explained in a very simple manner the gradual decay of religious faith. Religious zeal, said they, must necessarily fail the more generally liberty is established and knowledge diffused. Unfortunately, the facts by no means accord with their theory. There are certain populations in Europe whose unbelief is only equaled by their ignorance and debasement; while in America, one of the freest and most enlightened nations in the world, the people fulfill with fervor all the outward duties of religion.

On my arrival in the United States the religious aspect of the country was the first thing that struck my attention; and the longer I stayed there, the more I perceived the great political consequences resulting from this new state of things. In France I had almost always seen the spirit of religion and the spirit of freedom marching in opposite directions. But in America I found they were intimately united and that they reigned in common over the same country. My desire to discover the causes of this phenomenon increased from day to day. In order to satisfy it I questioned the members of all the different sects; I sought especially

the society of the clergy, who are the depositaries of the different creeds and are especially interested in their duration. As a member of the Roman Catholic Church, I was more particularly brought into contact with several of its priests, with whom I became intimately acquainted. To each of these men I expressed my astonishment and explained my doubts. I found that they differed upon matters of detail alone, and that they all attributed the peaceful dominion of religion in their country mainly to the separation of church and state. I do not hesitate to affirm that during my stay in America I did not meet a single individual, of the clergy or the laity, who was not of the same opinion on this point.
[. . .]

I am aware that at certain times religion may strengthen this influence, which originates in itself, by the artificial power of the laws and by the support of those temporal institutions that direct society. Religions intimately united with the governments of the earth have been known to exercise sovereign power founded on terror and faith; but when a religion contracts an alliance of this nature, I do not hesitate to affirm that it commits the same error as a man who should sacrifice his future to his present welfare; and in obtaining a power to which it has no claim, it risks that authority which is rightfully its own. When a religion founds its empire only upon the desire of immortality that lives in every human heart, it may aspire to universal dominion; but when it connects itself with a government, it must adopt maxims which are applicable only to certain nations. Thus, in forming an alliance with a political power, religion augments its authority over a few and forfeits the hope of reigning over all.

As long as a religion rests only upon those sentiments which are the consolation of all affliction, it may attract the affections of all mankind. But if it be mixed up with the bitter passions of the world, it may be constrained to defend allies whom its interests, and not the principle of love, have given to it; or to repel as antagonists men who are still attached to it, however opposed they may be to the powers with which it is allied. The church cannot share the temporal power of the state without being the object of a portion of that animosity which the latter excites.

The political powers which seem to be most firmly established have frequently no better guarantee for their duration than the opinions of a generation, the interests of the time, or the life of an individual. A law may modify the social condition which seems to be most fixed and determinate; and with the social condition everything else must change. The powers of society are more or less fugitive, like the years that we spend upon earth; they succeed each other with rapidity, like the fleeting cares of life; and no government has ever yet been founded upon an invariable disposition of the human heart or upon an imperishable interest.

As long as a religion is sustained by those feelings, propensities, and passions which are found to occur under the same forms at all periods of history, it may defy the efforts of time; or at least it can be destroyed only by another religion. But when religion clings to the interests of the world, it becomes almost as fragile a thing as the powers of earth. It is the only one of them all which can hope for immortality; but if it be connected with their ephemeral power, it shares their fortunes and may fall with those transient passions which alone supported them. The alliance which religion contracts with political powers must needs be onerous to itself, since it does not require their assistance to live, and by giving them its assistance it may be exposed to decay.

Source: A. de Tocqueville, *Democracy in America*,
Knopf, 1945, pp. 311, 345–6.

(d) Novak:
The Spirit of Democratic Capitalism

The classic text is: 'Give to Caesar the things that are Caesar's, and to God the things that are God's' (Matt. 22.21). In earlier chapters, we have already explored the importance of structural pluralism to democratic capitalism. This pluralism renders the mission of Christianity uniquely difficult. Some traditional societies imposed Christianity upon their citizens. Some socialist societies could conceivably do so. Under pluralism, no democratic capitalist society has a right to do so.

This means that the political system of democratic capitalism cannot, in principle, be a Christian system. Clearly, it cannot be a confessional system. But it cannot even be presumed to be, in an *obligatory* way, suffused with Christian values and purposes. Individual Christians and their organized bodies may legitimately work through democratic means to shape the will of the majority; but they must also observe the rights of others and, more than that, heed practical wisdom by respecting the consciences of others even more than law alone might demand. On the question of abortion, for example, no one is likely ever to be satisfied with the law, but all might be well advised not to demand in law all that their own conscience commands.

Dietrich Bonhoeffer has written about the impossibility of a Christian economy. For one thing, a market system must be open to all regardless of their religious faith. Economic liberty means that all must be permitted to establish their own values and priorities. The churches

180

and other moral-cultural institutions may seek to persuade persons to avoid some actions and to take others. Public authority properly forbids some practices, regulates others, commands others. Nonetheless, a wide range of economic liberties remains. This liberty is valued as the atmosphere most favorable to invention, creativity, and economic activism. To repress it is to invite stagnation.

For another thing, Christian values in their purity command a high level of charity that is not of this world. Christians are urged to moral behavior that seems counter-natural: to love enemies; to do good to those that hate them; when struck, to turn the other cheek. Such counsels are high standards by which to fault even our best daily practice. They are not rules cut to the expected behavior of most persons most of the time. Again, it is said: 'Love your neighbor as yourself' (Lev 19.18). It is not easy to love oneself. Escape from too much self often affords sorely needed relief. Often it is easier to love the poor and the oppressed than to love one's nextdoor neighbor. Part of the attraction of Christianity derives from the moral heroism to which such counsels call. Christianity in this sense is like a mountain peak. There is danger in such mountains. Christians who are not alpinists easily deceive themselves about their virtue.

No intelligent human order – not even within a church bureaucracy – can be run according to the counsels of Christianity. Not even saints in company assembled can bear such a regimen. Monasteries are designed for sinners, beginners, and backsliders. In the world at large, moreover, the consciences of all Christians are not identical. An economy based upon the consciences of some would offend the consciences of others. A free economy cannot – for all these reasons – be a Christian economy. To try to run an economy by the highest Christian principles is certain to destroy both the economy and the reputation of Christianity. Each Christian can and should follow his or her conscience, and cooperate in coalitions where consensus may be reached.

Liberty is a critical good in the economic sphere as well as in the sphere of conscience. Yet the guardians of the moral-cultural system are typically less concerned about liberty in the economic system than about their own liberty. Intellectuals insist upon a free market for their own work, but easily endorse infringements upon the liberty of economic activists. Journalists are quick to resist encroachments upon the laws which protect their own liberties; they are slow to protest – if they do not themselves encourage – infringements upon the liberties of industry and commerce. So it is and always was.

These different interests and different concerns illustrate the systematic distortions in human perception to which the doctrine of original sin draws attention. The perception of each of us is regularly more self-centered than our ideal selves can plausibly commend. We are not often as objective as we would like to be. That is why the separation of systems is appropriate to our weakness. At the heart of Judaism and Christianity is the recognition of sin, as at the heart of democratic capitalism is a differentiation of systems designed to squeeze some good from sinful tendencies.

[. . .]

To look upon human history as love-infused by a Creator who values others as others, who sees in those originating sources of insight and choice which we have come to know as 'persons' the purpose of his creation; and who in loving each as an individual creates of the contrarious many an unseen, hidden, but powerful community, is to glimpse a world in which the political economy of democratic capitalism makes sense.

In order to create wealth, individuals must be free to be other. They are not to be understood as fragments of a collective, members of a kinship group or ethnic enclave, but as individual others: originating sources of insight and choice. Such persons are not isolated and alien from one another. Sympathy, cooperation, and association are to them as natural, and as necessary, as breathing air. Yet when they form communities, they *choose* them, *elect* them, *contract* for them. The natural state of political community for persons is arrived at not by primordial belonging but by constitutional compact. Before the human race chose its communities, it had only a form of *pietas*, a type of *amor*, love of country. It had not yet glimpsed the possibility of *dilectio*. Even primordial love of country is good. But choice, compact, election, is better.

In this scheme, the individual is not atomic. Although the individual is an originating source of insight and choice, the fulfillment of the individual lies in a beloved community. Yet any community worthy of such love values the singularity and inviolability of each person. Without true individualism, there is no true community.

In the economic sphere, creation is to be fulfilled through human imitation of the Creator. Creation is no morality play. Nor is it a Panglossian perfect harmony. Many species perished in its evolutionary emergence, and within each species countless individuals have been untimely stricken. Winds have eroded fertile lands. Ice has covered the earth. Rushing waters have eaten away entire territories. Earthquakes, tornadoes, and volcanic ash have wreaked their havoc. The earth bears many scars that antedate the emergence of humankind. The beasts of the jungle are hardly kind to one another. Yet in the caves one is right to imagine that human beings loved one another as well as slew one another. Not so high as the angels, not so low as the beasts, the creation of humans is the most wondrous act of the Creator. Respecting liberty, the Creator allowed sin.

The problem for a system of economy is how to unleash human creativity and productivity while coping realistically with human sinfulness. To love humans as they are is to accept them in their sinfulness, while seeking a way to transform such sinfulness into creative action for the commonweal. Some argue that the best way to do this is to appeal to social solidarity and high moral ideals. They erect economic systems accordingly. Others hold that the common good is better served through allowing each individual to work as each judges best and to keep the rewards of such labor. For them, the profit motive is designed to inspire a higher level of common benefit by respecting the individual judgment of economic agents. The more the latter risk and invest, the greater return they may gather in. Most will not be selfish with this return; most will share it liberally. If they bury their talent, or squander it, that is their choice; they will hardly be thought to be good stewards. The idea is that greater incentives will stimulate greater economic activism. The more economically active most citizens are, the greater should be the common prosperity.

According to socialist theory, the rich get richer and the poor get poorer. The implication is that the poverty of the poor is caused by the wealth of the wealthy. The theory of democratic capitalism is quite different. It holds that economic activism creates wealth, and that the broader the stimulation of economic activism the greater the wealth created. It does not hold that economic activists are equal in talent, judgment, exertion, or luck, nor does it expect equal outcomes. Yet it does hold that economic activism, whether on the part of a few or on the part of many, benefits not only its agents but the entire community.

A system of political economy imitates the demands of *caritas* by reaching out, creating, inventing, producing, and distributing, raising the material base of the common good. It is based on realism. It respects individuals as individuals. It makes communal life more active, intense, voluntary, and multiple. An economic system which makes individuals dependent is no more an example of *caritas* than is a lover whose love encourages dependency. A collectivist system which does not respect individuals as originating sources of insight and choice is no more an example of *caritas* than is a beehive or a herd of cattle.

The highest goal of the political economy of democratic capitalism is to be suffused by *caritas*. Within such a system, each person is regarded as an originating source of insight, choice, action, and love. Yet each is also a part of all the others. The goal of the republic is to inspire in each and every citizen the desire to become all that each can become, as the motto of New York State – 'Excelsior!' – succinctly expresses. A cognate goal is to inspire the disciplines of realistic judgment: 'Confirm thy soul in self-control!' as the hymn puts it. The vision is that of a republic of independent, self-reliant, fraternal, and cooperative citizens, each of whose interests includes the interests of all in brotherhood 'from sea to shining sea'.

Under external assault and adversity, citizens forget petty contentions and are naturally drawn together. It is less easy for a pacific republic to maintain its unity. Under conditions of prosperity, the same diverse interests that defend all against the tyranny of the few tend to block the full unity of the many. Hence a democratic capitalist republic, in its pluralism, is nearly always in disequilibrium. Neither its political system nor its economic system nor its moral-cultural system can function as they are intended to function without the leadership which draws on the ideals of fraternity and community and inspires all to self-sacrifice for the common good.

Caritas is at one and the same time an ideal of individual autonomy – respecting the good of the other as other – and an ideal of community. It is the spiritual ideal which attracts from afar the only approximating drives of a democratic polity, a capitalist economy, and a liberal pluralist moral-cultural system. It is the spiritual ideal whose betrayal most injures the system in its every part. It is not an easy ideal to realize. That is why the institutions which try to approximate it in practice are best guided by the motto 'In God we trust', for no lesser source suffices for its full self-realization. Renewal, reform, and self-transformation are, in the light of that transcendent ideal always called for.

Source: M. Novak, *The Spirit of Democratic Capitalism*, Institute of Economic Affairs, 1991, pp. 351–3, 355–8.

Further reading

See the careful discussion in Mott, *A Christian Perspective on Political Thought*, Chapters 9 and 11 and Margaret Thatcher's account of the rather jejune Christianity which accords with her world outlook in Raban's *God, Man and Mrs. Thatcher*. There is an excellent study of the Christian background to Locke's thought in the book by Dunn. For a defence of market liberalism, see Novak's *The Spirit of Democratic Capitalism* and Gilder's *Wealth and Poverty*. For a more sceptical approach, consult Wogaman's *Christians and the Great Economic Debate* and the works by D. Meeks and by Stackhouse.

Chapter Thirteen

SOCIALISM

Introduction

Historically, Socialism is a phenomenon even more recent than Liberalism. The term 'socialism' itself dates only from the early nineteenth century and the socialist movement emerged as a response to the social and economic dislocations produced by the industrial revolution. Nevertheless elements in the socialist tradition go back further than the industrial revolution – at least as far as the original Christian community which, we are told, 'held all things in common'. This kind of social gospel has been part of the Christian tradition from many of the early Church Fathers, through the Franciscans, Thomas Münzer and the millenarian movements, the Diggers and Levellers of the English Civil War, the Jesuit Reductions in Paraguay, to contemporary forms such as the Christian Base Communities of Southern and Central America and the *Ujama* socialism of Julius Nyerere. Even some of the most militant socialist critics of Christianity such as Marx (in the extracts below) felt that Christianity contained certain ideas that it was Socialism's vocation to put into practice. A rather simple but powerful equation of Christian gospel with Socialism is well expressed in the writings of Dorothy Day.

Socialism as an explicit politico-economic doctrine was a French invention and early French socialists such as Lammenais, Leroux and Cabet proclaimed the identity of their views with Christianity. For them, Jesus Christ was the first communist and communism was just Christianity in practice. But this happy equation came under increasing pressure as the nineteenth century progressed. As capitalist social and economic relations spread, forms of Protestant Christianity closely associated with capitalism and based on an individualist ethos began to gain the upper hand: the more collectivist Catholicism (which in any

185

case became dramatically reactionary under Pius IX) was seen as distinctly *passé*. And socialism, too, became increasingly dominated by a rigid Marxist interpretation. The message of Marx and his followers was that socialism is a strictly secular doctrine which made Christianity irrelevant. Socialism might give substance to certain Christian ideals, but it thereby abolished the Christian religion.

The progress (or otherwise) of the twentieth century has shown such an equation of the advance of socialism with the retreat of religion to be much too facile. Marxism tended to generalize from the function of religion in mid-nineteenth-century Western Europe to the function of religion in all societies and to reduce the significance of religion to that of the economic conflicts it was held to reflect. Most socialists, particularly those influenced by Marxism, conserved a strong element of Enlightenment rationalism in their view of the world. This led them to underestimate the importance of non-rational modes of discourse. The religious mode, like the aesthetic, can refresh parts that more rational modes cannot reach. On this view some forms of socialism have had an inadequate grasp of human nature – not in the banal sense that socialist projects reflect some supposedly ineradicable self-interest, but in the more important and opposite sense that their conceptions are too narrow, too exclusive and too short-sighted in their views of human potential.

It is obvious that socialism and Christianity do share a number of themes. The socialist earthly kingdom in many ways mirrors the Christian Kingdom of God. But in the post-modern era both socialism and Christianity are becoming perforce more pluralist. Socialism is increasingly a site for the political struggles detailed in the next chapter and here specific forms of Christianity – black, green, feminist – will become more prominent.

(a) *Marx:* On Religion

The basis of irreligious criticism is: Man makes religion, religion does not make man. In other words, religion is the self-consciousness and self-feeling of man who has either not yet found himself or has already lost himself again. But man is no abstract being squatting outside the world. Man is the world of man, the state, society. This state, this society, produce religion, a reversed world-consciousness, because they are a reversed world. Religion is the general theory of that world, its encyclopaedic compendium, its logic in a popular form, its spiritualistic *point d'honneur*, its enthusiasm, its moral sanction, its solemn completion, its universal ground for consolation and justification. It is the fantastic realization of the human essence because the human essence has no true reality. The struggle against religion is therefore mediately the fight against the other world, of which religion is the spiritual aroma.

Religious distress is at the same time the expression of real distress and the protest against real distress. Religion is the sigh of the oppressed creature, the heart of a heartless world, just as it is the spirit of a spiritless situation. It is the opium of the people.

The abolition of religion as the illusory happiness of the people is required for their real happiness. The demand to give up the illusions about its condition is the demand to give up a condition which needs illusions. The criticism of religion is therefore in embryo the criticism of the vale of woe, the halo of which is religion.

Criticism has plucked the imaginary flowers from the chain not so that man will wear the chain without any fantasy or consolation but so that he will shake off the chain and cull the living flower. The criticism of religion disillusions man to make him think and act and shape his reality like a man who has been disillusioned and has come to reason, so that he will revolve round himself and therefore round his true sun. Religion is only the illusory sun which revolves round man as long as he does not revolve round himself.

The task of history, therefore, once the world beyond the truth has disappeared, is to establish the truth of this world. The immediate task of philosophy, which is at the service of history, once the saintly form of human self-alienation has been unmasked, is to unmask self-alienation in its unholy forms. Thus the criticism of heaven turns into the criticism of the earth, the criticism of religion into the criticism of right and the criticism of theology into the criticism of politics.

[. . .] The religious world is but the reflex of the real world. And for a society based upon the production of commodities, in which the producers in general enter into social relations with one another by treating their products as commodities and values, whereby they reduce their individual private labour to the standard of homogeneous human labour – for such a society, Christianity with its *cultus* of abstract man, more especially in its bourgeois developments, Protestantism, Deism, etc., is the most fitting form of religion. In the ancient Asiatic and other ancient modes of production, we find that the conversion of products into commodities, and therefore the conversion of men into producers of commodities, holds a subordinate place, which, however, increases in importance as the primitive communities approach nearer and nearer to their dissolution. Trading nations, properly so called, exist in the ancient world only in its interstices, like the gods of Epicurus in the Intermundia, or like Jews in the pores of Polish society. Those ancient social organisms of production are, as compared with bourgeois society, extremely simple and transparent. But they are founded either on the immature development of man individually, who has not yet severed the umbilical cord that unites him with his fellowmen in a primitive tribal community, or upon direct relations of subjection. They can arise and exist only when the development of the productive power of labour has not risen beyond a low stage, and when, therefore, the social relations within the sphere of material life, between man and man, and between man and nature, are correspondingly narrow. This narrowness is reflected in the ancient worship of nature, and in the other elements of the popular religions. The religious reflex of the real world can, in any case, only then finally vanish, when the practical relations of everyday life offer to man none but perfectly intelligible and reasonable relations with regard to his fellowmen and to nature.

> Sources: K. Marx and F. Engels, *On Religion*, Moscow, 1957, pp. 41–2;
> *Capital: A New Abridgement*, Oxford University Press, 1995, pp. 49–50.

(b) Rauschenbusch:
Christianizing the Social Order

When Jesus, at the beginning of his public career, came to the synagogue of his home city of Nazareth, they handed him the roll of the prophet Isaiah, and he singled out these words to read:

> The spirit of the Lord Jehovah is upon me,
> Because Jehovah hath anointed me to proclaim glad tidings to
> the poor;
> He hath sent me to bind up the broken-hearted,
>
> To proclaim liberty to the captives
> And the bursting of the prison to them that are bound;
> To proclaim the year of Jehovah's favor,
> And the day of vengeance of our God.

When these words were first written, they had promised an exiled nation freedom and restoration of its national life. Jesus declared that he found the purpose of his own mission in fulfilling this prophecy, and thereby he adopted it as the pronunciamento and platform of Christianity. The words reverberate with freedom, and wherever the Gospel has retained even a breath of the spirit of Jesus in it, it has been a force making for freedom. If its official exponents have ever turned it into a chain of the mind, may God forgive them.

Christianity necessarily must be on the side of freedom if it is to fulfill its twofold purpose of creating strong and saved characters, and of establishing a redeemed and fraternal social life, for neither of the two is possible without freedom.

Freedom is the life breath of a Christianized personality. A servile class or nation lacks virility. Slaves and flunkies cringe, lie, and steal. Oppressed peoples resort to conspiracies and assassinations. Free people organize. The general judgment of past ages that woman was a clog to the higher aspirations of able men was really true in large part. As long as women were a subject class, they had the vices of a subject class. Men kept them ignorant and oppressed, and then were cursed by pulling with unequal yoke-mates. Freedom is to character what fresh air is to the blood. This is the truth in Nietzsche's contempt for the morals of servility.

Freedom is also the condition of a Christianized social order. Men can have no fraternal relations until they face one another with a sense of freedom and of equal humanity. Despotism is always haunted by dread, and fear is not a symptom of the prevalence of fraternity. In tracing the moral evolution of the Family, the School, the Church and the State, we saw that every social organization is on the road to redemption when it finds the path of freedom.

We are told that democracy has proved a failure. It has in so far as it was crippled and incomplete. Political democracy without economic democracy is an uncashed promissory note, a pot without the roast, a form without substance. But in so far as democracy has become effective, it has quickened everything it has touched. The criminal law, for instance, has lost its bloody vindictiveness since the advent of democracy; men are now living who will see our penal institutions as agencies of human redemption and restoration. Democracy has even quickened the moral conscience of the upper classes. The most awful poverty has always existed before the eyes of the rich, yet they failed to see it till the lower classes became articulate through democracy. Is the cure of such blindness not a moral achievement?

Some forms of evil merely seem to multiply in a democracy because they get publicity there. Things that remain discreetly hidden in a despotism are dragged into the open by the impertinent curiosity of the plebs. What an aristocracy calls hereditary rights, a democracy calls scandalous graft. When Roman patricians or French seigneurs unloosed the anger of the common man, they could retire within the haughty class consciousness of a solid social group as into a bomb-proof shelter. In a democracy the extortionate rich must trust mainly to the thickness of their private skins.

The alternative for an aristocracy of superior persons is the democracy of labor. John Stuart Mill formulated the ideal of industrial democracy finely:

The form of association which, if mankind continue to improve, must be expected in the end to predominate, is not that which can exist between a capitalist as chief, and workpeople without a voice in the management, but the association of the laborers themselves on terms of equality, collectively owning the capital with which they carry on their operations, and working under managers elected and removable by themselves.

Two great movements are pushing toward the realization of this idea. The more radical of the two is Socialism. It stands in the midst of capitalistic society like a genuine republican party in a monarchical State, and seeks to lead the working class from 'the kingdom of compulsion into the republic of freedom'. The more conservative movement for industrial democracy is Trades-unionism. Just as a liberal party in a strong monarchy leaves the dynasty and its fundamental rights untouched, but demands parliamentary representation and the right to vote on the budget, so Trades-unionism recognizes the rights of the owner and employer under the present social order, but seeks constitutional guarantees and a Bill of Rights for the working class.
[. . .]
Democracy has become a spiritual hope and a religious force. It stands for the sanitation of our moral relations, and for the development of the human soul in freedom and self-control. In some future social order democracy may possibly stand for the right to be unequal. In our present social order it necessarily stands for more equality between man and man.

Men are unequal in their capacities, and always will be, and this inherent inequality of talent will inevitably be registered in some inequality of possessions. But beneath the superficial inequalities of intellect lies the fundamental endowment of human personality, and in that we are all equal. Wherever we get close enough to our fellows to realize their humanity, we feel an imponderable spiritual reality compared with which all wealth-getting gifts are trivial. Our children may differ widely in physical perfection and intellectual ability, but the strong child and the crippled child are alike life of our life, and the same mysterious human soul gazes at us out of their inscrutable baby eyes. Outsiders may rate the gifts of a husband and his wife very unequally, but the gifted partner often knows that all his cleverness is like autumn leaves and that in human worth his quiet mate outranks him. In the family it is love which acts as the revealer of this profound human dignity and equality. In society at large the Christian religion has been incomparably the strongest force in asserting the essential equality of all souls before God.

190

Democracy aids in Christianizing the social order by giving political and economic expression to this fundamental Christian conviction of the worth of man. We do not want absolute equality; we do want approximate equality. We can at least refrain from perpetuating and increasing the handicap of the feebler by such enormous inequalities of property as we now have. To assert that they really correspond to the actual differences in intellectual ability is idle talk, and it becomes more absurd with every year as we see the great fortunes grow. They are an institutionalized denial of the fundamental truths of our religion, and Democracy is the archangel whom God has sent to set his blazing foot on these icebergs of human pride and melt them down.

Men say that equality would hold ability down under a dead weight of mediocrity. If ability can be held down it is not very able. If the time ever comes when the strong are oppressed, I shall gladly join a crusade for their emancipation. Meantime I judge with the old German composer Zeller: 'A genius can do anything. A genius will shampoo a pig and curl its bristles.' Disciplined intellect will ask no odds except of the Almighty.

So, in the long run, it is the principles which men accept as the basis of their good organization which matter. And the principle which we have tried to put forward is that industry and property and economic activity should be treated as functions, and should be tested, at every point, by their relation to a social purpose. Viewed from that angle, issues which are insoluble when treated on the basis of rights may be found more susceptible of reasonable treatment. For a purpose is, in the first place, a principle of limitation. It determines the end for which, and therefore the limits within which, an activity is to be carried on. It divides what is worth doing from what is not, and settles the scale upon which what is worth doing ought to be done. It is, in the second place, a principle of unity, because it supplies a common end to which efforts can be directed, and submits interests, which would otherwise conflict, to the judgement of an over-ruling object. It is, in the third place, a principle of apportionment or distribution. It assigns to the different parties or groups engaged in a common undertaking the place which they are to occupy in carrying it out. Thus it establishes order, not upon chance or power, but upon a principle, and bases remuneration not upon what men can with good fortune snatch for themselves, nor upon what, if unlucky, they can be induced to accept, but upon what is appropriate to their function, no more and no less, so that those who perform no function receive no payment, and those who contribute to the common end receive honourable payment for honourable service.

Such a political philosophy implies that society is not an economic mechanism, but a community of wills which are often discordant, but which are capable of being inspired by devotion to common ends. It is, therefore, a religious one, and, if it is true, the proper bodies to propagate it are the Christian Churches. During the last two centuries Europe, and particularly industrial Europe, has seen the development of a society in which what is called personal religion continues to be taught as the rule of individual conduct, but in which the very conception of religion as the inspiration and standard of social life and corporate effort has been forgotten. The phenomenon is a curious one. To suggest that an individual is not a Christian may be libellous. To preach in public that Christianity is absurd is legally blasphemy. To state that the social ethics of the New Testament are obligatory upon men in the business affairs which occupy nine-tenths of their thought, or on the industrial organization which gives our society its character, is to preach revolution. To suggest that they apply to the relations of States may be held to be sedition. Such a creed does not find it difficult to obey the injunction: 'Render unto Caesar the things that are Caesar's and unto God the things that are God's.' To their first hearers the words must have come with a note of gentle irony, for to the reader of the New Testament the things which are Caesar's appear to be singularly few. The modern world is not seriously inconvenienced by rendering to God the things which are God's. They are not numerous, nor are they of the kind which it misses.

Hence the opinion, so frequently expressed, that the religion of a society makes no practical difference to the conduct of its affairs is not only contrary to experience, but of its very nature superficial. The creed of indifferentism, detached from the social order which is the greatest and most massive expression of the scale of values that is the working faith of a society, may make no difference, except to damn more completely those who profess it. But then, so tepid and self-regarding a creed is not a religion. Christianity cannot allow its sphere to be determined by the convenience of politicians or by the conventional ethics of the world of business. The whole world of human interests was assigned to it as its province. 'The law of divinity is to lead the lowest through the intermediate to the highest things.' In discharging its commission, therefore, a Christian Church will constantly enter the departments of politics and of economic relations, because it is only a bad modern convention which allows men to forget that these things, as much as personal conduct, are the sphere of the spirit and the expression of character. It will insist that membership in it involves obedience to a certain rule of life and the renunciation of the prizes offered by economic mastery.

Source: W. Rauschenbusch, *Christianizing the Social Order*, Macmillan, 1912, pp. 353–64.

(c) *Tawney:* The Acquisitive Society

'He hath put down the mighty from their seat, and hath exalted the humble and meek.' A society which is fortunate enough to possess so revolutionary a basis, a society whose Founder was executed as the enemy of law and order, need not seek to soften the materialism of principalities and powers with mild doses of piety administered in an apologetic whisper. It will teach as one having authority, and will have sufficient confidence in its Faith to believe that it requires neither artificial protection nor judicious under-statement in order that such truth as there is in it may prevail. It will appeal to mankind, not because its standards are identical with those of the world, but because they are profoundly different. It will win its converts, not because membership involves no change in their manner of life, but because it involves a change so complete as to be ineffaceable. It will expect its adherents to face economic ruin for the sake of their principles with the same alacrity as, not so long ago, it was faced by the workman who sought to establish trade unionism among his fellows. It will define, with the aid of those of its members who are engaged in different trades and occupations, the lines of conduct and organization which approach most nearly to being the practical application of Christian ethics in the various branches of economic life, and, having defined them, will censure those of its members who depart from them without good reason. It will rebuke the open and notorious sin of the man who oppresses his fellows for the sake of gain as freely as that of the drunkard or adulterer. It will voice frankly the judgement of the Christian conscience on the acts of the State, even when to do so is an offence to nine-tenths of its fellow-citizens. Like Missionary Churches in Africa to-day, it will have as its aim, not merely to convert the individual, but to make a new kind, and a Christian kind of civilization.

Such a religion is likely to be highly inconvenient to all parties and persons who desire to dwell at ease in Zion. But it will not, at any rate, be a matter of indifference. The marks of its influence will not be comfort, but revolt and persecution. It will bring not peace, but a sword. Yet its end is peace. It is to harmonize the discords of human society, by relating its activities to the spiritual purpose from which they derive their significance.

> Brother, the virtue of our heavenly love,
> tempers our will and makes us want no more
> than what we have – we thirst for this alone.
>
> If we desired to be higher up,
> then our desires would not be in accord

with His will Who assigns us to this sphere.

Indeed, the essence of this blessed state
is to dwell here within His holy will,
so that there is no will but one with His;

Then it was clear to me that every where
of Heaven is Paradise, though there the light
of Grace Supreme does not shine equally.

The famous lines in which Piccarda explains to Dante the order of
Paradise are a description of a complex and multiform society which is
united by overmastering devotion to a common end. By that end all
stations are assigned and all activities are valued. The parts derive their
quality from their place in the system, and are so permeated by the
unity which they express that they themselves are glad to be forgotten,
as the ribs of an arch carry the eye from the floor from which they
spring to the vault in which they meet and interlace.

Such a combination of unity and diversity is possible only to a society
which subordinates its activities to the principle of purpose. For what
that principle offers is not merely a standard for determining the relations of different classes and groups of producers, but a scale of moral
values. Above all, it assigns to economic activity itself its proper place
as the servant, not the master, of society. The burden of our civilization
is not merely, as many suppose, that the product of industry is ill-
distributed, or its conduct tyrannical, or its operation interrupted by
embittered disagreements. It is that industry itself has come to hold a
position of exclusive predominance among human interests, which no
single interest, and least of all the provision of the material means of
existence, is fit to occupy. Like a hypochondriac who is so absorbed in
the processes of his own digestion that he goes to his grave before he
has begun to live, industrialized communities neglect the very objects
for which it is worth while to acquire riches in their feverish preoccu-
pation with the means by which riches can be acquired.

That obsession by economic issues is as local and transitory as it is
repulsive and disturbing. To future generations it will appear as pitiable
as the obsession of the seventeenth century by religious quarrels appears
to-day; indeed, it is less rational, since the object with which it is concerned is less important. And it is a poison which inflames every
wound and turns every trivial scratch into a malignant ulcer. Society
will not solve the particular problems of industry which afflict it until
that poison is expelled, and it has learned to see industry itself in the
right perspective. If it is to do that, it must rearrange its scale of values.
It must regard economic interests as one element in life, not as the

whole of life. It must persuade its members to renounce the opportunity of gains which accrue without any corresponding service, because the struggle for them keeps the whole community in a fever. It must so organize its industry that the instrumental character of economic activity is emphasized by its subordination to the social purpose for which it is carried on.

Source: R. Tawney, *The Acquisitive Society*, Bell, 1921, pp. 126–7, 131–5.

(d) Cort: Christian Socialism

What can we conclude from this long, long story, from Moses to the present moment, the story of those who have reflected on the imperatives of the Judeo-Christian tradition and sought to apply them to the temporal order?

Let me deal with that question by responding to some questions raised by a Christian who read most of this manuscript and still disagreed with the idea that a Christian could, not to mention should, be a socialist.

1. 'Can you extract a political program from the gospel? Is feeding the hungry and clothing the naked identical to the systematic redistribution of wealth? Can the spirit of Christian love ever be reduced to a political imperative?'

Answer: Concentrate the mind on the old saw: 'Give a man a fish and you feed him for a day; teach him how to fish and you feed him for a lifetime.' Then ask yourself, 'Which is more in keeping with the spirit of the gospel?' The answer is obvious. From there it is a short step in logic to a further conclusion: even more in keeping with the letter and spirit of the gospel, especially in the modern era, is the construction of a political economy that makes it possible for every man or woman who needs a job to work at a decent job so that he or she may feed, clothe and shelter him or her self and his or her children. The physical, psychological, spiritual, economic, and political advantages of this reading of the gospel – as opposed to one that is exclusively personal and individual – seem too obvious to need further repetition. The simpler reading *may* have been appropriate for Jesus' time. There is evidence that it was not appropriate even then. It is certainly not appropriate for our time.

Several quotes from the Catholic bishops' pastoral letter on the US economy are relevant:

> The responsibility for alleviating the plight of the poor falls upon all members of society. As individuals, all citizens have a duty to assist the poor through acts of charity and personal commitment. But

195

private charity and voluntary action are not sufficient. *We also carry out our moral responsibility to assist and empower the poor by working collectively through government to establish just and effective public policies* (189, emphasis added).

And from the very last paragraph:

Jesus taught us to love God and one another and that the concept of neighbor is without limit . . . Love implies concern for all – especially the poor – and *a continued search for those social and economic structures that permit everyone to share in a community that is part of a redeemed creation* (Rom. 8.21–3) (365, emphasis added).

The 'spirit of Christian love' cannot be reduced to a political imperative, granted, but it most certainly has a political dimension. Feeding the hungry and clothing the naked are not precisely identical with a systematic redistribution of wealth, but in the present situation of gross inequality, obscene wealth and wretched poverty, they most certainly cry to heaven for both systematic and unsystematic redistribution.

2. 'What is it that you are for? How is the "socialization" of property to be effected without the Marxist solution of a strong central government ("the vanguard of the proletariat")? What is the engine of your implementation of the social gospel?'

Answer. There is no need to socialize all forms of property. There should be more rather than fewer people who enjoy the benefits of private property, both productive and consumer property, than we presently have, even in the United States, where property is so concentrated in the hands of a small minority.

There is no one 'engine' for the implementation of the social gospel, unless it be called Democratic Process. An old saw is relevant here: 'Never underestimate the intelligence of the average, ordinary person and never overestimate his or her knowledge.' Democratic process, democracy, is based on the assumption that *given the facts*, the ordinary person will make the right decisions most of the time. Another part of the democratic assumption is that the ordinary person not only has enough intelligence, but he or she also has enough basic human decency. A few more relevant quotes, some of which have appeared before, but can bear repetition:

Reinhold Niebuhr: 'Man's capacity for justice makes democracy possible, but man's inclination to injustice makes democracy necessary.'

Winston Churchill: 'Democracy is the worst form of government except for all those other forms that have been tried from time to time.'

E. B. White: 'Democracy is the recurrent suspicion that more than half the people are right more than half the time. It is the feeling of privacy in the voting booths, the feeling of communion in the libraries, the feeling of vitality everywhere ... It is an idea that hasn't been disproved yet, a song the words of which have not gone bad.'

Lord Acton: 'Power tends to corrupt and absolute power corrupts absolutely.' This saying holds both in political and economic life. Therefore power – whether political or economic – must be well distributed. The best, most effective form of distribution in economic life is the producer cooperative – one-person-one-vote. Just as it is the most democratic form of productive enterprise, it is also, like democracy, one of the most difficult. However, we now have enough examples of successful cooperative enterprise to use this particular 'engine' with some confidence. Of these the most sensationally successful is the Mondragón Group in the Basque country of Spain.

Full implementation of economic democracy calls for democratic structures at the level of the individual enterprise, such as the producer cooperative, but at many other levels as well, the industry level, the state, regional and national economic level. Guild socialism had some good insights. So did the vocational group plan of Heinrich Pesch and Pius XI. So did the CIO Industry Council Plan. So does the West German practice of *Mitbestimmung* (co-determination: worker representation on boards of directors) and the French practice of *autogestion* (self-management). So do a number of American experiments with worker participation in management – joint production committees, quality-of-life circles – which have proven so attractive to both labor and management that even corporations like General Motors and unions like the United Auto Workers have accepted them. Every trade union, incidentally, every union contract, is an 'engine' for the implementation of the social gospel.

One of the major curiosities of economic and political discourse in the 1980s is the selection of John Stuart Mill as an ideological hero by Michael Novak, the Catholic champion of 'democratic capitalism', the oxymoron to end all oxymorons. (Oxymoron: 'A rhetorical figure in which an epigrammatic effect is created by the conjunction of incongruous or contradictory terms; for example, "a mournful optimist"' (*American Heritage Dictionary*).) Mill not only identified himself finally as a socialist, but in the very work that Novak memorializes as some sort of justification for capitalism Mill gave one of the most eloquent arguments for pre-Marxian socialism, now well on the way to becoming post-Marxian socialism as well. Interestingly enough, this was published in 1848, the same year as Marx and Engels's *Communist Manifesto*. Mill speaks first of the advantages of 'an association of the laborers themselves on terms of equality, collectively owning the capital with which they carry on their operations'. He continues:

The mode in which cooperation tends . . . to increase the productiveness of labor, consists in the vast stimulus given to productive energies by placing the laborers, as a mass, in a relation to their work that would make it their principle and their interest (at present it is neither) to do the utmost, instead of the least possible, in exchange for their remuneration. It is scarcely possible to rate too highly this material benefit, which yet is as nothing compared with the moral revolution in society that would accompany it: the healing of the standing feud between capital and labor; the transformation of human life, from a conflict of classes struggling for opposite interests, to a friendly rivalry in the pursuit of a good common to all; the elevation of the dignity of labor; a new sense of dignity and independence in the laboring class; and the conversion of each human being's daily occupation into a school of the social sympathies and the practical intelligence.

What am I for? I am for all the things that the popes (and the World Council of Churches) have been for. I call it 'democratic socialism' and call to the witness stand the Socialist International to support that designation.

In the last manifestation of his annual book production my old friend Michael Novak does me the honor of associating my name with this kind of democratic socialism. Then he quotes Ludwig von Mises:

If anyone likes to call a social idea which retains private ownership of the means of production socialistic, why, let him! A man may call a cat a dog and the sun the moon if it pleases him.

To which I respond, 'Same to you, Ludwig, and the same to you, Michael! If anyone likes to call capitalism democratic, socialism communism and communism socialism, if anyone chooses to ignore all pre-Marxian socialism and all post-Marxian socialism, if anyone chooses to deny that the Socialist International has some faint claim to define what socialism really is, why, let him! A man may call a cat a dog and the sun the moon if it pleases him.'

The fear of God is the beginning of wisdom, but the fear of communism has too often been the beginning of foolishness. If the Novaks and the Miseses really feared communism in a sensible way, they would be more appreciative of the Socialist International and those who are concerned about freedom for the affluent, within reason, but also and primarily, as Christ taught us, about justice for the poor.

Cardinal Arns said it very well and with magnificent brevity:

One thing is clear . . . we must reject capitalism, which is based on selfishness. We believe in the right of workers to own their own land

and to keep their profits for themselves, and therefore we incline toward socialism.

Socialism has been defined in many ways, many of them inaccurate, but many accurate and not necessarily contradictory. 'Socialism is the opposite of individualism.' This was the definition of Alexandre Vinet, the French Protestant who used the word for the first time in 1831. 'Production for use and not for profit' is all right, but a rewording, 'Production primarily for use and only secondarily for profit' would be more in keeping with the definition of the Socialist International. 'Socialism is the extension of democratic process from the political to the economic sphere.' Excellent. 'Socialism is the vision of a pluralist society in which the advantages of competition, a free market and political democracy are reconciled with the maximum socialization of production and the demands of justice, full employment and the realization of that minimum of worldly goods for all which Thomas Aquinas told us is necessary for a life of virtue.' If I have to pick one definition among them, let it be that, but I like the idea of retaining all of them.

3. 'If Christian socialism is grounded ultimately on faith . . . how is that socialism viable in a pluralist, secular democracy?'

Answer: Despite the trace of skeptical condescension in what I wrote about the natural-law reasoning of Cathrein, Pesch and Nell-Breuning, I do agree fundamentally with them that there is in human nature, on average, a kind of unwritten law of decency – Niebuhr's 'capacity for justice'. All the basic tenets of Christian, democratic socialism can find some motivation and support in that unwritten law.

In the United States, Christian socialism starts – or restarts – with an additional advantage. The *New York Times* for 11 December, 1984, ran the following news item:

> In recent years researchers have consistently found that about 40 percent of Americans attend religious services weekly, three-quarters of them pray at least once a day, and more than 90 percent profess belief in God.

Most of these people get whatever religion they have from the Bible. The reactionary preachers who dominate the television screen tell them that the Bible teaches us that 'government should get off the back of business', that the nuclear bomb is the Christian's best friend, that our present economy is the best possible economy in the world. They are wrong. The Bible teaches nothing of the sort. All we have to do is to tell them what the Bible really teaches, persuade them to believe it, and – who knows? – the kingdom of God may yet come on earth as it is in heaven, at least insofar as poor, weak human nature is capable, with the help of God. This is precisely what Jesus taught us to pray for, and work to make real. He also told us that God, our God, would indeed help us. As Eberhard Arnold said to the religious socialists at Tambach in 1919, responding to the discouragements of Barth, 'Karl Barth is right. Human action goes nowhere. But if God tells us to do something, is that just human action?'

And God has told us to do something.

Source: J. Cort, *Christian Socialism*, Orbis, 1988, pp. 352–6.

Further reading

For a short, measured reflection see Mott, *A Christian Perspective on Political Thought*, Chapters 12 and 13. Lengthier and more enthusiastic is Cort's eminently readable *Christian Socialism*. For the Marxist critique of Christianity see McLellan, *Marxism and Religion* and McGovern's *Marxism: An American Christian Perspective*. There is a good discussion of what recent Christian thinkers have been led to say about socialism in Dorrien, *The Democratic Socialist Vision*. See also Tawney's *Equality* and Day's autobiography. For the Christian roots of socialism, see Rowland's *Radical Christianity* and for the common humanist Utopia in both socialism and Christianity, see Marsden, *Marxian and Christian Utopianism*.

Chapter Fourteen

NEW SOCIAL MOVEMENTS

Introduction

The last third of the twentieth century has seen the rise of what have been called new social movements which have expressed concerns not represented in traditional forms of political thought and action. With the increasing importance of information and services in the economy, the old struggles for participation in the political system and a redistribution of economic resources have been challenged by movements which concentrate on the meaning and quality of life in the social process as a whole. The economic success of industrial society has created problems to which its ideological offspring liberalism and socialism cannot provide an answer because they are too universal in their approach and too blind to the specific difficulties of particular groups in society. In face of the tendency of the purely instrumental reason of late capitalism to colonize all aspects of life, the social movements involved with the environment, nuclear power, ethnic and gender relations, peace and human rights have tried to restore a sense of solidarity based on consensual values. As such, these movements contain a broad spiritual dimension and have often found sustenance in a reformulated Christian discourse.

This interaction between Christian symbolism and new forms of politics is at its clearest in the development of black political theology in North America and South Africa. Whereas the latter emphasizes redemptive suffering, reconciliation and non-violence, the black theology of North America, reflecting the experience of slavery and being uprooted, has been more confrontational. Re-reading the Bible against this background, black theology has found a powerful gospel of the oppressed. By contrast, the link between feminism as a political movement and Christianity emerges from an anti-patriarchal viewpoint. The writings of such theologians as Ruether and Fiorenza suggest new forms of community based on relationships of nurture and solidarity. Traditional Christianity has been accused of using nature as badly as it has used women. The burden of Lynn White's article is that Christianity is guilty, through its doctrine of creation as being at the disposal of human beings, of encouraging the despoliation of nature through the industrial revolution. It follows that any profound change in popular consciousness about environmental concerns is going to involve a radical reassessment of the relation of human beings to nature – from one of domination to one of stewardship.

(a) Cone:
Ecumenism, Liberation and Black Theology

From the time of its origin in slavery to the present, black religious thought has been faced with the question of whether to advocate integration into American society or separation from it. The majority of the participants in the black churches and the civil rights movement have promoted integration, and they have interpreted justice, liberation, love, suffering, and hope in the light of the goal of creating a society in which blacks and whites can live together in a 'beloved community'.

While integrationists have emphasized the American side of the double consciousness of African-Americans, there have also been nationalists who rejected any association with the United States and instead have turned towards Africa. Nationalists contend that blacks will never be accepted as equals in a white racist church and society. Black freedom can be achieved only by black people separating themselves from whites – either by returning to Africa or by forcing the government to set aside a separate state within the United States so blacks can build their own society.

The nationalist perspective on the black struggle for freedom is deeply embedded in the history of black religious thought. Its prominent advocates include Bishop Henry McNeal Turner of the AME Church; Marcus Garvey, the founder of the Universal Negro Improvement Association; and Malcolm X of the religion of Islam. Black nationalism is centered on blackness, a repudiation of all of the values of white culture and religion. Proponents reverse the values of the dominant society by attributing to black history and culture what whites have said about theirs. For example, Bishop Turner claimed that 'We have as much right biblically and otherwise to believe that God is a Negro . . . as you . . . white people have to believe that God is a fine looking, symmetrical and ornamented white man.' Marcus Garvey held a similar view: 'If the white man has the idea of a white God, let him worship his God as he desires . . . We Negroes believe in the God of Ethiopia, the everlasting God – God the Father, God the Son and God the Holy Ghost, the One God of all ages.'

The most persuasive interpreter of black nationalism during the 1960s was Malcolm X, who proclaimed a challenging critique of King's philosophy of integration, nonviolence, and love. Malcolm X advocated black unity instead of the 'beloved community', self-defense in lieu of nonviolence, and self-love in place of turning the other cheek to whites.

[. . .]

During the first half of the 1960s, King's interpretation of justice as equality with whites, liberation as integration, and love as nonviolence dominated the thinking of the black religious community. However after the riot in Watts in August 1965, black clergy began to take another look at Malcolm's philosophy, especially his criticisms of Christianity and American society. Malcolm X's contention that America was a nightmare and not a dream began to ring true to many black clergy as they watched their communities go up in flames as young blacks shouted in jubilation, 'burn, baby, burn'.

It was during the James Meredith 'march against fear' in Mississippi in June 1966 (after Malcolm had been assassinated in February 1965) that some black clergy began to openly question King's philosophy of love, integration, and nonviolence. When Stokely Carmichael proclaimed 'Black Power', it sounded like the voice of Malcolm X. Though committed to the Christian gospel, black clergy found themselves moving slowly from integration to separation, from Martin Luther King to Malcolm X.

The rise of Black Power created a decisive turning point in black religious thought. Black Power forced black clergy to raise the theological question about the relation between black faith and white religion. Although blacks have always recognized the ethical heresy of white Christians, they have not always extended it to Euro-American theology. With its accent on the cultural heritage of Africa and political liberation 'by any means necessary', Black Power shook black clergy out of their theological complacency.

Unable to ignore or reject Black Power, a small group of black clergy, mostly from the North, separated themselves from King's absolute commitment to nonviolence. Nevertheless, like King and unlike Black Power advocates, these black clergy were determined to remain within the Christian community. They were faced with the dilemma of how to reconcile Christianity and Black Power, Martin Luther King and Malcolm X.

In their attempt to resolve their dilemma, an ad hoc National Committee of Negro Churchmen (later the National Conference of Black Churchmen – NCBC) published a statement on 'Black Power' in the *New York Times*, 31 July 1966. The publication of the 'Black Power' statement represented the beginning of a process in which a radical group of black clergy in both black and white denominations made a sharp separation between their understanding of the Christian gospel and the theology of white churches. Addressing the leaders of white America (especially the churches) and the black community, black clergy endorsed the positive elements in Black Power.

In the debate that followed, the clergy of the NCBC became certain that their theological orientation in black history and culture created in them a view of the gospel radically different from that of white Christians. The term 'liberation' emerged as the dominant theme in black theology, and justice, love, hope, and suffering were interpreted in the light of its political implications. Black clergy were determined that they would not allow the theology of white racists to separate them from their solidarity with suffering blacks in the urban ghettos. That was why they found Malcolm X more useful than King, even though they were as determined as King not to separate themselves from the latter.

[. . .]

Although black theologians debated among themselves about liberation and reconciliation, African religion and Christianity, liberation and suffering, they agreed that white religion is racist and therefore un-Christian. In black theologians' attack on white religion and in their definition of the gospel as liberation, they moved toward a close solidarity with liberation theologians in Africa, Asia, Latin America, and the oppressed in the United States. In the early seventies, the dialogues between black and Third World theologians began – first with Africans, then with Latin Americans, and lastly with Asians. The dialogues with Third World theologians on other continents created a realization of the need for dialogue between blacks and other oppressed minorities in the United States and with an emerging feminist consciousness in all Christian groups.

The dialogues with other liberation theologians has revealed both the strengths and weaknesses of black theology. For example, Africans pointed out the gaps in the knowledge of American black theologians about African culture; Latin theologians revealed their lack of class analysis; Asian theologians showed the importance of a knowledge of religions other than Christianity; feminist theologians revealed the sexist orientation of black theology; and other minorities in the United

States showed the necessity of a coalition in the struggle for justice in the United States and around the globe.

A black feminist theology has already begun to emerge with the work of such persons as Paula Murray, Jackie Grant, Katie Cannon, Delores Williams, and Kelly Brown. It is clear that black theology will develop radically new directions when a fully developed feminist consciousness emerges. It will deepen its analysis of racism and also protect it from the worst aspects of sexism.

The impact of Third World theologians has already pushed black theology in the direction of a consideration of Marxism and socialism. This exploration has taken place in the context of the Ecumenical Association of Third World Theologians (EAT-WOT), which held its organizing meeting in Dar es Salaam, Tanzania, in 1976. Since that time meetings have been held in Ghana (1977), Sri Lanka (1979), Brazil (1980), India (1981), and Geneva (1983). Black theologians have also had a positive impact on Third World theologians in accenting the importance of the problem of racism. These dialogues have also established the category of liberation as the heart of the gospel for many Third World theologians here and abroad.

> Source: J. Cone, *Speaking the Truth: Ecumenism, Liberation and
> Black Theology*, Eerdmans, 1986, pp. 102–3, 104–5, 108–10.

(b) Chopp:
Christianity, Democracy and Feminist Theology

I want to suggest that not only does a consideration of Christianity and democracy enable us to understand feminist theology in the United States, but also that American feminist theology offers one of the most fruitful and challenging points of contact between a disestablished Christianity and a democracy seeking a multicultural and non-patriarchal transformation. That is to say, I do not think one can truly understand feminist theology in the United States unless one puts it in the locus between Christianity and democracy. This claim holds true both historically and currently. I want to argue further than feminist theology can be seen as a resource for a new relationship between Christianity and democracy. This new relationship entails a transformation of 'public' theology towards a prophetic theology that offers specific resources, both practically and theoretically, for a new interpretation of democracy as non-patriarchal and constituted through narratives, practices, and visions of multiculturalism.

Allow me to state some assumptions in order to move into the burden of my argument. First, I am most concerned with democracy in the sense of a democratic culture, that is the institutions, habits, narratives, and practices that form participation in political, personal, and cultural self-determination. Democracy, in the United States, is by no means simply a set of laws and principles, but the ongoing phenomena of producing new practices and narratives of what constitutes American democracy. Christianity has played an extremely important role in this vision of democracy, most notably, by providing physical spaces for development of citizenry, by forming the moral character of citizens, and by shaping communal norms and cultural practices. From the distinct debates on who is included in citizenship practices such as voting, to more broad-reaching concerns of the continual reinterpretation of American identity, to the present crisis of definition of public and private (long a foundation for one historical practice of democracy), we might say that democracy itself involves, in the United States, the continual process of reinterpreting the nature, narratives, and practices of democracy. In light of this historical process that is itself American democracy, I am most concerned with addressing two present historical problems: the crisis of patriarchy, manifested in the division of public and private along gender lines, and the crisis of multiculturalism, manifested, among other places, in the disestablishment of any one dominant narrative of what it is to be a woman.

My second assumption shifts the focus to feminist theology, which I will find necessary to relate to both feminist theory and Christian theology. I recognize that feminist theorists, by and large, neglect feminist theology, not because it is feminist, but because it is theology. This is always of some interest to me, for such neglect accepts and continues the public/private distinction in which objective knowledge opposes the sentimentality of religion, and it simply ignores the many women in this country for whom Christianity is a space of flourishing as well as oppression. Despite feminist theory's perpetuation of the Enlightenment rejection of religion, feminist theology is, in practice and theory, deeply related to the movements of feminist theory.

Third, feminist theology is also a form of Christian theology in the United States and, I shall argue, is best represented as a form of 'prophetic pragmatism', a term I borrow from Cornel West. One of my concerns is to suggest that there is something other than liberal Christianity and conservative Christianity. Indeed, I think there is plenty of evidence to suggest another 'form' of Christianity, one that is best understood as a quite different paradigm of Christianity than that of liberal or conservative Christianity. Hermeneutically speaking, I am attempting to draw attention to a reality of Christianity in the United States that lacks a media tag or a theoretical label. In some ways, my move parallels Christopher Lasch's attempt in his recent volume *The*

True and Only Heaven to reconstruct populism as an anti-progressive democratic tradition. My project is parallel to Lasch's both in its hermeneutical strategy to redraw the political, cultural, and narrative terrain and in its reliance upon thinkers such as Edwards, Emerson, Dewey, Peirce, the Niebuhr brothers, and Martin Luther King (as well as many others, including Elizabeth Cady Stanton, W. E. B. DuBois, Audre Lourde, and Marge Piercy). In a more direct way, I see this essay as dependent upon and committed to the project Cornel West identifies in *The American Evasion of Philosophy*, in which he reconstructs pragmatism as 'a reconception of philosophy as a form of cultural criticism that attempts to transform linguistic, social, cultural, and political traditions for the purposes of increasing the scope of individual development and democratic operations'.

[. . .] feminist theology, with its locus in prophetic pragmatism, serves as one resource for forming new discourses, practices, and habits for a new multicultural democracy in the United States. Due to its social locus as a broad-based movement, its radical reconstruction of Christian traditions, and its creative blending of aesthetics, ethics, and analytics, feminist theology can serve as one productive resource for reinterpreting democratic culture in the United States. In this section I give three illustrative discourses in which I see feminist theology contributing to ongoing conversations about American democracy.

First, feminist theology offers a necessary form of critical theory through its critiques of patriarchal democracy as a form of monotheistic ordering – that is, the invocation of patriarchy as fundamentally a spiritual-political practice of securing identity of the one, in this case of man, over the difference and subjugation of the other, woman. Patriarchy is a set of social practices that structures man's power and value over that of woman's, but feminist theology maintains it is also a certain ordering of one's identity through the difference and subjugation of all others. Quite literally, patriarchy, as practised in contemporary culture, is not merely dependent upon binary metaphysics but also upon an ordering that we can call monotheistic, that is the setting up of those in power as God. This monotheistic patriarchy is a political, cultural, and psychological system, with profound spiritual ramifications. What I mean by spiritual, in this sense, is the sense of wholeness of the self as well as the connectedness of the self to all that is. What is important about the theological critique is to show how, in the logic of monotheistic patriarchy, the very identity of the self gets constructed through a pattern of posing the 'other', e.g., woman, as different and inferior. Thus patriarchy cannot be addressed adequately until a logic not only uncovers such ordering but also provides new forms of identity. In feminist theology, this takes at least three dimensions: (1) multicultural identities that substantially move beyond binary opposition; (2) the decentering of the self in relation to God (or some notion of the whole, the ultimate or the absolute), earth and others; and (3) the construction of identity not as a fixed ontological ordering but as a process, journey, or horizon that is continually renegotiated and transformed. To construct this new sense of identity, feminist theology draws upon both current feminist practices as well as many traditions of Christian spirituality that offer images of the self as constructed through terms of connectedness, process, and relatedness.

Second, feminist theology contributes to the empowerment of new ways of being, and thus new habits of citizenship, through the formulation of new narratives for women's lives. On a quite practical level, this is one of the greatest survival needs at present for women in culture. Women, across class and race lines, have undergone massive changes in lifestyle in the last twenty years. Yet the dominant narratives for women, as testified to in women's magazines, are still to put women in charge of the private realm and to extend her responsibility for personal relations to the public working place. In other words, the virtues given to women in this culture still stress her inferiority, the virtues of passivity and self-negating service, and the basic closure of a woman's life.

Feminist theology creates new narratives for women's lives that substantially move beyond both the patriarchal story of what it is to be a woman and toward an elaboration of women's stories in a multicultural context. Such narratives, resisting the patriarchal ordering of public and private, men and women, focus on the multiplicity of narratives for women. Indeed, of central concern in feminist and womanist theology is the lifting to public consciousness of the differences between narratives for black women and white women as in Jacqueline Grant's *White Woman's Christ, Black Woman's Jesus* and Katie Cannon's *Black Womanist Ethics*. Asian-American theologian Rita Nakashima Brock, Asian theologian Chung Hyun Kyun, and Hispanic-American theologian Ada Maria Isasi-Diaz provide narratives for women's lives out of their particular cultural contexts.

Part of the real emphasis on new narratives will be empowerment of women, including the formation of such virtues as self-respect and human dignity. Feminist theologians turning to issues of physical abuse with women often find themselves involving the long tradition of Christianity of placing dignity as gift from God rather than human surroundings. And it is here that I want to underscore the importance of transcendence or God claims. If modern theologies of culture found it necessary to invoke God to relativize culture, feminist theologies invoke God to point within culture to the dignity of every human being and to demand and require cultural empowerment of all persons.

Perhaps feminist theology can serve as one of the greatest alternatives to the American practice of determining value by the money one makes or marries.

Deeply related to this is concern for fundamental attitudes needed for ongoing cultural transformation of democracy. Americans, as the authors of the recent volume *The Good Society* suggest, have a fundamental attitude of fear and need to move to one of trust and, I would add, openness. But where are sources for trust? One place is the emergent tradition of prophetic pragmatism, which combines a reading of Christian tradition in which an attitude of fundamental trust replaces the fear invoked and sustained in patriarchal monotheism. And, certainly, feminist theology is greatly concerned to create a certain type of openness to the world, one that does not negate the self but opens the self to encounters with those who are different. Such concern for new narratives of women's lives is matched, in feminist theology, with the concern for new practices and visions of community.

Third, feminist theology contributes to ongoing democratic transformation by offering discourses that envision new forms of community. Feminist theologians are critical of both the individual autonomy that is so dominant in contemporary democracy but also of the communitarian critique that is so often lifted up as the only real alternative. The autonomous individual, in view of most feminist theologians, is neither an adequate description of women's lives nor a value to be sought for democracy. But the communitarian position tends to retrieve a past form of community that is dependent upon patriarchal ordering in which women had few, if any, rights of self determination. Again out of feminist religious practice and feminist readings of Christian traditions, theologians explore what new substantial forms of community might look like. American feminist theologians such as Catherine Keller and Rosemary Radford Ruether envision forms of community in which individual selves can be nurtured through communal relations. Biblical scholar Elisabeth Schussler Fiorenza has researched forms of community in the New Testament and proposes a model of community as the 'ekklesia of women' to name 'the assembled gathering of free citizens to determine their own spiritual-political affairs'. I have suggested a model of the community of emancipatory transformation drawing upon the symbol of communion, forming community through open rhetorical practices, and providing the nurture of ongoing spirituality through virtues of justice, creativity, wisdom, and love (where, for instance, love is the willingness to engage in open, free conversation, to let one's mind be changed, to make one's own opinion, argument, and knowledge available). Given the general rubric of Christian prophetic pragmatism, the particular contributions and challenges of American feminist theology are not provided in any dogmatic sense. Indeed, the relationship between Christianity and democracy is not one in which Christianity can assume, any longer, that it is the dominant cultural tradition but one, to use a metaphor favored among feminists, of a quilt where one of the contributing pieces is feminist theology. I by no means think feminist theology is or will be the dominant center; indeed, I prefer the power of its voice as a prophetic margin. Nonetheless, as in a quilt where a well-pieced strand of color can transform the pattern of the quilt, so also does feminist theology have important constructive contributions to make to the ongoing reinterpretation of democracy in the United States.

Source: R. Chopp, 'Christianity, Democracy and Feminist Theology', in
Christianity and Democracy in Global Context, ed. J. Witte,
Westview, 1993, pp. 111–13, 126–9.

(c) *White:* Christianity and Ecological Crisis

Especially in its Western form, Christianity is the most anthropocentric religion the world has seen. As early as the 2nd century both Tertullian and St Irenaeus of Lyons were insisting that when God shaped Adam he was foreshadowing the image of the incarnate Christ, the Second Adam. Man shares, in great measure, God's transcendence of nature. Christianity, in absolute contrast to ancient paganism and Asia's religions (except, perhaps, Zoroastrianism), not only established a dualism of man and nature but also insisted that it is God's will that man exploit nature for his proper ends.

At the level of the common people this worked out in an interesting way. In Antiquity every tree, every spring, every stream, every hill had its own *genius loci*, its guardian spirit. These spirits were accessible to men, but were very unlike men; centaurs, fauns, and mermaids show their ambivalence. Before one cut a tree, mined a mountain, or dammed a brook, it was important to placate the spirit in charge of that particular situation, and to keep it placated. By destroying pagan animism, Christianity made it possible to exploit nature in a mood of indifference to the feelings of natural objects.

It is often said that for animism the Church substituted the cult of saints. True; but the cult of saints is functionally quite different from animism. The saint is not *in* natural objects; he may have special shrines, but his citizenship is in heaven. Moreover, a saint is entirely a man; he can be approached in human terms. In addition to saints, Christianity of course also had angels and demons inherited from Judaism and perhaps, at one remove, from Zoroastrianism. But these were all as mobile as the saints themselves. The spirits *in* natural objects, which formerly had protected nature from man, evaporated. Man's effective monopoly on spirit in this world was confirmed, and the old inhibitions to the exploitation of nature crumbled.

When one speaks in such sweeping terms, a note of caution is in order. Christianity is a complex faith, and its consequences differ in differing contexts. What I have said may well apply to the medieval West, where in fact technology made spectacular advances. But the Greek East, a highly civilized realm of equal Christian devotion, seems to have produced no marked technological innovation after the late 7th century, when Greek fire was invented. The key to the contrast may perhaps be found in a difference in the tonality of piety and thought which students of comparative theology find between the Greek and the Latin Churches. The Greeks believed that sin was intellectual blindness, and that salvation was found in illumination, orthodoxy – that is, clear thinking. The Latins, on the other hand, felt that sin was moral evil, and that salvation was to be found in right conduct. Eastern theology has been intellectualist. Western theology has been voluntarist. The Greek saint contemplates; the Western saint acts. The implications of Christianity for the conquest of nature would emerge more easily in the Western atmosphere.

The Christian dogma of creation, which is found in the first clause of all the Creeds, has another meaning for our comprehension of today's ecologic crisis. By revelation, God had given man the Bible, the Book of Scripture. But since God had made nature, nature also must reveal the divine mentality. The religious study of nature for the better understanding of God was known as natural theology. In the early Church, and always in the Greek East, nature was conceived primarily as a symbolic system through which God speaks to men: the ant is a sermon to sluggards; rising flames are the symbol of the soul's aspiration. This view of nature was essentially artistic rather than scientific. While Byzantium preserved and copied great numbers of ancient Greek scientific texts, science as we conceive it could scarcely flourish in such an ambience.

However, in the Latin West by the early 13th century natural theology was following a very different bent. It was ceasing to be the decoding of the physical symbols of God's communication with man and was becoming the effort to understand God's mind by discovering how his creation operates. The rainbow was no longer simply a symbol of hope first sent to Noah after the Deluge: Robert Grosseteste, Friar Roger Bacon, and Theodoric of Freiberg produced startlingly sophisticated work on the optics of the rainbow, but they did it as a venture in religious understanding. From the 13th century onward, up to and including Leibnitz and Newton, every major scientist, in effect, explained his motivations in religious terms. Indeed, if Galileo had not been so expert an amateur theologian he would have got into far less trouble: the professionals resented his intrusion. And Newton seems to have regarded himself more as a theologian than as a scientist. It was not until the late 18th century that the hypothesis of God became unnecessary to many scientists.

It is often hard for the historian to judge, when men explain why they are doing what they want to do, whether they are offering real reasons or merely culturally acceptable reasons. The consistency with which scientists during the long formative centuries of Western science said that the task and the reward of the scientist was 'to think God's thoughts after him' leads one to believe that this was their real motivation. If so, then modern Western science was cast in a matrix of Christian theology. The dynamism of religious devotion, shaped by the Judeo-Christian dogma of creation, gave it impetus.

We would seem to be headed toward conclusions unpalatable to many Christians. Since both *science* and *technology* are blessed words in our contemporary vocabulary, some may be happy at the notions, first, that, viewed historically, modern science is an extrapolation of natural theology and, second, that modern technology is at least partly to be explained as an Occidental, voluntarist realization of the Christian dogma of man's transcendence of, and rightful mastery over, nature. But, as we now recognize, somewhat over a century ago science and technology – hitherto quite separate activities – joined to give mankind powers which, to judge by many of the ecologic effects, are out of control. If so, Christianity bears a huge burden of guilt.

I personally doubt that disastrous ecologic backlash can be avoided simply by applying to our problems more science and more technology. Our science and technology have grown out of Christian attitudes toward man's relation to nature which are almost universally held not only by Christians and neo-Christians but also by those who fondly regard themselves as post-Christians. Despite Copernicus, all the cosmos rotates around our little globe. Despite Darwin, we are *not*, in our hearts, part of the natural process. We are superior to nature, contemptuous of it, willing to use it for our slightest whim. The newly elected Governor of California, like myself a churchman but less troubled than I, spoke for the Christian tradition when he said (as is alleged), 'when you've seen one redwood tree, you've seen them all'. To a Christian a tree can be no more than a physical fact. The whole concept of the sacred grove is alien to Christianity and to the ethos of the West. For nearly two millennia Christian missionaries have been chopping down sacred groves, which are idolatrous because they assume spirit in nature.

212

What we do about ecology depends on our ideas of the man–nature relationship. More science and more technology are not going to get us out of the present ecologic crisis until we find a new religion, or rethink our old one. The beatniks, who are the basic revolutionaries of our time, show a sound instinct in their affinity for Zen Buddhism, which conceives of the man–nature relationship as very nearly the mirror image of the Christian view. Zen, however, is as deeply conditioned by Asian history as Christianity is by the experience of the West, and I am dubious of its viability among us.

Possibly we should ponder the greatest radical in Christian history since Christ: St Francis of Assisi. The prime miracle of St Francis is the fact that he did not end at the stake, as many of his left-wing followers did. He was so clearly heretical that a General of the Franciscan Order, St Bonaventura, a great and perceptive Christian, tried to suppress the early accounts of Franciscanism. The key to an understanding of Francis is his belief in the virtue of humility – not merely for the individual but for man as a species. Francis tried to depose man from his monarchy over creation and set up a democracy of all God's creatures. With him the ant is no longer simply a homily for the lazy, flames a sign of the thrust of the soul toward union with God; now they are Brother Ant and Sister Fire, praising the Creator in their own ways as Brother Man does in his.

Later commentators have said that Francis preached to the birds as a rebuke to men who would not listen. The records do not read so: he urged the little birds to praise God, and in spiritual ecstasy they flapped their wings and chirped rejoicing. Legends of saints, especially the Irish saints, had long told of their dealings with animals but always, I believe, to show their human dominance over creatures. With Francis it is different. The land around Gubbio in the Apennines was being ravaged by a fierce wolf. St Francis, says the legend, talked to the wolf and persuaded him of the error of his ways. The wolf repented, died in the odor of sanctity, and was buried in consecrated ground.

What Sir Steven Runciman calls 'the Franciscan doctrine of the animal soul' was quickly stamped out. Quite possibly it was in part inspired, consciously or unconsciously, by the belief in reincarnation held by the Cathar heretics who at that time teemed in Italy and southern France, and who presumably had got it originally from India. It is significant that at just the same moment, about 1200, traces of metempsychosis are found also in western Judaism, in the Provençal *Cabbala*. But Francis held neither to transmigration of souls nor to pantheism. His view of nature and of man rested on a unique sort of pan-psychism of all things animate and inanimate, designed for the glorification of their transcendent Creator, who, in the ultimate gesture of cosmic humility, assumed flesh, lay helpless in a manger, and hung dying on a scaffold.

I am not suggesting that many contemporary Americans who are concerned about our ecologic crisis will be either able or willing to counsel with wolves or exhort birds. However, the present increasing disruption of the global environment is the product of a dynamic technology and science which were originating in the Western medieval world against which St Francis was rebelling in so original a way. Their growth cannot be understood historically apart from distinctive attitudes toward nature which are deeply grounded in Christian dogma. The fact that most people do not think of these attitudes as Christian is irrelevant. No new set of basic values has been accepted in our society to displace those of Christianity. Hence we shall continue to have a worsening ecologic crisis until we reject the Christian axiom that nature has no reason for existence save to serve man.

The greatest spiritual revolutionary in Western history, St Francis, proposed what he thought was an alternative Christian view of nature and man's relation to it: he tried to substitute the idea of the equality of all creatures, including man, for the idea of man's limitless rule of creation. He failed. Both our present science and our present technology are so tinctured with orthodox Christian arrogance toward nature that no solution for our ecologic crisis can be expected from them alone. Since the roots of our trouble are so largely religious, the remedy must also be essentially religious, whether we call it that or not. We must rethink and refeel our nature and destiny. The profoundly religious, but heretical, sense of the primitive Franciscans for the spiritual autonomy of all parts of nature may point a direction. I propose Francis as a patron saint for ecologists.

Source: L. White, 'The Historical Roots of Our Ecological Crisis', *Science*, vol. 155 (March 1967), pp. 1205–7.

Further reading

For a general introduction see Beckford's *Religion and Advanced Industrial Society*, Chapter 6.

For a short introduction to black theology, see the article by Kalilombe in the collection edited by Ford. Also the various books by Cone and the collection *Black Theology: A Documentary History*, by Wilmore and Cone.

For feminist political theology, see the article by Harrison in Loades's reader *Feminist Theology*. See also the remarkable re-reading of the New Testament in Fiorenza's *In Memory of Her*, and the new forms of community outlined in Ruether's books *Sexism and God-Talk* and *Women-Church,* and Chopp's *The Power to Speak.*

For green political theology, see Osborne's *Stewards of Creation,* Spretnak's incisive *The Spiritual Dimension of Green Politics* and the suggestive work of McFague, *Models of God.* There is substantial theological reflection in Moltmann's *God in Creation.*

Chapter Fifteen

A DISTINCTLY
CHRISTIAN POLITICS?

Introduction

As the excerpts below from the pioneering work of Max Weber demon-strate, it is difficult to make generalizations about the comparative political impact of the major world religions. After all, as the foregoing chapters have amply shown, the political impact of Christianity itself is extremely diverse. Nevertheless, the work of Weber and his followers do suggest some contrasts that may be illuminating. The most evident is that Christianity has always espoused the principle of the separation of religion and politics, of Church and State: however intertwined they may have become in the post-Constantinian settlement they remained, in principle, separable. In Islamic and Hindu societies, for example, religious and political leadership was in the hands of the same people; and in China the Confucian outlook was at the heart of the govern-mental system. Buddhism, it is true, stereotyped strongly autonomous and self-contained religious organizations but its other worldly orien-tation tended to diminish its impact on politics. And traditional Hindu thought was not wedded to any particular political framework, the task of government being simply to ensure that each individual could dis-charge his or her particular caste obligations.

Another contrast worth pondering is between the semitic religions of the Book and those further East. The loose tolerant religious ideology of Hinduism, for example, meant that unity was preferred by the caste system rather than any strictly religious conceptions. Judaism, Christianity and Islam, by contrast, had from the beginning a written orthodoxy. It is therefore arguable that only the semitic religions can be truly fundamentalist.

What appears to be the political legacy of Christianity is its tendency towards the secularization of the political sphere. Islam aspires to have a universal nation in which politics is infused with religious principles. In Christianity, by contrast, the Protestant ethic (in Weber's famous thesis) has given birth to an economic order and a concomitant liberal democracy whose operations have emancipated themselves from any religious sanction.

(a) *Weber:* Politics and Religion

The conflict of ascetic ethics, as well as of the mystically oriented temper of brotherly love, with the apparatus of domination which is basic to all political institutions has produced the most varied types of tension and compromise. Naturally, the polarity between religion and politics is least wherever, as in Confucianism, religion is equivalent to a belief in spirits or simply a belief in magic, and ethics is no more than a prudent accommodation to the world on the part of the educated man. Nor does any conflict between religion and politics exist wherever, as in Islam, religion makes obligatory the violent propagation of the true prophecy which consciously eschews universal conversion and enjoins the subjugation of unbelievers under the dominion of a ruling order dedicated to the religious war as one of the basic postulates of its faith, without recognizing the salvation of the subjugated. For this is obviously no universalistic salvation religion. The practice of coercion poses no problem, as God is pleased by the forcible dominion of the faithful over the infidels, who are tolerated once they have been subjugated.

Inner-worldly asceticism reached a similar solution to the problem of the relation between religion and politics wherever, as in radical Calvinism, it represented as God's will the domination over the sinful world, for the purpose of controlling it, by religious virtuosi belonging to the 'pure' church. This view was fundamental in the theocracy of New England, in practice if not explicitly, though naturally it became involved with compromises of various kinds. Another instance of the absence of any conflict between religion and politics is to be found in the intellectualistic salvation doctrines of India, such as Buddhism and Jainism, in which every relationship to the world and to action within the world is broken off, and in which the personal exercise of violence as well as resistance to violence is absolutely prohibited and is indeed without any object. Mere conflict between concrete demands of a state and concrete religious injunctions arises when a religion is the pariah faith of a group that is excluded from political equality but still believes in the religious prophecies of a divinely appointed restoration of its social level. This was the case in Judaism, which never in theory rejected the state and its coercion but, on the contrary, expected in the Messiah their own masterful political ruler, an expectation that was sustained at least until the time of the destruction of the Temple by Hadrian.

Wherever congregational religions have rejected all employment of force as an abomination to God and have sought to require their members' avoidance of all violence, without however reaching the consistent conclusion of absolute flight from the world, the conflict between religion and politics has led either to martyrdom or to passive anti-political sufferance of the coercive regime. History shows that religious anarchism has hitherto been only a short-lived phenomenon, because the intensity of faith which makes it possible is in only an ephemeral charisma. Yet there have been independent political organizations which were based, not on a purely anarchistic foundation, but on a foundation of consistent pacifism. The most important of these was the Quaker community in Pennsylvania, which for two generations actually succeeded, in contrast to all the neighboring colonies, in existing side by side with the Indians, and indeed prospering, without recourse to violence. Such situations continued until the conflicts of the great colonial powers made a fiction of pacifism. Finally, the American War of Independence, which was waged in the name of basic principles of Quakerism (though the orthodox Quakers did not participate because of their principle of non-resistance), led to the discrediting of this principle even inwardly. Moreover, the corresponding policy of the tolerant admission of religious dissidents into Pennsylvania brought even the Quakers there to a policy of gerrymandering political wards, which caused them increasing uneasiness and ultimately led them to withdraw from co-responsibility for the government.

Typical examples of completely passive indifference to the political dimension of society, from a variety of motives, are found in such groups as the genuine Mennonites, in most Baptist communities, and in numerous other sects in various places, especially Russia. The absolute renunciation of the use of force by these groups led them into acute conflicts with the political authorities only where military service was demanded of the individuals concerned. Indeed, attitudes toward war, even of religious denominations that did not teach an absolutely anti-political attitude, have varied in particular cases, depending upon whether the wars in question were fought to protect the religion's freedom of worship from attack by political authority or fought for purely political purposes. For these two types of war, two diametrically opposite slogans prevailed. On the one hand, there was the purely passive sufferance of alien power and the withdrawal from any personal participation in the exercise of violence, culminating ultimately in personal martyrdom. This was of course the position of mystical apoliticism, with its absolute indifference to the world, as well as the position of those types of inner-worldly asceticism which were pacifistic in principle. But even a purely personal religion of faith frequently generated political indifference and religious martyrdom, inasmuch as it recognized neither a rational order of the outer world pleasing to God, nor a rational domination of the world desired by God. Thus, Luther completely rejected religious revolutions as well as religious wars.

The other possible standpoint was that of violent resistance, at least to the employment of force against religion. The concept of a religious revolution was consistent most with a rationalism oriented to an ascetic mastery of mundane affairs which taught that sacred institutions and institutions pleasing to God exist within this world. Within Christianity, this was true in Calvinism, which made it a religious obligation to defend the faith against tyranny by the use of force. It should be added, however, that Calvin taught that this defense might be undertaken only at the initiative of the proper authorities, in keeping with the character of an institutional church. The obligation to bring about a revolution in behalf of the faith was naturally taught by the religions that engaged in wars of missionary enterprise and by their derivative sects, like the Mahdists and other sects in Islam, including the Sikhs – a Hindu sect that was originally pacifist but passed under the influence of Islam and became eclectic.

The representatives of the two opposed viewpoints just described sometimes took virtually reverse positions toward a political war that had no religious motivation. Religions that applied ethically rationalized demands to the political realm had necessarily to take a more fundamentally negative attitude toward purely political wars than those religions that accepted the institutions of the world as 'given' and relatively indifferent in value. The unvanquished Cromwellian army petitioned Parliament for the abolition of forcible conscription, on the ground that a Christian should participate only in those wars the justice of which could be affirmed by his own conscience. From this standpoint, the mercenary army might be regarded as a relatively ethical institution, inasmuch as the mercenary would have to settle with God and his conscience as to whether he would take up this calling. The employment of force by the state can have moral sanction only when the force is used for the control of sins, for the glory of God, and for combating religious evils – in short, only for religious purposes. On the other hand, the view of Luther, who absolutely rejected religious wars and revolutions as well as any active resistance, was that only the secular authority, whose domain is untouched by the rational postulates of religion, has the responsibility of determining whether political wars are just or unjust. Hence, the individual subject has no reason to burden his own conscience with this matter if only he gives active obedience to the political authority in this and in all other matters which do not destroy his relationship to God.

The position of ancient and medieval Christianity in relation to the state as a whole oscillated or, more correctly, shifted its center of gravity from one to another of several distinct points of view. At first there was a complete abomination of the existing Roman empire, whose existence until the very end of time was taken for granted in Antiquity by everyone, even Christians. The empire was regarded as the dominion of Anti-Christ. A second view was complete indifference to the state, and hence passive sufferance of the use of force, which was deemed to be unrighteous in every case. This entailed active compliance with all the coercive obligations imposed by the state, e.g., the payment of taxes which did not directly imperil religious salvation. For the true intent of the New Testament verse about 'rendering unto Caesar the things which are Caesar's' is not the meaning deduced by modern harmonizing interpretations, namely a positive recognition of the obligation to pay taxes, but rather the reverse: an absolute indifference to all the affairs of the mundane world.

Two other viewpoints were possible. One entailed withdrawal from concrete activities of the political community, such as the cult of the emperors, because and insofar as such participation necessarily led to sin. Nevertheless, the state's authority was accorded positive recognition as being somehow desired by God, even when exercised by unbelievers and even though inherently sinful. It was taught that the state's authority, like all the institutions of this world, is an ordained punishment for the sin brought upon man by Adam's fall, which the Christian must obediently take upon himself. Finally, the authority of the state, even when exercised by unbelievers, might be evaluated positively, due to our condition of sin, as an indispensable instrument, based upon the divinely implanted natural knowledge of religiously unilluminated heathens, for the social control of reprehensible sins and as a general condition for all mundane existence pleasing to God.

Of these four points of view, the first two mentioned belong primarily to the period of eschatological expectation, but occasionally they come to the fore even in a later period. As far as the last of the four is concerned, ancient Christianity did not really go beyond it in principle, even after it had been recognized as the state religion. Rather, the great change in the attitude of Christianity toward the state took place in the medieval church, as the investigations of Troeltsch have brilliantly demonstrated. But the problem in which Christianity found itself involved as a result, while not limited to this religion, nevertheless generated a whole complex of difficulties peculiar to Christianity alone, partly from internal religious causes and partly from the operation of non-religious factors. This critical complex of difficulties concerned the relationship of so-called 'natural law' to religious revelation on the one hand, and to positive political institutions and their activities on the other.

We shall advert again to this matter briefly, both in connection with our exposition of the forms of religious communities and in our analysis of the forms of domination. But the following point may be made here regarding the theoretical solution of these problems as it affects personal ethics: the general schema according to which religion customarily solves the problem of the tension between religious ethics and the non-ethical or unethical requirements of life in the political and economic structures of power within the world is to relativize and differentiate ethics into 'organic' (as contrasted to 'ascetic') *ethics of vocation.* This holds true whenever a religion is dominant within a political organization or occupies a privileged status, and particularly when it is a religion of institutional grace.

Christian doctrine, as formulated by Aquinas for example, to some degree assumed the view, already common in animistic beliefs regarding souls and the world beyond, that there are purely natural differences among men, completely independent of any effects of sin, and that these natural differences determine the diversity of status destinies in this world and beyond. Troeltsch has correctly stressed the point that this formulation of Christian doctrine differs from the view found in Stoicism and earliest Christianity of an original golden age and a blissful state of anarchic equality of all human beings.

At the same time, however, religion interprets the power relationships of the mundane world in a metaphysical way. Human beings are condemned – whether as a result of original sin, of an individual causality of *karma,* or of the corruption of the world deriving from a basic dualism – to suffer violence, toil, pain, hate, and above all differences in class and status position within the world. The various callings or castes have been providentially ordained, and each of them has been assigned some specific, indispensable function desired by God or determined by the impersonal world order, so that different ethical obligations devolve upon each. The diverse occupations and castes are compared to the constituent portions of an organism in this type of theory. The various relationships of power which emerge in this manner must therefore be regarded as divinely ordained relationships of authority. Accordingly, any revolt or rebellion against them, or even the raising of vital claims other than those corresponding to one's status in society, is reprehensible to God because they are expressions of creaturely self-aggrandizement and pride which are destructive of sacred tradition. The virtuosi of religion, be they of an ascetic or contemplative type, are also assigned their specific responsibility within such an organic order, just as specific functions have been allocated to princes, warriors, judges, artisans, and peasants. This allocation of responsibilities to religious virtuosi is intended to produce a treasure of supernumerary good works which the institution of grace may thereupon distribute. By subjecting himself to the revealed truth and to the correct sentiment of love, the individual will achieve, and that within the established institutions of the world, happiness in this world and reward in the life to come.

For Islam, this organic conception and its entire complex of related problems was much more remote, since Islam rejected universalism, regarding the ideal status order as consisting of believers and unbelievers or pariah peoples, with the former dominating the latter. Accordingly, Islam left the pariah peoples entirely to themselves in all matters which were of indifference to religion. It is true that the mystical quest for salvation and ascetic virtuoso religion did conflict with institutional orthodoxy in the Muslim religion. It is also true that Islam did experience conflicts between sacred and profane law, which always arise when positive sacred norms of the law have developed. Finally, Islam did have to face certain questions of orthodoxy in the theocratic constitution. But Islam did not confront the ultimate problem of the relationship between religious ethics and secular institutions, which is a problem of religion and natural law.

On the other hand, the Hindu books of law promulgated an organic, traditionalistic ethic of vocation, similar in structure to medieval Catholicism, only more consistent, and certainly more consistent than the rather thin Lutheran doctrine regarding the *status ecclesiasticus, politicus*, and *oeconomicus*. As we have already seen, the status system in India actually combined a caste ethic with a distinctive doctrine of salvation. That is, it held that an individual's chances of an ever higher ascent in future incarnations upon earth depend on his having fulfilled the obligations of his own caste, be they ever so disesteemed socially. This belief had the effect of inducing a radical acceptance of the social order, especially among the very lowest castes, which would have most to gain in any transmigration of souls.

On the other hand, the Hindu theodicy would have regarded as absurd the medieval Christian doctrine, as set forth for example by Beatrice in the *Paradiso* of Dante, that the class differences which obtain during one's brief span of life upon earth will be perpetuated into some 'permanent' existence in the world beyond. Indeed, such a view would have deprived the strict traditionalism of the Hindu organic ethic of vocation of all the infinite hopes for the future entertained by

222

the pious Hindu who believed in the transmigration of souls and the possibility of an ever more elevated form of life upon this earth. Hence, even from the purely religious point of view, the Christian doctrine of the perpetuation of class distinctions into the next world had the effect of providing a much less secure foundation for the traditional stratification of vocations than did the steel-like anchorage of caste to the altogether different religious promises contained in the doctrine of metempsychosis.

The medieval and the Lutheran traditionalistic ethics of vocation actually rested on a general presupposition, one that is increasingly rare, which both share with the Confucian ethic: that power relationships in both the economic and political spheres have a purely personal character. In these spheres of the execution of justice and particularly in political administration, a whole organized structure of personal relations of subordination exists which is dominated by caprice and grace, indignation and love, and most of all by the mutual piety and devotion of masters and subalterns, after the fashion of the family. Thus, these relationships of domination have a character to which one may apply ethical requirements in the same way that one applies them to every other purely personal relationship.

Yet as we shall see later, it is quite certain that the 'masterless slavery' (Wagner) of the modern proletariat, and above all the whole realm of the rational institution of the state – that 'rascal the state' (*Racker von Staat*) so heartily abominated by romanticism – no longer possess this personalistic character. In a personalistic status order it is quite clear that one must act differently toward persons of different status. The only problem that may arise on occasion, even for Thomas Aquinas, is how this is to be construed. Today, however, the *homo politicus*, as well as the *homo oeconomicus*, performs his duty best when he acts without regard to the person in question, *sine ira et studio*, without hate and without love, without personal predilection and therefore without grace, but sheerly in accordance with the impersonal duty imposed by his calling, and not as a result of any concrete personal relationship. He discharges his responsibility best if he acts as closely as possible in accordance with the rational regulations of the modern power system. Modern procedures of justice impose capital punishment upon the malefactor, not out of personal indignation or the need for vengeance, but with complete detachment and for the sake of objective norms and ends, simply for the working out of the rational autonomous lawfulness inherent in justice. This is comparable to the impersonal retribution of *karma*, in contrast to Yahweh's fervent quest for vengeance.

The use of force within the political community increasingly assumes the form of the *Rechtsstaat*. But from the point of view of religion, this

223

is merely the most effective mimicry of brutality. All politics is oriented to *raison d'état*, to realism, and to the autonomous end of maintaining the external and internal distribution of power. These goals, again, must necessarily seem completely senseless from the religious point of view. Yet only in this way does the realm of politics acquire a peculiarly rational mystique of its own, once brilliantly formulated by Napoleon, which appears as thoroughly alien to every ethic of brotherliness as do the rationalized economic institutions.

The accommodation that contemporary ecclesiastical ethics is making to this situation need not be discussed in detail here. In general the compromise takes form through reaction to each concrete situation as it arises. Above all, and particularly in the case of Catholicism, the accommodation involves the salvaging of ecclesiastical power interests, which have increasingly become objectified into a *raison d'église*, by the employment of the same modern instruments of power employed by secular institutions.

The objectification of the power structure, with the complex of problems produced by its rationalized ethical provisos, has but one psychological equivalent: the vocational ethic taught by asceticism. An increased tendency toward flight into the irrationalities of apolitical emotionalism in different degrees and forms, is one of the actual consequences of the rationalization of coercion, manifesting itself wherever the exercise of power has developed away from the personalistic orientation of heroes and wherever the entire society in question has developed in the direction of a national 'state'. Such apolitical emotionalism may take the form of a flight into mysticism and an acosmistic ethic of absolute goodness or into the irrationalities of non-religious emotionalism, above all eroticism. Indeed, the power of the sphere of eroticism enters into particular tensions with religions of salvation. This is particularly true of the most powerful component of eroticism, namely sexual love. For sexual love, along with the 'true' or economic interest, and the social drives toward power and prestige, is among the most fundamental and universal components of the actual course of interpersonal behavior.

Source: M. Weber, *Economy and Society*, ed. G. Roth and G. Wittich, University of California Press, 1978, pp. 593–601.

(b) *Weber:* The Rise of Christianity

[. . .] In the last analysis the factor which produced capitalism is the rational permanent enterprise, with its rational accounting, rational technology and rational law, but again not these alone. Necessary complementary factors were the rational spirit, the rationalization of the conduct of life in general and a rationalistic economic ethic.

The earliest form of economic ethics, and of the economic relations which result from it, is the sanctity of tradition.

[. . .] Primitive traditionalism may undergo essential intensification through two circumstances. In the first place, material interests may be tied up with the maintenance of tradition. When, for example, in China an attempt was made to change certain roads or to introduce more rational means or routes of transportation, the perquisites of certain officials were threatened; and the same was the case in the Middle Ages in the West, and in modern times when railroads were introduced. Such vested interests of officials, landholders and merchants contributed decisively to stifling a tendency toward rationalization. Stronger still is the stereotyping of business on magical grounds, stemming from a deep repugnance towards undertaking any change in the established conduct of life because supernatural evils are feared. Commonly a defence of some economic privilege is also involved, but its effectiveness depends on a general belief in the potency of the magical processes which are feared.

Such traditional obstructions cannot be overcome by the economic impulse alone. It is an erroneous notion that our rationalistic and capitalistic age is characterized by a stronger economic interest than other periods, since the moving spirits of modern capitalism are not possessed of a stronger acquisitive drive than, for example, an Oriental trader. The unleashing of pure greed has produced only irrational results; such men as Cortez and Pizarro, who were perhaps its strongest embodiment, were far from having an idea of a rationalistic economic life. As the economic impulse is universal, the interesting question is under which circumstances it becomes rationalized so as to produce rational institutions of capitalistic enterprise.

At the start two opposite attitudes towards the pursuit of gain exist in combination. Inside the community there is attachment to tradition and pietistic relations with fellow members of tribe, clan and household which exclude unrestricted quest for gain within the circle of those bound together by religious ties; externally absolutely unrestricted pursuit of gain is permitted, as every foreigner is an enemy to whom no ethical considerations apply. Thus the ethics of internal and external relations are completely distinct. The course of development involves on the one hand the bringing of calculation into the relations of traditional brotherhood, displacing the old religious relationship . . . At the same time there is a tempering of the unrestricted quest for gain in relations with foreigners.

[. . .] The antipathy of Catholic ethics, and following that the Lutheran, towards every capitalistic tendency stems essentially from a repugnance towards the impersonality of human relations entailed by a capitalist economy, which places certain human actions beyond the influence of the church and prevents the latter from penetrating them and moulding them along ethical lines. The relations between the master and the slave could be regulated ethically, whereas it would be exceedingly difficult, if not impossible, to introduce moral considerations into the relations between the mortgage creditor and the property which was pledged for the debt, or between an endorser and the issuer of a bill of exchange. The consequence of the position adopted by the church was that medieval economic ethics excluded over-pricing and free competition, and relied on the principle of just price to assure everyone of a chance to gain a livelihood.

The Jews cannot be made responsible for the breaking up of this circle of ideas. Their situation during the Middle Ages may be compared sociologically with that of an Indian caste in a world without other castes; they were an outcast people. However, the difference is that according to the promise of the Indian religion the caste system is valid for eternity. The individual may in the course of time reach heaven through a series of reincarnations, the length of time this takes depending upon his deserts; but this is possible only within the caste system. The caste organization is eternal, and anyone who attempted to leave it would be accursed and condemned to pass in hell into the bowels of a dog. The Jewish religion, on the contrary, promises a reversal of caste relations in the future world. In the present world the Jews are branded as an outcast people, either as punishment for the sins of their fathers, as Deutero-Isaiah holds, or for the salvation of the world, which is the presupposition of the mission of Jesus of Nazareth; from which position they are to be released by a social revolution. In the Middle Ages the Jews were a guest people standing outside political society; they could not be received into citizenship because they could not participate in the communion of the Lord's Supper, and hence could not belong to the oath-bound fraternity.

The Jews were not the only guest people. The Caursines, for example, occupied a similar position. These were Christian merchants who dealt in money and in consequence were, like the Jews, under the protection of the princes, and on consideration of a payment enjoyed the privilege of carrying on monetary dealings. What distinguished the Jews in a striking way from the Christian guest peoples was the impossibility in their entering into convivial and matrimonial relations with the Christians. Originally the Christians did not hesitate to accept Jewish

hospitality, in contrast to the Jews who feared that their ritual prescriptions about food would not be observed by their hosts. On the
occasion of the first outbreak of medieval anti-semitism the faithful
were warned by the synods not to conduct themselves unworthily and
hence not to accept offerings from the Jews who on their side despised
the hospitality of the Christians. Marriage with non-Jews was strictly
excluded from the time of Ezra and Nehemiah.

A further ground for the outcast position of the Jews was the fact
that agriculture could not be reconciled with the requirements of their
ritual. Ritual considerations were responsible for the Jewish predilection
for monetary dealings. Jewish piety demanded knowledge of the law
and continuous study which were easier to combine with trade than
with other occupations. Moreover, the prohibition of usury by the
church entailed a condemnation of the exchange dealings indispensable to trade, and the Jews were not subject to ecclesiastical law.

Finally, Judaism had maintained the originally universal dualism of
internal and external morality which allowed them to accept interest
from foreigners who did not belong to the brotherhood or the community. This dualism legitimized other irrational types of business,
especially tax farming and political financing of various kinds. In the
course of the centuries the Jews acquired a special skill in these matters
which made them useful and in demand. But all this was pariah capitalism, not rational capitalism such as developed in the West.
Consequently, few Jews can be found among the creators of the modern economy, the large entrepreneurs; this type was Christian and only
conceivable in Christendom. The Jewish manufacturer, in contrast, is a
more recent phenomenon. The Jews could not have played a part in the
establishment of rational capitalism because they were outside the craft
organizations, even where, as in Poland, they had command over a
numerous proletariat which they might have organized in the capacity
of entrepreneurs in domestic industry or as manufacturers. Anyway,
the Jewish ethic is traditionalist, as the Talmud shows. The pious Jew's
horror of any innovation is as great as that of any primitive people
steeped in magic.

Nevertheless, Judaism was of considerable importance for modern
rational capitalism, in so far as it transmitted to Christianity its hostility
towards magic. Apart from Judaism and Christianity, and two or three
Oriental sects (one of which is in Japan), no religion is characterized by
such a clear hostility towards magic. This hostility probably arose when
the Israelites found in Canaan the magic of the agricultural god Baal,
while Jahveh was a god of volcanoes, earthquakes and pestilences. The
struggle between the two priesthoods and the victory of the priests of

Jahveh discredited the fertility magic of the priests of Baal and stigmatized it as decadent and godless. Having made Christianity possible and given it the character of a religion essentially free from magic, Judaism played an important role in economic history, because the dominance of magic outside the Christian world constitutes one of the most serious obstacles to the rationalization of economic life, as magic involves a stereotyping of technology and economic relations. When attempts were made to build railroads and factories in China a conflict with geomancy ensued, as the latter required that the location of structures on certain mountains, in forests, by rivers and on cemetery hills should not disturb the spirits' peace.

Only great reforming and rationalizing prophets could ever break the power of magic and establish a rational conduct of life ... The prophets have released the world from magic and in doing so have created the basis for our modern science and technology, and for capitalism. No such prophets sprang up in China.

India, however, did produce a religion of salvation, and in contrast with China it has known great and prophetic missionary activities. But the typical Hindu prophet, such as Buddha, lives an exemplary life which leads to salvation, but does not regard himself as sent by God to insist upon everybody's obligation to follow his example, taking the position that whoever wishes for salvation can choose freely. Many may reject salvation, as it is not the destiny of everyone to enter at death into *nirvana*. Only philosophers imbued with hatred of this world are prepared to make the stoical resolution and withdraw from life.

The result was that Hindu prophets influenced only the intellectual classes who produced forest hermits and poor monks ... Consequently Buddhism in its pure form was confined to a thin stratum of monks, while the laity found no ethical precepts according to which life should be led. True, Buddhism had its decalogue, but in distinction from that of the Jews it contained no binding commands, only recommendations. The most important good deed was to maintain the monks. Such a religious spirit could never displace magic, but only replace one kind by another.

In contrast to the ascetic religion of salvation of India and its weak influence on the masses, Judaism and Christianity were from the beginning plebeian religions and have deliberately remained such. The struggle of the ancient church against the Gnostics was nothing else but a struggle against the aristocracy of the intellectuals, such as is common in ascetic religions, with the object of preventing their seizing the leadership in the church. This struggle was crucial for the success of Christianity among the masses, and hence for the fact that magic was suppressed among the general population to the greatest possible extent. True, it has not been extirpated even today, but it was degraded to the status of something unholy, and diabolic.

The germ of this change in the position of magic is found far back in ancient Jewish ethics, which is much concerned with matters which we also find treated in the proverbs and the so-called prophetic texts of the Egyptians. But the most important prescriptions of Egyptian ethics were futile because by laying a scarab on the region of the heart one could prepare a dead man to conceal successfully the sins he had committed, deceive the judge of the dead and thus enter into paradise. Jewish ethics knows no such sophisticated subterfuges and neither does Christianity. In the Eucharist the latter has indeed sublimated magic into the form of a sacrament, but it gave its adherents no means for evading the final judgement such as were provided by the Egyptian religion. To study the influence of a religion on life one must distinguish between its official teachings and the actual behaviour upon which in reality it places a premium in this world or the next.

We must also make a distinction between the religion of the adepts and the religion of the masses. Virtuoso religion affects everyday life only as an ideal; its claims are the highest, but they fail to determine everyday ethics. The relation between the two varies in different religions. In Catholicism they are brought into harmonious union in so far as the claims of the religious virtuoso are held up alongside the duties of the laymen as counsels of perfection. The truly perfect Christian is the monk; but his mode of life is not imposed on everyone, although some of his virtues in a modified form are held up as ideals. The advantage of this combination was that ethics was not split asunder as in Buddhism, where the divergence between monastic ethics and mass ethics meant that the most worthy individuals in the religious sense withdrew from the world to establish a separate community.

Christianity was not alone in respect of this tendency, which recurs fairly frequently in the history of religions. The example of Tibet shows how enormous achievements can be made possible by an ascetically oriented methodical conduct of life. The country seems condemned by nature to be an eternal desert; but a community of celibate ascetics has carried out colossal construction works in Lhassa and moulded the country in accordance with the doctrines of Buddhism. In the Middle Ages in the West the monk is the first human being who lives rationally and works methodically and by rational means towards a goal, namely, the future life. Only for him did the clock strike, only for him were the hours of the day divided. The economic life of the monastic communities was also rational. The monks furnished a part of the officials during the early Middle Ages. The power of the doges of Venice collapsed when struggles about the investiture deprived them of the possibility of employing churchmen for overseas tasks.

However, the rational mode of life remained restricted to monastic circles. True, the Franciscan movement attempted to extend it to the laity through the institution of the tertiaries, but the institution of the confessional was a barrier to such an extension. The church domesticated the peoples of medieval Europe by means of its system of confession and penance. For the men of the Middle Ages the possibility of unburdening themselves through a confessional after they had rendered themselves liable to punishment meant a release from the consciousness of sin which the teachings of the church had instilled. The unity and strength of the methodical conduct of life were thus in fact broken up. In its knowledge of human nature the church did not rely on ethical consistency of the individual but steadfastly held to the view that in spite of the warnings of the confessional and of penances, no matter how severe, he would fall morally again and again. The church, therefore, shed its grace on the just as well as the unjust.

The Reformation made a decisive break with this system. The dropping of monastic ideals by the Lutheran Reformation meant the disappearance of the dualistic distinction between a universally binding morality and an especially demanding code for virtuosi. The other-worldly asceticism came to an end. The fervently religious individuals who would have gone into monasteries had now to practise their religion in ordinary life. Protestantism created an adequate ethic for such an asceticism within the world. Celibacy was not required provided that the pursuit of riches did not lead one astray into wanton enjoyment. Thus Sebastian Franck was correct in summing up the spirit of the Reformation when he said: 'You think you have escaped from the monastery, but now everyone must be a monk throughout his life.'

The tremendous significance of this transformation of the ascetic ideal can still be seen in the lands saturated by Protestant ascetic religiosity. The role of the religious denominations in America shows it vividly. Despite the separation of state and church, until fifteen or twenty years ago no banker or physician could take up a residence or establish connections without being asked to what religious community he belonged, and his prospects were good or bad according to his answer. Acceptance into a sect was preceded by a strict inquiry into one's ethical conduct. Membership of a sect which did not recognize the Jewish distinction between internal and external moral codes guaranteed one's business honour and reliability which in turn guaranteed success. This is the root of the principle 'honesty is the best policy' and of the ceaseless repetition among the Quakers, Baptists and Methodists of the saying based on experience that 'God would take care of his own'. 'The Godless cannot trust each other across the road; they turn to us when they want to do business; piety is the surest road to wealth.'

It is true that the accumulation of wealth, due to piety, led to a dilemma similar to that which the medieval monasteries repeatedly had to face: religious austerity led to wealth, wealth to fall from grace, and this again to the necessity of reconstruction. Calvinism sought to avoid this difficulty through the idea that man was only an administrator of what God had given him; it condemned enjoyment, yet permitted no flight from the world and regarded working with others under a rational discipline as the religious duty of the individual. Out of this system of ideas came our word 'vocation', which is known only to the languages influenced by the Protestant translations of the Bible. It expresses the value placed upon activity carried on according to the rational capitalist principle regarded as the fulfilment of a God-given task. Here lay also the deepest roots of the contrast between the Puritans and the Stuarts, despite the fact that both were capitalistically minded. For the Puritan the Jew was likewise repugnant because he devoted himself to irrational and illegal occupations such as giving war loans, tax farming and leasing of offices, in the manner of the court favourite.

The idea of vocation gave to the modern entrepreneur a plentiful supply of industrious workers and crystal-clear conscience in exploiting them, while the latter were offered the prospect of eternal salvation as the reward of their ascetic devotion to work. In an age when ecclesiastical discipline controlled the whole of life to an extent inconceivable now, this idea had an impact quite different from any it might have today. Like the Catholic, the Lutheran churches recognized and practised ecclesiastical discipline. But in the Protestant ascetic communities admission to the Lord's Supper depended on ethical fitness which was identified with respectability in business, while no one inquired into the content of one's faith. Such a powerful, unconsciously refined organization for the production of capitalistic individuals has never existed in any other church or religion, and in comparison with it what the Renaissance did for capitalism shrinks into insignificance. Its faithful occupied themselves with technical problems and were first-class experimenters. From art and mining, experimentation was introduced into science. Although it did not transform the soul of man as did the innovations of the Reformation, the Renaissance view of the world exercised the main influence on the policy of rulers. Almost all the great scientific discoveries of the sixteenth century and even the beginning of the seventeenth were made in the environment of Catholicism. Copernicus was a Catholic, while Luther and Melanchthon condemned his discoveries. Scientific progress and Protestantism must not

231

be unquestioningly identified. The Catholic Church has indeed on various occasions obstructed scientific progress; but the ascetic sects of Protestantism were equally inclined to have nothing to do with science, except in situations where material requirements of everyday life were involved. On the other hand it is Protestantism's specific contribution to have placed science in the service of technology and economics.

Source: M. Weber, *On Capitalism, Bureaucracy and Religion,*
ed. S. Andreski, Allen & Unwin, 1983, pp. 128–37.

Further reading

There is a good overview in Moyser's introduction to his *Politics and Religion in the ModernWorld.* On Islam see the chapter in the same book by Perry, Enayat's *Modern Islamic Political Thought,* and Esposito's *The Islamic Threat – Myth or Reality?.* For Buddhism, see Ling's stimulating *Buddha, Marx and God* and for Hindu political thought see Talbot's chapter in the Moyser book.

There are good general surveys in Mews, *Religion in Politics: A World Guide* and in Merkl and Smart, *Religion and Politics in the Modern World.* For a more sociological approach see Hadden and Shupe, *Prophetic Religions and Politics: Religion and the Political Order, Vol. 1.* For good discussions of Weber, see Eisenstadt, *The Protestant Ethic and Modernization.*

BIBLIOGRAPHY

Aquinas, Thomas, *The Political Ideas of Saint Thomas Aquinas*. Ed. D. Bigongiari, New York, Hafner, 1953.

Aquinas, Thomas, *Selected Political Writings*. Ed. A. D'Entrèves, Oxford, Blackwell, 1959.

Badham, Paul, *The Contribution of Religion to the Conflict in Northern Ireland*. Canterbury, Centre for the Study of Religion and Society, 1987.

Badham, Paul, ed., *Religion, State and Society in Modern Britain*. Lewiston, Mellen Press, 1989.

Bailyn, Bernard, *The Ideological Origins of the American Revolution*. Cambridge, Harvard University Press, 1992.

Bammel, Ernst and Moule, C. D. F., eds., *Jesus and the Politics of His Day*. Cambridge, Cambridge University Press, 1984.

Barbour, Ian, ed., *Western Man and Environmental Ethics: Attitudes Towards Nature and Technology*. Reading, Addison-Wesley, 1973.

Baumgart, William and Regan, Richard, eds., *St. Thomas on Law, Morality and Politics*. Indianapolis, Hachett, 1988.

Baum, Gregory and Coleman, John, eds., *The Church and Christian Democracy*. Edinburgh, T. & T. Clark, 1987.

Beckford, James, *Religion and Advanced Industrial Society*. Boston, Unwin Hyman, 1989.

Bellah, Robert, *The Broken Covenant: American Civil Religion in the Time of Trial*. 2nd edn, Chicago, Chicago University Press, 1992.

Berryman, Phillip, *Liberation Theology: Essential Facts about the Revolutionary Movement in Latin America and Beyond*. London, Tauris, 1987.

Bieler, Andre, *The Social-Humanism of Calvin*. Richmond, John Knox Press, 1964.

Black, Anthony, *Political Thought in Europe 1250–1450*. Cambridge, Cambridge University Press, 1992.

Boff, Leonardo, *Ecclesiogenesis: The Base Communities Reinvent the Church.* London, Collins, 1986.

Boff, Leonardo, *Introducing Liberation Theology.* Tunbridge Wells, Burns and Oates, 1987.

Bonino, José, *Towards a Christian Political Ethics.* London, SCM Press, 1983.

Bonino, José, *Christians and Marxists: The Mutual Challenge to Revolution.* London, Hodder and Stoughton, 1976.

Bowsma, William, *John Calvin: A Sixteenth Century Portrait.* New York, Oxford University Press, 1988.

Brandon, S., *Jesus and the Zealots: A Study of the Political Factor in Primitive Christianity.* Manchester, Manchester University Press, 1967.

Brown, Peter, *Augustine of Hippo: A Biography.* London, Faber, 1967.

Bruce, Steve, *The Rise and Fall of the New Christian Right: Conservative Protestant Politics in America 1978–1988.* Oxford, Clarendon Press, 1988.

Bruce, Steve, *God Save Ulster! The Religion and Politics of Paisleyism.* Oxford, Oxford University Press, 1986.

Burns, J. H., ed., *Mediaeval Political Thought c.350–c.1450.* Cambridge, Cambridge University Press, 1988.

Burns, J. H. and Goldie, D., eds., *The Cambridge History of Modern Political Thought 1450–1700.* Cambridge, Cambridge University Press, 1991.

Cargill Thompson, W., *The Political Thought of Martin Luther.* Brighton, Harvester, 1984.

Carman, John and Juergensmeyer, Mark, eds., *A Bibliographic Guide to the Comparative Study of Ethics.* New York, Cambridge University Press, 1991.

Chadwick, Owen, *The Christian Church in the Cold War.* Harmondsworth, Allen Lane, 1992.

Chopp, Rebecca, *The Power to Speak: Feminism, Language, God.* New York, Crossroad, 1989.

Clements, Keith, *A Patriotism for Today: Dialogue with Dietrich Bonhoeffer.* London, Collins, 1986.

Cochrane, Charles, *Christianity and Classical Culture: A Study of Thought and Action from Augustus to Augustine.* London, Oxford University Press, 1954.

Cohn-Sherbok, Dan and McLellan, David, *Religion in Public Life.* Basingstoke, Macmillan, 1992.

Coleman, John, ed., *One Hundred Years of Catholic Social Thought: Celebration and Challenge.* Maryknoll, Orbis, 1991.

Cone, James, *Speaking the Truth: Ecumenism, Liberation and Black Theology.* Grand Rapids, Eerdmans, 1986.

Cone, James, *For My People: Black Theology and the Black Church.* Maryknoll, Orbis, 1984.

Cort, John, *Christian Socialism*. Maryknoll, Orbis, 1988.

Court, John, *Myth and History in the Book of Revelation*. London, SPCK, 1979.

Cullman, Oscar, *The State in the New Testament*. London, SCM Press, 1967.

Davis, Charles, *Theology and Political Society*. Cambridge, Cambridge University Press, 1980.

Day, Dorothy, *Loaves and Fishes*. London, Victor Gollancz, 1963.

Deane, Herbert, *The Political and Social Ideas of St. Augustine*. New York, Columbia University Press, 1963.

De Gruchy, John, *Liberating Reformed Theology*. Grand Rapids, Eerdmans, 1991.

Dickens, Arthur, *Martin Luther and the Reformation*. London, English Universities Press, 1967.

Dooyeweerd, Herman, *Roots of Western Culture: Pagan, Secular and Christian Options*. Toronto, Wedge, 1979.

Dorr, Donal, ed., *Option for the Poor: A Hundred Years of Vatican Social Teaching*. Maryknoll, Orbis, 1983.

Dorrien, Gary, *The Democratic Socialist Vision*. Totowa, Rowman, 1986.

Dunn, John, *The Political Thought of John Locke*. London, Cambridge University Press, 1969.

Dvornik, Francis, *Early Christians and Byzantine Political Philosophy: Origins and Background*. Harvard, Trustees for Harvard University, 1966.

Edwards, David, *Christians in a New Europe*. London, Collins, 1990.

Eisenstadt, S. N., ed., *The Protestant Ethic and Modernization: A Comparative View*. New York, Basic Books, 1968.

Ellul, Jacques, *The Political Illusion*. New York, Vintage, 1967.

Ellul, Jacques, *The Meaning of the City*. Grand Rapids, Eerdmans, 1970.

Enayat, H., *Modern Islamic Political Thought: The Response of Shi'i and Sunni Muslims to the Twentieth Century*. London, Macmillan, 1982.

d'Entrèves, A. P., *The Notion of the State: an Introduction to Political Theory*. Oxford, Clarendon Press, 1967.

Esposito, John, *The Islamic Threat: Myth or Reality?*. New York, Oxford University Press, 1992.

Everett, William, *God's Federal Republic: Reconstructing Our Governing Symbol*. New York, Paulist Press, 1988.

Fiorenza, Elisabeth Schüssler, *In Memory of Her: A Feminist Theological Reconstruction of Christian Origins*. London, SCM Press, 1983.

Fogarty, Michael, *Christian Democracy in Western Europe 1820–1953*. London, Routledge and Kegan Paul, 1957.

Ford, David, ed., *The Modern Theologians*. Oxford, Blackwell, 1989.

Forrester, Duncan, *Theology and Politics*. Oxford, Blackwell, 1988.

Frend, W., *The Rise of Christianity*. London, Darton, Longman & Todd, 1984.

Friesen, Abraham, *Thomas Münzer, a Destroyer of the Godless: the Making of a Sixteenth Century Religious Revolutionary*. Berkeley, University of California Press, 1990.

Garrow, David, *Bearing the Cross: Martin Luther King Jr and the Southern Christian Leadership Conference*. New York, Random House, 1988.

Gilby, Thomas, *Principality and Pity. Aquinas and the Rise of State Theory in the West*. London, Longmans, 1958.

Gilder, George, *Wealth and Poverty*. New York, Buchan and Enright, 1982.

Griffith, Carol, ed., *Christianity and Politics: Catholic and Protestant Perspectives*. Washington, D.C., Ethics and Public Policy Center, 1981.

Gritsch, Eric, *Thomas Münzer: A Tragedy of Errors*. Minneapolis, Fortress Press, 1989.

Guttiérez, Gustavo, *A Theology of Liberation: History, Politics and Salvation*. Maryknoll, Orbis, 1988.

Guttiérez, Gustavo, *The Power of the Poor in History: Selected Writings*. Maryknoll, Orbis, 1983.

Habgood, John, *Church and Nation in a Secular Age*. London, Darton, Longman & Todd, 1983.

Habiger, Matthew, *Papal Teaching on Private Property*. New York, University Press of America, 1990.

Hadden, Jeffrey and Shupe, Anson S., eds., *Prophetic Religions and Politics: Vol. 1, Religion and the Political Order*. New York, Paragon House, 1986.

Hancock, Ralph, *Calvin and the Foundations of Modern Politics*. Ithaca, Cornell University Press, 1989.

Hargrove, Eugene, ed., *Religion and Environmental Crisis*. Athens, University of Georgia Press, 1986.

Hastings, Adrian, *Church and State: The English Experience*. Exeter, University of Exeter Press, 1991.

Hatch, Nathan, *The Democratization of American Christianity*. New Haven, Yale University Press, 1989.

Hawkesworth, M. E., *Beyond Oppression: Feminist Theory and Political Strategy*. New York, Continuum, 1990.

Hennelly, Alfred, ed., *Liberation Theology: A Documentary History*. Maryknoll, Orbis, 1990.

Hooker, Richard, *Of the Laws of Ecclesiastical Polity*. London, Dent, 1907.

Höpfl, Harro, *The Christian Polity of John Calvin*. London, Cambridge University Press, 1982.

James, W., *The Christian in Politics*. Oxford, Oxford University Press, 1962.

Johnston, Douglas and Sampson, Cynthia, eds., *Religion, the Missing Dimension of Statecraft*. Oxford, Oxford University Press, 1995.

Kaufman, Peter, *Redeeming Politics*. Princeton, Princeton University Press, 1990.

Kee, Alastair, *Marx and the Failure of Liberation Theology*. Philadelphia, Trinity Press, 1990.

King, Ursula, *Religion in Europe*. Amsterdam, Kok Pharos, 1995.

Kingdom, Robert and Linder, Robert, eds., *Calvin and Calvinism: Sources of Democracy?*. Lexington, D. C. Heath, 1970.

Kirk, Russell, *The Conservative Mind: From Burke to Eliot*. 7th edn, Chicago, Regency, 1986.

Klostermaier, Klaus, *A Survey of Hinduism*. Albany, State University of New York Press, 1994.

Lerner, R. and Mahdi, M., eds., *Mediaeval Political Philosophy: A Sourcebook*. New York, Free Press, 1963.

Lewis, Ewart, ed., *Mediaeval Political Ideas*. London, Routledge, 1954.

Lindsay, A. D., *The Churches and Democracy*. London, Epworth, 1934.

Ling, T., *Buddha, Marx and God. Some Aspects of Religion in the Modern World*. New York, St. Martin's Press, 1966.

Loades, Ann, *Feminist Theology: A Reader*. London, SPCK, 1990.

McClendon, James, *Ethics: Systematic Theology*, vol. 1. Nashville, Abingdon Press, 1986.

MacDonald, Michael, *Children of Wrath: Political Violence in Northern Ireland*. Cambridge, Polity Press, 1986.

McFague, Sally, *Models of God: Theology for an Ecological, Nuclear Age*. Philadelphia, Fortress, 1987.

McGovern, Arthur, *Marxism: An American Christian Perspective*. Maryknoll, Orbis, 1980.

McLellan, David, *Marxism and Religion*. London, Macmillan, 1987.

McManners, John, *Church and State in France 1870–1914*. London, SPCK, 1972.

Maritain, Jacques, *Christianity and Democracy*. San Francisco, Ignatius Press, 1986.

Markus, Robert, *Saeculum. History and Society in the Theology of St. Augustine*. London, Cambridge University Press, 1970.

Marsden, John, *Marxian and Christian Utopianism*. New York, Monthly Review, 1991.

Medhurst, Kenneth and Moyser, George, eds., *Church and Politics in a Secular Age*. Oxford, Clarendon Press, 1988.

Meeks, Douglas, *God the Economist. The Doctrine of God and Political Economy*. Minneapolis, Fortress, 1989.

Meeks, Wayne, *The First Urban Christians*. New Haven, Yale University Press, 1983.

Merkl, Peter and Smart, Vivian, *Religion and Politics in the Modern World*. New York, New York University Press, 1983.

Mews, Stuart, ed., *Religion in Politics: A World Guide*. Chicago, St. James Press, 1989.

Michel, Patrick, *Politics and Religion in Eastern Europe*. Oxford, Polity, 1991.

Micklem, Nathaniel, *The Idea of a Liberal Democracy*. London, Oxford University Press, 1957.

Milbank, John, *Theology and Social Theory: Beyond Secular Reason*. Oxford, Blackwell, 1990.

Misner, Paul, *Social Catholicism in Europe: From the Onset of Industrialization to the First World War.* London, Darton, Longman & Todd, 1991.

Moltmann, Jürgen, *On Human Dignity: Political Theology and Ethics.* London, SCM Press, 1984.

Moltmann, Jürgen, *God in Creation: A New Theology of Creation and the Spirit of God.* New York, Harper & Row, 1985.

Montefiore, Hugh, *Christianity and Politics.* London, Macmillan, 1990.

Mott, Charles, *A Christian Perspective on Political Thought.* New York, Oxford University Press, 1993.

Moyser, George, ed., *Politics and Religion in the Modern World.* London, Routledge, 1991.

Moyser, George and Medhurst, Keith, eds., *Church and Politics in a Secular Age.* New York, Oxford University Press, 1988.

Mullett, Michael, *Radical Religious Movements in Early Modern Europe.* London, Allen and Unwin, 1980.

Myers, Ched, *Binding the Strong Man: A Political Reading of Mark's Story of Jesus.* Maryknoll, Orbis, 1988.

Neuhaus, Richard, *The Naked Public Square: Religion and Democracy in America.* Grand Rapids, Eerdmans, 1984.

Nicholls, David, *Deity and Domination: Images of God and State in the Nineteenth and Twentieth Centuries.* New York, 1989.

Nisbet, Robert, *Conservatism: Dream and Reality.* Milton Keynes, Open University Press, 1986.

Noll, Mark, ed., *Religion and American Politics from the Colonial Period to the 1980s.* New York, Oxford University Press, 1990.

Novak, Michael, *The Spirit of Democratic Capitalism.* London, IEA Health and Welfare Unit, 1991.

O'Brien, David and Shannon, Thomas, *Catholic Social Thought: The Documentary Heritage.* Maryknoll, Orbis, 1992.

Osborne, Lawrence, *Stewards of Creation: Environmentalism in the Light of Biblical Teaching.* Oxford, Latimer House, 1990.

Paris, Peter, *The Social Teaching of the Black Churches.* Philadelphia, Fortress, 1985.

Plamenatz, John, *Man and Society.* Vol. I, 2nd edn, London, Longman, 1993.

Quinton, Anthony, *The Politics of Imperfections: The Religious and Secular Traditions of Conservative Thought in England from Hooker to Oakshott.* London, Faber, 1978.

Raban, Jonathan, *God, Man and Mrs. Thatcher.* London, Chatto and Windus, 1989.

Robbins, Thomas and Anthony, Dick, eds., *In Gods We Trust: New Patterns of Religious Pluralism in America.* New Brunswick, Transaction Publishers, 1991.

Rose, Richard, *Northern Ireland: Time of Choice.* Washington, American Enterprise Institute, 1976.

Rossiter, Clinton, *Conservatism in America: The Thankless Persuasion.* New York, Knopf, 1962.

Rowland, Christopher, *Radical Christianity: A Reading of Recovery.* Cambridge, Polity, 1988.

Rowland, Christopher, *Christian Origins.* London, SPCK, 1986.

Rowland, Christopher and Corner, Mark, *Liberating Exegesis: The Challenge of Liberation Theology to Biblical Studies.* London, SPCK, 1990.

Ruether, Rosemary Radford, *Sexism and God-Talk: Toward a Feminist Theology.* London, SCM Press, 1983.

Ruether, Rosemary Radford, *Women-Church: Theology and Practice of Feminist Liturgical Communities.* San Francisco, Harper & Row, 1985.

Sandoz, Ellis, *A Government of Laws: Political Theory, Religion and the American Founding.* Baton Rouge, Louisiana State University Press, 1990.

Scott, Peter, *Theology, Ideology and Liberation.* Cambridge, Cambridge University Press, 1995.

Segundo, Jan Luis, *The Liberation of Theology.* Dublin, Gill & Macmillan, 1977.

Segundo, Jan Luis, *The Community called Church.* London, Gill & Macmillan, 1980.

Segundo, Jan Luis, *Faith and Ideologies,* 3 vols. Maryknoll, Orbis, 1984.

Sigmund, Paul, *Liberation Theology at the Crossroads.* New York, Oxford University Press, 1990.

Skinner, Quentin, *The Foundations of Modern Political Thought,* 2 vols. Cambridge, Cambridge University Press, 1978.

Sobrino, Jon, *Jesus the Liberator: A Historical-theological Reading of Jesus of Nazareth.* London, Burns and Oates, 1994.

Spretnak, Charlene, *The Spiritual Dimension of Green Politics.* Santa Fe, Bear & Co., 1986.

Spretnak, Charlene, *The Politics of Women's Spirituality.* New York, Anchor, 1982.

Stackhouse, Max, *Public Theology and Political Economy: Christian Stewardship in Modern Society.* Grand Rapids, Eerdmans, 1987.

Stackhouse, Max, *Creeds, Society and Human Rights: A Study in Three Cultures.* Grand Rapids, Eerdmans, 1984.

Tawney, Richard, *Equality.* London, Unwin, 1964.

Tillich, Paul, *Perspectives on Nineteenth and Twentieth Century Protestant Theology,* ed. C. Braaten. New York, Harper & Row, 1967.

Troeltsch, Ernst, *Protestantism and Progress: the Significance of Protestantism for the Rise of the Modern World.* Philadelphia, Fortress, 1986.

Ullmann, Walter, *A History of Political Thought: The Middle Ages*. Penguin, Harmondsworth, 1970.

Villa-Vicencio, Charles, *A Theology of Reconstruction: Nation-Building and Human Rights*. Cambridge, Cambridge University Press, 1992.

Wald, Kenneth, *Religion and Politics in the United States*. New York, St. Martin's Press, 1987.

Wallace, Ronald, *Calvin, Geneva and the Reformation*. Edinburgh, Scottish Academic Press, 1988.

Walsh, Michael and Davies, Brian, eds., *Proclaiming Justice and Peace: Documents from John XXIII to John Paul II*. London, Collins, 1984.

Walzer, Michael, *The Revolution of the Saints: A Study in the Origin of Radical Politics*. London, Weidenfeld and Nicholson, 1966.

Weil, Simone, *The Need for Roots*. London, Routledge, 1952.

Wills, Gary, *Under God: Religion and American Politics*. New York, Simon and Schuster, 1990.

Wilmore, G. S., *Black Religion and Black Radicalism: An Interpretation of the Religious History of Afro-American People*. Maryknoll, Orbis, 1983.

Wilmore, Gayraud and Cone, James, *Black Theology: A Documentary History 1966–1979*. Maryknoll, Orbis, 1979.

Wink, Walter, *Naming the Powers: The Language of Power in the New Testament*. Philadelphia, Fortress, 1984.

Witte, John, ed., *Christianity and Democracy in Global Context*. Boulder, Westview Press, 1993.

Wogaman, Philip, *Christians and the Great Economic Debate*. London, SCM Press, 1972.

Wogaman, Philip, *Christian Perspectives on Politics*. Minneapolis, Fortress, 1988.

Wood, James, ed., *Readings on Church and State*. Waco, Baylor University Press, 1989.

Wuthnow, Robert, *Communities of Discourse: Ideology and Social Structure in the Reformation, the Enlightenment, and European Socialism*. Cambridge, Harvard University Press, 1989.

Wuthnow, Robert, *The Restructuring of American Religion: Society and Faith since World War II*. Princeton, Princeton University Press, 1988.

Yoder, John, *The Politics of Jesus*. Grand Rapids, Eerdmans, 1972.

Zuck, Lowell, *Christianity and Revolution: Radical Christian Testimonies 1520–1650*. Philadelphia, Temple University Press, 1975.

INDEX OF NAMES